Made in L.A. 2025

MADE IN L.A. 2025

Essence Harden Paulina Pobocha

HAMMER MUSEUM, UNIVERSITY OF CALIFORNIA, LOS ANGELES

DELMONICO BOOKS • D.A.P. NEW YORK

Contents

Biennials are special projects. While the exhibitions are experienced by the public every other year, they are an ever-present condition for the organizing institution. As one iteration concludes, the next is already in preparation. Made in L.A., now in its seventh edition, has become an integral part of the Hammer's identity, embedded in the fabric of the museum and emblematic of our role as a proving ground for artists and ideas. This charge feels even more important at a time when federal support for the arts is under threat, and there is pressure for institutions to reject the very values of open exchange, equitable access, and creative freedom that the Hammer holds most dear.

While I have had the great joy of curating a biennial in the past, this is my first experience with one as a director. Since my arrival at the Hammer in early 2025, I have felt the significance of Made in L.A. to the communities of our city and witnessed the ways that the Hammer is uniquely situated to support this important project. Made in L.A. is an essential forum that spotlights the breadth of creativity that emanates from within our city. Looking back at the previous iterations of the exhibition at the Hammer, I am inspired by the expansiveness and histories of artistic communities across Los Angeles. I feel fortunate to assume oversight for a biennial that captures a city's creative spirit across geographies and generations, with each edition building on the legacy of those that came before.

Made in L.A. 2025 features twenty-eight participants. Their practices span painting, sculpture, ceramics, photography, moving image, and mural making but also include experimental theater, music, archival work, and live performance. They truly represent the expansive artistic practices found across the city, and I sincerely congratulate the curators, Essence Harden and Paulina Pobocha. They accepted the enormous task of traversing the city's many artistic communities and in so doing developed a selection of work that embodies our topographic and creative landscape. I am also grateful for the hard work of curatorial assistant Jennifer Buonocore-Nedrelow for her dedication to the visions of this year's artists. Similarly, I would like to acknowledge Andie Kimura, our late, beloved Hammer colleague who advanced the early phases of this year's biennial. Together, the curatorial team has assembled a group of vibrant, critical, and resilient artists whose practices sit in conversation with the reverberations of the city.

We are deeply honored to continue the awards that are presented as part of Made in L.A. through the generosity of Jarl and Pamela Mohn. Two are selected by a jury of curators: the Mohn Award for artistic excellence, for which the awardee receives $100,000 and a book of their

8

work published by the Hammer; and the $25,000 Career Achievement Award, which recognizes an artist in the biennial who has been practicing in Los Angeles for decades. A third award, the $25,000 Public Recognition Award, will be determined through votes cast by visitors to the exhibition. All three are underwritten by the Mohn Family Foundation, which provides additional support for the exhibition. I sincerely appreciate the Mohns' ongoing partnership and the warm welcome that they extended to me as I entered this remarkable partnership.

The Hammer Circle has grown with each Made in L.A. biennial as an engaged and enthusiastic community of inspired collectors interested in emerging talent. Since the start of Made in L.A. in 2012, the Hammer Circle has provided an essential foundation of financial support for the biennial, and we are grateful for their continued endorsement of this iteration. Special thanks to the Hammer Circle's chair, Tracy O'Brien, for her dedication and leadership.

I offer deepest gratitude to our friends of the Hammer for their support and belief in the vision of Made in L.A. 2025. Major support has been provided by The Billy and Audrey L. Wilder Foundation, Miky Lee, and Mark Sandelson. Generous funding for Made in L.A. has been provided by The Fran and Ray Stark Foundation; Bill Hair; Susan Genco and Mitch Kamin; J.P. Morgan; Dori Peterman Mostov and Charles Mostov; and Orange Barrel Media. Additional support has been provided by The Buddy Taub Foundation, Dennis A. Roach and Stephanie Roach, Directors; McCrea Foundation; the Pasadena Art Alliance;

The Rhonda S. Zinner Foundation and Jonathan Segal; and Michael Silver. My heartfelt thanks to each funder for sharing our commitment to uplifting the voices of these extraordinary artists. On behalf of the curators, I would like to extend our deepest thanks to the lenders, who generously shared works from their collections in support of the exhibition. Their names can be found on page 336.

I am thrilled to continue the indelible legacy of my predecessor, Ann Philbin, in spearheading our shared belief in championing the artists who make up the dynamic creative ecosystem of Los Angeles. Every edition of Made in L.A. has offered complex ideas that are presented within even more complex installations. Organizing a biennial is a monumental undertaking that could not be possible without the extraordinary talents and labor of our staff at every level of the museum, who are recognized on pages 339–340. I am deeply appreciative of the work every person offers to ensure the success of our exhibitions and programs; Made in L.A. is no exception.

I would lastly like to extend my deepest gratitude to all the artists for entrusting their work to us. It is a profound honor to share your contributions at the Hammer locally, nationally, and internationally. I look forward to welcoming the conversations and exchanges that stem from these projects and am eager to see how this work contributes to the evolving legacy of Made in L.A. for years to come.

Zoë Ryan, Director

Curatorial Acknowledgments

Made in L.A. 2025 reflects our shared belief that Los Angeles is a complex and unfolding landscape through which artists think, feel, and speculate. We approached this exhibition without a fixed thesis, allowing the city, its artists, and their practices to guide us. What emerged is a show shaped by intuition, trust, and the rhythms of conversation—what we've called a "no-methodology methodology." The vastness of Los Angeles extends far beyond its physical borders; it is a terrain of invention, as Kellie Jones notes in *South of Pico: African American Artists in Los Angeles in the 1960s and 1970s* (Duke University Press, 2017), shaped by layered histories of migration, improvisation, and self-making. Its contradictions—spatial, cultural, economic—don't constrain it but animate it.

The result: a field of overlapping temporalities, vernacular aesthetics, domestic architectures, public forums, and, most importantly, communities. Everything we encountered during our research fed our thinking. The art in this show could not have been made anywhere besides

Los Angeles, and that, perhaps, is the most defining characteristic of Made in L.A. 2025.

We extend our greatest appreciation to the hundreds of artists who welcomed us to their studios over the last two years. This exhibition results from the conversations that making art engenders and the cumulative knowledge that the extraordinary artists of this city offered with fervor, generosity, and goodwill. While the Hammer Museum's galleries are not large enough to hold even a small portion of the unforgettable works we encountered over the course of planning, Los Angeles certainly is. We urge the visitors to this exhibition to follow their curiosities and share in the art that vigorously animates so much of the city.

When, in 2012, Ann Philbin, former director of the Hammer Museum, initiated the very first Made in L.A., she gave form to the creative energies of this city. Thirteen years later, the vibrant art scene of Los Angeles would be impossible to imagine without Made in L.A. as an anchor. Ann also had the prescience to set the two of us up on a professional blind date—the best blind date we've ever been on. Thank you, Ann, for the magnitude of your vision and the scrupulous attention you devote to each and every detail of all that crosses your path.

Zoë Ryan assumed the directorship of the Hammer in the middle of our planning, as Los Angeles was on fire. Her unflappable composure set the tone for her stewardship of this exceptional institution. To this exhibition, she has offered indispensable insight with humility, wisdom, and tact, from our first meeting to our last.

12

This show would not have moved forward without the wholehearted support of Cynthia Burlingham, former deputy director for curatorial affairs; she has been a part of the Hammer from its inauguration, and her familiarity with all iterations of Made in L.A. is without equal. The leadership of Fred Yeries, deputy director of external affairs, made funding this exhibition possible. Todd Quinn and Michael Harrison offered steadfast support through a turbulent period of local and global distress as, respectively, the Hammer's interim and former deputy directors of finance, operations, and administration.

The Hammer Museum's Board of Directors have displayed their unwavering commitment to Made in L.A. time and again. Marcy Carsey, chair; Eric Esrailian, vice-chair; and Michael Rubel, president, led the board during the preparation of this year's exhibition with dependable intelligence and savvy. We are also grateful to Dr. Julio Frenk, UCLA chancellor and member of the Hammer board, for his dedication to the artist and arts-worker communities of the university.

A generosity of spirit, boundless curiosity, and deep belief in the power of art distinguishes Jarl and Pamela Mohn. Their largesse has enabled us to explore all the art that this city has to offer and share what we learned in the pages of this publication and on the walls of the museum. The Hammer Circle and its many members offered major support for this exhibition. We also relied on major support from The Billy and Audrey L. Wilder Foundation, Miky Lee, and Mark Sandelson. Generous support was provided by The Fran and Ray Stark Foundation; Bill Hair; Susan Genco and Mitch Kamin; J.P. Morgan; Dori Peterman Mostov and Charles Mostov; and Orange Barrel Media. Additional support was provided by The Buddy Taub Foundation, Dennis A. Roach and Stephanie Roach, Directors; McCrea Foundation; the Pasadena Art Alliance; The Rhonda S. Zinner Foundation and Jonathan Segal; and Michael Silver.

Made in L.A. is a show assembled from objects and images coming directly from artists' studios. In only a handful of instances, we asked for loans from private individuals. Their willingness to temporarily part with beloved works from their collections underscores the care and seriousness of their custodianship. We would like to thank the estate of Alonzo Davis, especially Dale Brockman Davis as well as Christopher Heijnen of Parrasch Heijnen for their enthusiastic support of re-creating on the museum's walls Davis's iconic mural conceived and made in Los Angeles for the 1984 Olympics. Our appreciation also extends to all the galleries that work with the artists in this presentation, large and small. They are crucial to the art ecosystem of this city.

Like all institutions, the Hammer Museum is not an abstract monolith but a community of art professionals who, in their jobs, exceed all standards of excellence. Fred Yeries, deputy director for external affairs; Nicole Berry, senior director of donor engagement; Aiza Keesey, chief development officer; and their talented team including Bryan Alfaro, Courtney Raterman Casal, Paula Conde-Porto,

Teresa Fleming, Renato Gontijo, Beth Harker, Sophie Helm, Isabella Kefgen, Dylan King, Brennen Ogawa, and Jade Wisansky, orchestrated the extensive fundraising and outreach needed to realize a project as ambitious as this. We would like to thank all of the members of the Hammer's curatorial team. Erin Christovale, curator, shared her wisdom and offered critical input at every juncture. Her infectious laughter kept us going. Pablo José Ramírez, curator, who had just opened *Made in L.A. 2023: Acts of Living* as we embarked on the 2025 edition, offered crucial insight built on his immediate experience throughout the planning process. We relied on former interim chief curator Aram Moshayedi's institutional knowledge to orient us to this project and to the museum.

Designing an exhibition where much of the artwork has not yet been made requires an extraordinarily talented and flexible team. We acknowledge the tireless creativity of Adam Peña, manager of exhibition design and production, and Maribel Ruiz, coordinator of exhibition design and production. Their sensitivity to space is palpable throughout the galleries. Portland McCormick, director of registration and collections management, has been indispensable to this presentation. Portland, together with Shira Abramsohn, Julie Dickover, Susan Hersey, Alexandra Moran, and Emma Rudman, shouldered every challenge and intricacy of this project with uncompromising attention to the care of the works in the show. Their precision and rigor was mirrored by the preparatory team of Angelica Perez-Aguirre, Jason Pugh, Michael Terzano, and Chris

Zickefoose. Scott Tennent, chief communications officer, and Vanessa Arizmendi, Nathalie Chybik, Lisa Davis, Ramon Espinosa, Lauren Graycar, Ashley Kruythoff, Philip Leers, Tara Morris, Gabriel Noguez, and Santiago Pazos created the platform for sharing the exhibition's many stories with the public; Claudia Bestor, director of public programs, and Shannon Cynowa, manager of public programs, developed public programs that give vitality to the exhibition; Hallie Scott, associate director of academic programs, with Sonja Cayetano, Alice Kaufman, Kai Monet, and Rachel Regalado, facilitated access and interpretation; and Lauren Coryell, Lionel Deatherage, Madicyn Herbst, Malaya Johnson, Alexis Tongue, and their many team members in Visitor Services and Gallery Operations staffed the galleries and made them welcoming to all the Hammer's visitors. Too many to name, our colleagues in the Facilities and Security departments have met the many unusual demands presented by this exhibition with zeal.

The achievements of this catalogue are the product of collective brilliance. First, we offer profound thanks to the authors of the illuminating texts this publication contains. Thank you to Taylor Aldridge, Sampada Aranke, Giampaolo Bianconi, Annika Bohanec, Jennifer Buonocore-Nedrelow, Kate Durbin, David Getsy, Esti Giordani, Chinaka Hodge, Suzanne Hudson, Summer Kim Lee, Todd Lerew, Ali Liebegott, Henoch Moore, Terence Nance, Kate Nesin, Leigh Raiford, Heidi Schreck, and Robeson Taj Frazier. Douglas Fogle gamely joined us in the conversation printed in these pages. Domenick Ammirati, the editor

16

of this volume, has been a trusted collaborator. The book's designers, Folder Studio, bestowed order and elegance to what at the start seemed unruly. We extend our thanks to Karen Kelly and Barbara Schroeder of Dancing Foxes; our conversations gave form to this publication.

To think that Made in L.A. 2025 would be possible without Michael Nock, director, exhibition and publication management, would be an exercise of hubris. Previous iterations of this exhibition counted at least one of the curators as an employee of the museum. Not this time—Michael was our "in-house" advocate. He shouldered every challenge and intricacy of this project with intelligence, creativity, and grace. His contributions reverberate across this catalogue and throughout the museum's galleries. Jennifer Buonocore-Nedrelow, curatorial assistant, shepherded this show from start to finish. We relied on her deep knowledge, eager spirit, and organizational acumen time and again. She was assisted in her efforts by Juan Silverio, curatorial assistant, who joined the curatorial team in the final phases and made sure we crossed the finish line. Exhibition coordinator Andie Kimura's steady hand, precision, and humor belied the difficult task she had of organizing and managing a terrifyingly complex schedule of studio visits. She made sure we were on time, focused, and fed when everything felt in flux and the project ahead seemed nearly insurmountable. We are honored to have worked with Andie and miss her presence daily.

We extend our deepest gratitude to the twenty-eight artists of Made in L.A. 2025. Their works not only reflect the diverse and dynamic spirit of Los Angeles but also challenge and inspire us to see the world anew. Collaborating with each artist has been an honor, and their contributions are the heartbeat of this biennial. We are profoundly thankful for their trust, creativity, and the dialogues that have enriched this journey.

—Essence Harden and Paulina Pobocha

To Paulina Pobocha, who has made this process absolutely fun, engaging, rigorous, and possible. As I've said to anyone who will listen, our arranged marriage became a love marriage upon meeting, and I cannot wait to continue collaborating together in the decades to come.

To my forever collaborators and thought partners in art—Taylor Renee Aldridge, Se Young Au, Sadie Barnette, Erin Christovale, Meg Fransee, Esti Giordani, Yeshi Gusfield, Kyle Halle-Earby, Lauren Halsey, Naima J. Keith, Rena Karefa-Johnson, Kyla McMillan, Christine Messineo, Bianca Moran, Diana Nawi, Leigh Raiford, Adee Roberson, Martine Syms—thank you for your brilliance, generosity, and constant exchange.

To my love, Jihaari Terry, who champions, celebrates, and is always willing to talk through anything with me, and my baby girl, Ozell, who makes life's pursuits worth it.

Lastly, to my generational home—California, and especially Oakland, Berkeley, and Los Angeles—I love you.

—EH

Eleven months into the planning of Made in L.A., I assumed the position of chair and curator of modern and contemporary art at the Art Institute of Chicago. From the first, I had the unflinching support of James Rondeau, President and Eloise W. Martin Director. James believes in the importance of Made in L.A. and shared in my enthusiasm to see this project through its completion. In the months since, I have flown back and forth from Los Angeles to Chicago more times than I can count. I am indebted to the patience and support of my colleagues at AIC, especially Sarah Guernsey, deputy director and senior vice president for curatorial affairs, and the Department of Modern and Contemporary Art.

Many people in L.A. have become wonderful friends. I am especially grateful for the engaging and insightful conversations I've shared with Doug Aitken, Jack Bankowsky, John Knight, Silvia Gaspardo Moro, Charles Ray, and Shaun Regen.

Essence Harden, consider this exhibition and accompanying publication a love letter. It has been an honor to work alongside you.

Greg and Matilda, I am indebted to you most of all. This exhibition, every exhibition that has preceded it, and all those that will follow are built on your support, selflessness, love, and fearless ability to remind me of what planet I live on.

—PP

Essence Harden and Paulina Pobocha

in conversation with Douglas Fogle

PAULINA POBOCHA   This will probably come up in the conversation, because I say it over and over, but we have no ideas. And I think that's good.

DOUGLAS FOGLE   Let's not hold that thought.

ESSENCE HARDEN   Yeah, well, I like to feel a bit meandering, because that's actually how this process has worked—

D.F.   Are we recording yet, by the way? We are? Okay.

E.H.   And my hope is that you get a sense of how me and Paulina actually are, and that it doesn't feel too didactic or dry. I want it to feel useful, but also process-y. And natural. And caffeinated. I prepared nothing so that I could just see how my brain responds to the time we're in. Right?

D.F.   Okay.

P.P.   Back to the whole "We have no ideas" thing: We came to this project with no preconceived plan to show this type of artist, or focus on this community of artists. While there are actually surprising undercurrents that connect almost everyone, those came to the surface after the fact.

Of course, saying that we have no ideas underplays or—what's the word?—belies the fact we find some things more interesting than others. Right?

E.H.   When I hear "no ideas," I always think of *Seinfeld* and Larry David. I think it's funny to say it that way, and it aligns with how I do the curatorial thing, coming from a non-art-historian background.

The process was organic. There's a lot of trust in both of our practices, and in each other. Having that trust meant that we could say, "It will resolve itself naturally." Part of that is *our* relationship—feeling connected, spending time with each other, chatting about all kinds of shit. Paulina and I are so different on paper, but we have a shared sensibility about the work itself.

It's about the object, performance, material, etc.; the art, whatever it is, is primary rather than us using someone's biography as a strategy to foreground our ideas. We were more intrigued by how we felt when we were in the studio with the work and our conversations with these artists about their practice.

22

D.F.   How did you collectively decide which artists to visit?

P.P.   This is actually really uninteresting. The Hammer has a list that's, like, two thousand people long, and we reviewed it. And that's how we arrived at our first round of visits, then after a certain point, it was really suggestions of friends, suggestions of other artists that we met along the way—a Rube Goldberg, domino effect.

E.H.   Paulina and I talk at weird hours, often at 4 and 5 a.m. So, I don't remember us ever having this kind of conversation directly, but we realized that it wasn't going to be, "You get to have a couple of people, and I get to have a couple of people, and we're going to agree on 75 percent." It was, "No. We have to agree on everything."

P.P.   There was no veto. That just seemed antithetical to the whole operation.

E.H.   It means that we talk a lot; "What do you think about this? Does this make sense?"

P.P.   It's about introducing ideas. Right? Like when you brought up Black House Radio. You're just like—

E.H.   "I don't know what this is."

D.F.   I know in the first press release I read, "We're focusing on emerging." But clearly, from your list, there's a beautiful texture of different generations.

P.P.   Just to backtrack, because I think it all funnels into the same place, I moved to Los Angeles in January 2024. I had visited plenty, but getting here, I realized I really don't know this city, and it functions very differently from the types of cities that I'm used to. I lived in New York for twenty-six years, and my other touchstones are European cities.

So, I think the type of work that I was most interested in somehow engaged the city itself, took the city as a subject matter. Some of the artists are working in what we consider the conventional art world. Some, not at all. But almost everyone touches on the character of the city. I think the work that is on the checklist couldn't have been made anywhere else. I don't think that that's necessarily true for previous versions of Made in L.A.—or I dunno, maybe I'm wrong in that assessment.

E.H.   I've lived here for ten years, but I grew up in the Bay Area. When you are from California, you generally have a relationship with Los Angeles because you have to.

It was really cool to have Paulina move here in the beginning of this process. She didn't know the city, and it made me stretch myself in ways. I don't do certain things because it takes a long time to get there. And with this, you have to. So, I thought "This is really good for my brain to

24

remember that the geography and the county itself is gigantic." The experience of Made in L.A. is actually exploring the county.

 Glendale! I went to Glendale on a Saturday to visit a gallery and very clearly remember how abstract the whole experience was: "Now I'm in Glendale." For whatever reason, it was such a strange moment—Where am I in life? I'm in Glendale.

Anyway, I love Glendale.

From the idea of Made in L.A., one would think it was a horizontal survey, but L.A. isn't just about city planning it, and it isn't just a horizontal place. It's a place with history. You're moving across the landscape physically but also conceptually, left to right, right to left, up and down, through time. Sometimes it felt upside down—artists envisioning a future, and artists building on the long history of art making in the city. All that was important to us.

This is a bit of a side note, but when I was working at MoMA with Robert Gober, he once said something that has stayed with me. He said that he's often asked *who* his influences are; *who* are other artists you're influenced by? But few really considered the fact that *what* you're influenced by is maybe what you read in the newspaper in the morning, maybe what you had for breakfast—the fact that you didn't have your blueberry muffin.

I think a lot of these studio visits are a reflection of not just some sort of grand art-historical idea but reacting to the day-to-day, to the time in which we're living, to the

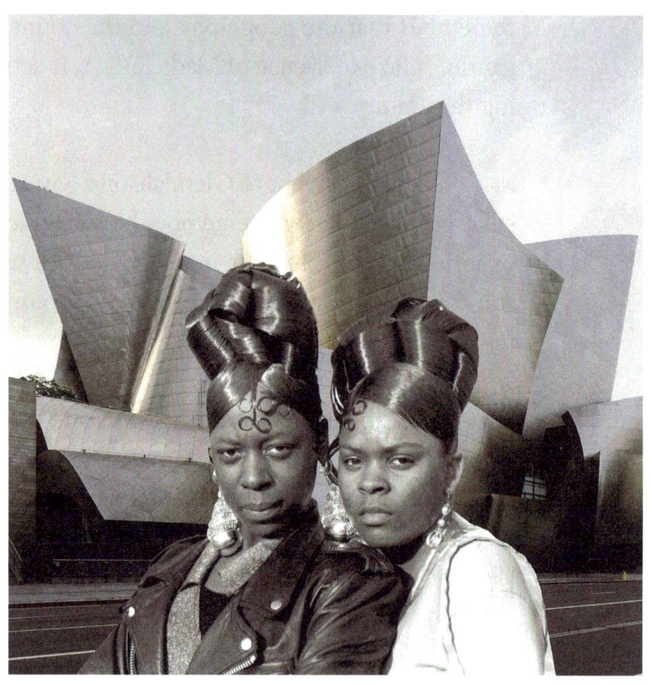

Jerald Cooper, *Baltimore Girls*, 2022. Photo collage. 12 × 12 in. (30.5 × 30.5 cm)

fact that you were stuck behind a train for an hour and a half and you could not make it across that intersection. That gives you a lot of time to think—I'd never really seen a freight train—not in a way that registered. Everyday occurrences inevitably filter into the context of the studio visit, and the things that come to the surface during those conversations.

D.F.   So many have defined Los Angeles as this completely horizontal cultural and physical landscape. Reyner Banham, the British architectural historian who loved the city, used to tell this story. When scholars wanted to read Dante, they learned Italian. When they wanted to learn about Los Angeles, they had to learn to drive to experience it.

What I see in what you two have put together is diagonality—vectors rather than any kind of woven tapestry. I'm thinking about the visual artists, and how they're punctuated on your list by groups like Black House Radio, and also dealing with time-based work, or the New Theater Hollywood and the theatrical thing.

I'm very interested in how as curators you came upon them, and then realized how you might bring them all together within the white cube, because many of these are organic practices that happen in the world and involve people in different kinds of settings.

E.H.   For Black House Radio, and for Hood Century, I followed them on Instagram. I've been following Hood Century for years, and thought the online presence was very interesting. It's an archive; it deals with L.A. but also other cities. Here, they organize tours of homes in historically Black neighborhoods, like Ladera Heights and Baldwin Hills and what we would broadly call South Central. It's about making a connection between modernism and Black life in this and other cities.

With Black House Radio, I didn't really know what it was. My spouse plays records for a living, and he introduced me to a recorded session. What I saw was a living room being filmed in a single frame. The shot of the space included a bunch of Black family portraits on the wall, an older couch covered in plastic, and a DJ sitting and spinning on said couch with a party happening around them. When I see something and wonder, "What exactly is this?" it's my inclination to ask for a studio visit.

Michael Donte, who founded Black House Radio, is trying to connect his generation with a historical arc of music making that has been central to queer Black people. And he's doing it by putting it back into this domestic site. It centers this question around architecture and domesticity, and Black Los Angeles, the same thread we saw with Hood Century.

P.P.   We just came from a meeting about the floor plan, and about how we're going to have Michael DJ parties at the museum, which is something that's happened during Made in L.A.'s past. But when the space is, let's say, dormant, when there aren't live DJ sets happening, there might be a lot of speakers, and maybe some TVs streaming archived

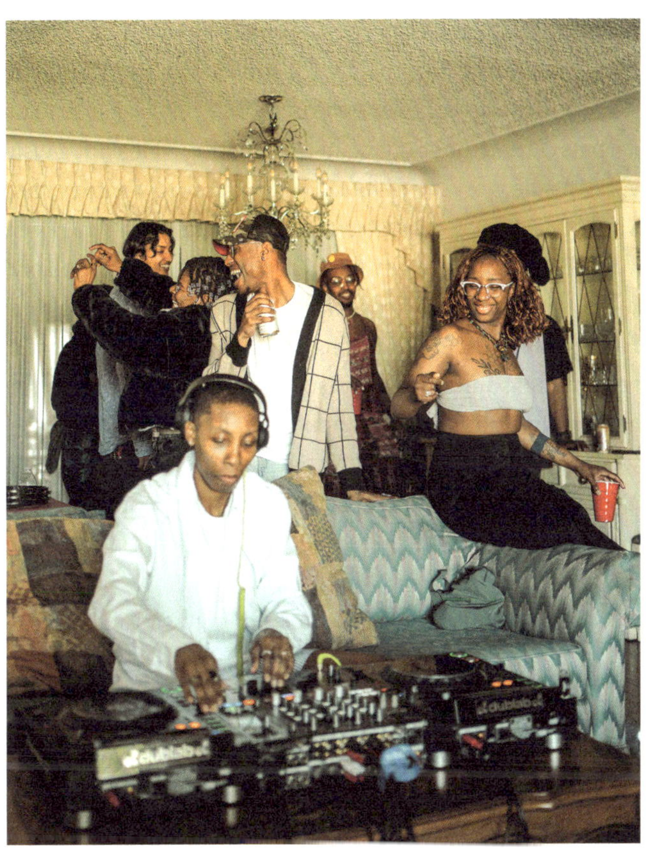

Black House Radio event, Los Angeles, April 2024

footage of these dance parties, to give some sense of it. We'll have some carpeting, mainly for sound, but also to nod at domestic space. When we were talking about what kind of carpets, I remember saying in the meeting, "He's not a visual artist—he works with music. It doesn't really matter what kind of carpets. Let's just get some carpets from wherever."

Because the point here is not to create a simulacra of the space where Michael hosts his parties; it's not about faking some space, presenting a couch covered in plastic, re-creating something that isn't here. It's about the music, and community, and it's about giving people access, the way that we experienced it, from afar—well, except not on a computer but on a larger screen, so more people can see it at once. Logistics!

E.H.   It's a sensation we are after, not replication.

P.P.   Right. We're not bringing in plastic-covered couches.

E.H.   It's cool to work with people who don't do this; the museum, the false sentiment of a neutral space, is not his jam. Maybe it will be afterward, but this is his first exploration into it. And so, we get to be in this really exciting conversation of how we distill what he's doing for a museum audience.

P.P.   The only thing we're "reproducing" is the experience of watching this stream online but we're doing this, by necessity, in a public space.

30

D.F.   What about New Theater Hollywood? How did
that happen, and how will it manifest itself within the
gallery space?

P.P.   I've spent a lot of time in Germany. Over probably the
last nine years, I would go maybe every four months, working on a long-term exhibition project. While I was mainly
in the Rhineland, I would go to Berlin to visit friends. And
so, I had known about New Theater for some time, which
started in Berlin (though Max and Calla are both from the
United States; they met at Cooper Union, if I'm remembering correctly). A lot of the artists would perform there.

They moved to Hollywood right around the time
that I did. And it was just so bizarre to me that you would
take something that to me seems so German, so Dada, and
all of this that is built on Berlin's very particular, more than
a century-long history of avant-garde experimental theater,
and move it to Los Angeles, where historical precedent
doesn't seem to exist and yet "theater" is the heart of the entertainment industry. There are actors everywhere.

D.F.   This all came from Weimar. Most of what we experience as the entertainment business and the cinema came
from the huge influx of immigrants because of the war, and
even before the war.

P.P.   And this history, this not-so-obvious history, under-
mines this idea that in Los Angeles the culture is very thin,
that it's horizontal. Theodor Adorno lived here in the 1930s,

31

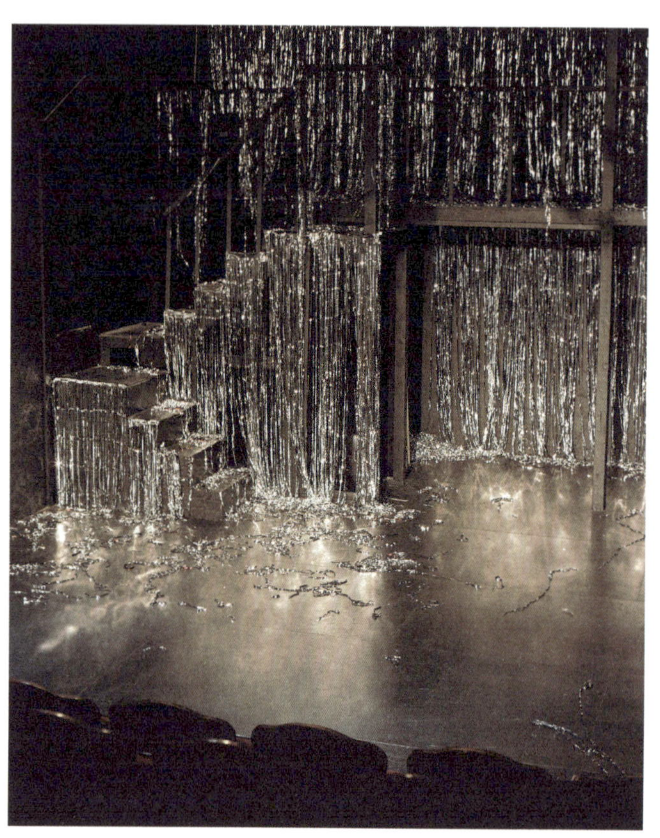

New Theater Hollywood

32

and then came back in the 1950s. William Faulkner wrote for Hollywood. All of the entertainment industry here is built on such a rich past that's largely unknown to most. There was an interesting tension around the idea of New Theater Hollywood and well, Hollywood—Tinseltown, yeah?—because avant-garde theater isn't really part of the culture anymore, if it ever was. Maybe the closest thing would be drag clubs, or experimental music venues, or comedy—Pee-Wee Herman came from somewhere. How do you start something that comes with a ready-made audience in a place like Berlin here in Los Angeles?

Leilah [Weinraub]'s writing a play about growing up in L.A. that's going to be staged at New Theater. Max and Calla are producing her play, but just to complicate matters, they also have been making an episodic, fictionalized TV series where they play themselves producing New Theater productions.

D.F.   Meta. Meta. Meta. But not in that bad way.

P.P.   In a way that makes me ask, "What are you thinking?"…I love it.

D.F.   Could you talk a little bit about the more senior artists who are in Made in L.A., the range of work, and their legacies in this town, and how that feeds into what you've been thinking about?

P.P.   Well…architectural history, looking at urban planning. Immediately John Knight came to mind as someone who was born in Hollywood, has lived in Los Angeles his entire life, who was trained as an architect, but very quickly pivoted to conceptual art. He's *theeee* conceptual artist in the show, and maybe—alongside Michael Asher, though he's dead—in the city.

The work that we're showing is from the 1970s. It's called *Quiet Quality* (1974); it is an electric blanket and a text pulled from the *Los Angeles Real Estate Supplement* published sometime in the 1970s. He had been collecting these texts from the paper, clipping things out, and gathering them in a box.

The work from this period is about the expansion of L.A.'s suburbs, and that too relates to race, class, economics. It's after the Watts Uprisings, white flight from the city, and the absurd strategies of these developers, and the way that these new housing developments were marketed to middle-class and upper-middle-class white people as oases outside of the city. So John's work just seemed like a perfect complement to what Hood Century was doing. And then here is someone who approaches a very similar subject but in a way that's *almost* completely dematerialized (save, in this case, for the electric blanket).

E.H.   Another artist who's making work about Los Angeles, maybe less directly, is Pat O'Neill. I knew him as an experimental filmmaker. But in his studio there were these sculptures, and this series of photographs that he had

34

made over a long period of time, actually between here and New York and the Bay Area—

P.P.   And New Jersey. I'm from New Jersey.

E.H.   New Jersey. Don't forget!

P.P.   Don't even think about it.

E.H.   The sculptures, which are from the 1960s and 1970s, were about cityscapes, car culture, the urban chaos of these places at these particular moments. They use fiberglass and car paint, which are elements very present around the vintage cars he collected, or his father's cars that are all in his yard. They're these incredible abstract forms, and they were just so casually sitting in the studio. Light was streaming in from the glass door onto the sculptures, so we got that pop, like automotive paint in the sun.

We were obsessed. When he went to UCLA with Carl [Cheng] in the 1950s, there wasn't an MFA program, and because they're both from the Los Angeles area, they used materials of, broadly speaking, the aerospace and auto industries.

That thing of someone making in a place for a really long period, even if it's not widely known in its time…It seeds the Earth. Other people can create sculpture that builds on legacies that may be invisible to them, that they might not even know about. But Pat's work seeds the ideas, the presentation, the relationship to technology. Just using the tools and materials around you, to have something to say about the particular histories and realities of *this* place.

It did the same thing to me when I was talking to Carl, and when we were talking about John—I realized, "Holy shit. These people are foundational to everything I'm looking at right now."

p.p.   One thing with Pat is that—and I'm speculating here—because of his success as an experimental filmmaker, his work in sculpture seemed to be overlooked.

For me, in the space of the exhibition, it nicely points to the whole generation, his generational cohort of artists like Craig Kaufman and Larry Bell and Robert Irwin and DeWain Valentine, sculptors who are working with the same or similar materials whose work is widely known and who are so closely associated with L.A. This is all part of that same history.

e.h.   My favorite exhibitions are the ones where I say to myself, "I have no clue what's going to be happening here. That's great." When people come to the exhibition, being surprised should be part of the experience. I want people to feel excited about what they thought they were going to see, and think, "Oh, I never knew of this work. I forgot about this work. I didn't realize that this person did this."

Pat's studio really did that to me. We were just there recently, picking work, and I thought, "Fucking Christ. This is so good." After you see art like that, you feel kind of

36

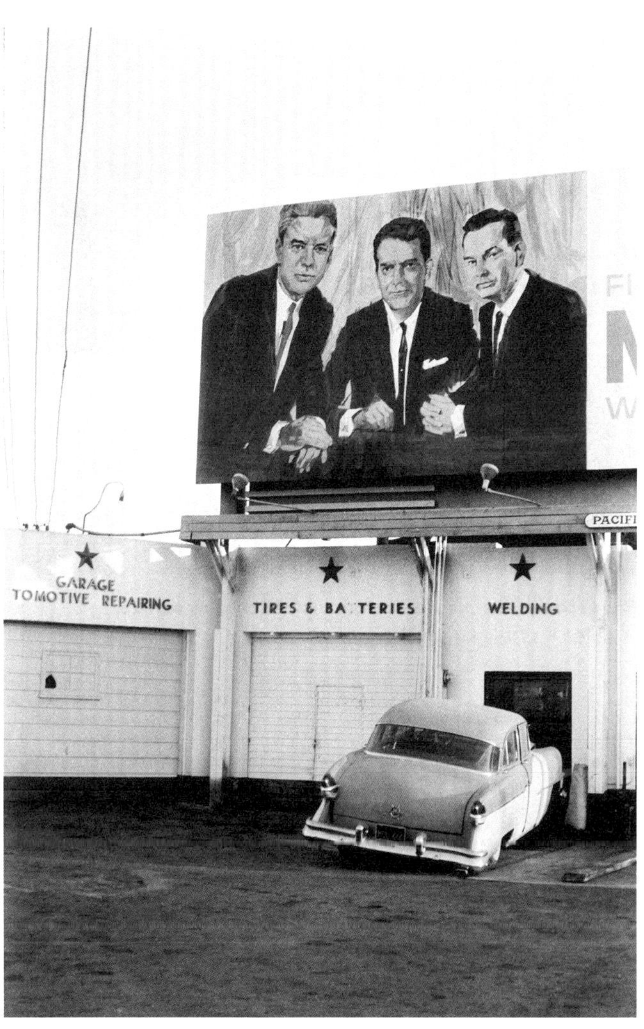

Pat O'Neill, *Los Angeles*, from the series *Cars and Other Problems*, ca. 1960s. Printed and published by Curatorial Inc. Archival pigment print. Frame: 24 ½ × 20 ½ in. (62.2 × 50 cm)

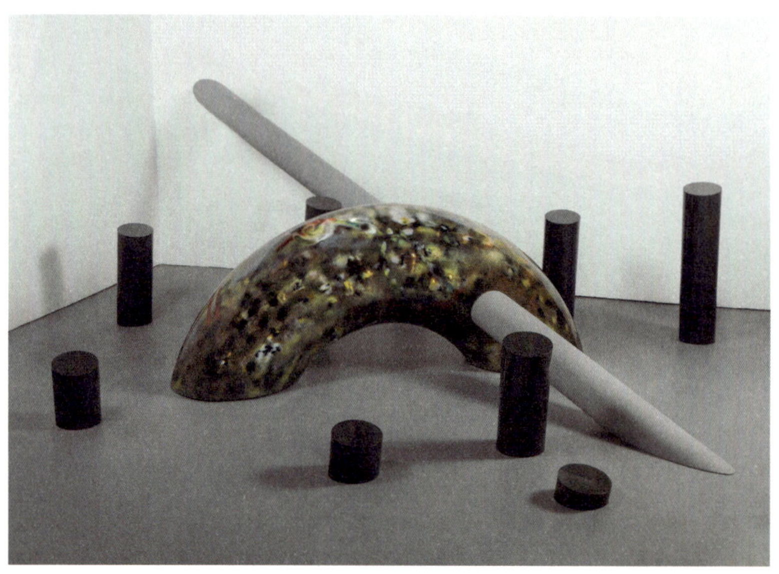

Pat O'Neill, *British Columbia Sweep*, 1970. Fiberglass, wood, lacquer surface.
144 × 180 × 48 in. (365.8 × 457.2 × 121.9 cm)

high, like you had eight coffees. Or the best meal of your life, or twelve martinis, or something.

p.p.   Maybe not twelve.

e.h.   Maybe four.

d.f.   I would love for you both to talk a little bit about the painters in the exhibition. How did you balance people working in different styles? Was it just the hunch and the feeling of the work? Were you thinking about figurative painting versus abstract?

e.h.   Uh-uh.

d.f.   Nothing?

p.p.   No.

d.f.   Who is the youngest artist working in that medium?

e.h.   Ali Eyal, probably.

p.p.   Ali was a really early visit. He's a very good painter. I tend to avoid art that relies too much on biography. But his work strongly draws on his personal history as an Iraqi who lived through the US invasion of Iraq and lost a large part of his family, I think his father among others. His paintings in many ways deal with his own trauma.

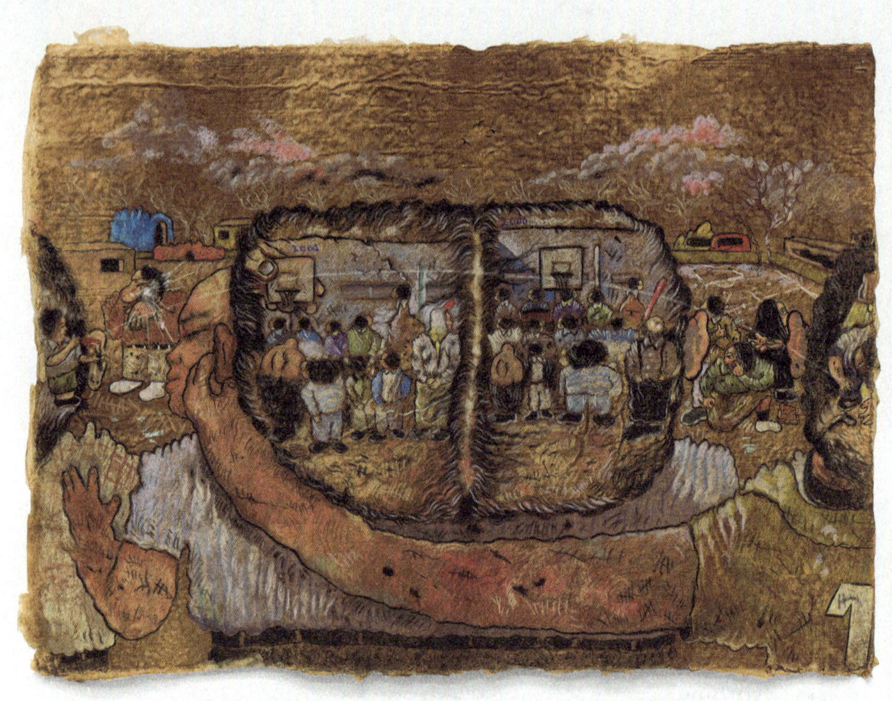

Ali Eyal, *Just a group school photo, but…*, 2024. Pastel on Japanese paper. 21 × 30 in. (53.3 × 76.2 cm)

40

And yet he's able to take that and digest it in a way that it is not singular to him. When you're looking at his paintings, you have these vignettes of different things that he remembers stitched together. I think the way that he represents images on the canvas is very similar to how memory works, where you have these disparate moments colliding, and maybe not fully making narrative sense. It reaches far beyond his personal experiences to something that everyone can relate to, even if it's maybe only structural, a representation of how images flow in and out of your head and collide or fall away from each other, or part ways.

He's also dealing with the tropes of narrative. He'll represent a ripped page on the edges of the canvas. First, you're looking at what seems to be a straightforward representation of some scene, but then you realize that it's already filtered through not only his own personal memory but also how memory gets transcribed on paper or canvas—it also addresses the limits of painting. The style is cartoonish and grotesque. It's figurative, it's representational, but his style is very loose, and a level of abstraction comes through in his paint application.

I don't know. I think it was just, like, he's a good painter.

D.F.   Did he go to school here?

P.P.   He went to school in Baghdad. I know another artist, who lives in London—nothing to do with the show—who also went to school in Baghdad, and they had the most conventional training. Both of them could paint a room without referencing photography just by walking in, looking around, leaving, going to their studio, and painting it with photographic realism. That is extraordinary training—which you then unlearn.

E.H.   I remember he said something about using Disney characters to learn how to draw as a kid.

P.P.   That's everyone, by the way.

E.H.   Disneyland came up a gazillion times. I've never thought about Disneyland as much in my life.

P.P.   At the start, I said, "There's going to be so much about Disney." And Essence replied, "No. There's not."

D.F.   How did he end up in Los Angeles?

P.P.   His wife goes to UCLA. But I'm not quite sure if that is the reason they came to L.A., or even how long they've been here.

E.H.   The Hammer didn't give us any requirements about the longetivity of your being here. And that's really useful, because it's a real city. People come here, they move here, they change places all of the time.

I wanted to consider the work of Will Rawls, who I think moved here probably the most recently of anyone—he teaches at UCLA now and he was in New York for

42

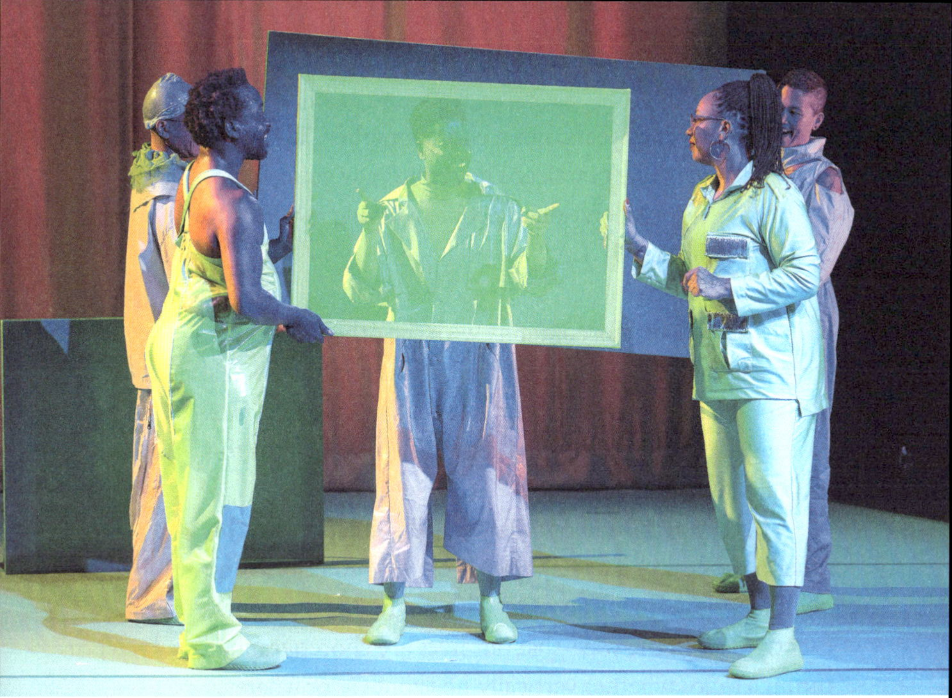

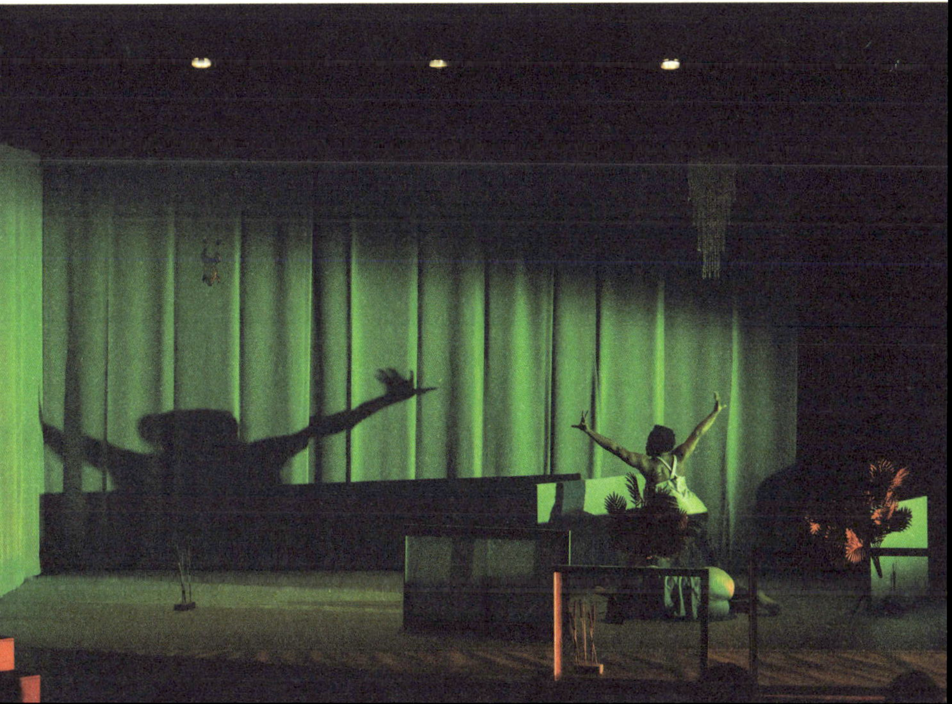

Will Rawls, *[siccer]*, 2023. Performance and installation diptych

twenty years; he's a choreographer. This person has an incredible practice. They're literally going to be teaching the next generation of people working in performance coming out of UCLA.

D.F.   The idea of choreography with the other things you were talking about, from DJ culture to even John's electric blanket, really frames this idea beautifully. Los Angeles exploiting itself, and Ali coming across Disney…there's this global connectivity.

But if you think about that book on Situationism, that title, "A passage of a few people through a rather brief moment in time"—I'm misquoting—choreography is, of course, exactly that, in the ways that our lives are choreographed through a city, whether vertically, horizontally, or whatever.

E.H.   Will has a relationship to space. He asked about the layout of the exhibition in the earlier stages of planning. So, just like painting or sculpture, Will is a part of the layout as well. It's not ancillary to what we're doing.

D.F.   Are there any other nooks and crannies of the show, and other artists that come to mind that you both would like to talk about?

E.H.   Greg Breda. The plant life in his backyard is featured in almost every painting—the flowers, the way that light moves through the work. His interest in spirituality around it feels so specific to growing up in Inglewood, his

44

relationship with his mother, the passing of time, the passing of light in his studio.

P.P.   Similarly—but then not at all—there's Beaux Mendes. They're a plein air painter. Like, who is a plein air painter? It sounds so anachronistic. Almost every weekend they leave the city with their truck, go to Angeles National Forest, and paint the landscape there.

And then you go to the studio, and you see these paintings of gnarled trees, and other observations of nature that, in fact, look like nothing you would expect from a plein air painter, if you even think about conventional plein air painting. Meaning that the images are representational, but these objects in nature, their identities are barely legible. If no one tells you that this is some part of the tree, it could be an image of body parts entwining, it could be mitochondrial DNA, it could just be an abstract painting— and maybe it's everything all at once, or in succession, changing as you're looking, completely unstable.

D.F.   Widline Cadet is someone I'm intrigued by. She's a photographer and sculptor, Haitian, born and raised in New York, and was teaching at UCLA when she first moved here a few years ago.

E.H.   Widline's interpretation of Los Angeles mirrors lots of Haitian elements, like the architecture. She's fascinated by the breezeway structures that we have all over the city for apartment buildings and homes and how those

45

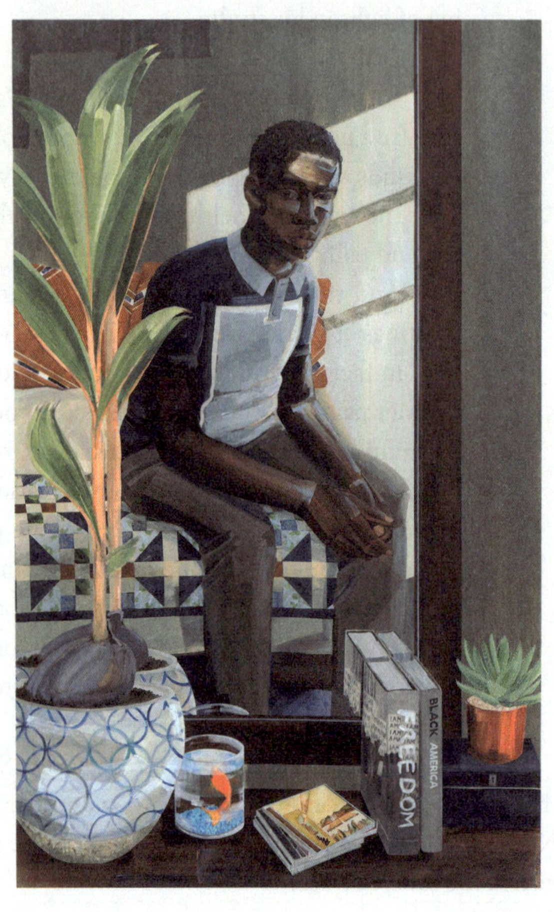

Greg Breda, *A Ladder*, 2018. Acrylic on vellum. 63 × 40 in. (160 × 101.6 cm)

46

are omnipresent in Haiti as well. People reduce California as not belonging to anywhere else. But it's really fascinating to me when artists move here, and they say, "Oh, this thing that's from very far away reminds me of some element of home."

P.P.   That just made me think of Freddy Villalobos. He said something really interesting during our studio visit. He was an AV tech here at the Hammer, and one of the art handlers said, "Go visit Freddy." OK, we're going to go visit Freddy. I went, and his project was super interesting. So, first of all, you'll see a film that he shot. Please someone remind me of the street—I'm still new.

D.F.   Figueroa.

P.P.   Figueroa. So, it's in the neighborhood where he grew up, and it's just him driving down Figueroa to the place where Sam Cooke was murdered. The sound is a Sam Cooke recording slowed down with low end hertz like he used a low pass filter. And then also in the installation are these Donald Judd-esque boxes filled with concrete. The subwoofer plays at such a low frequency, it's not so much that you hear it, but you feel it. And then over the course of the exhibition, the concrete starts breaking apart. In the studio, even in the short time that this subwoofer was playing, its vibrations caused…

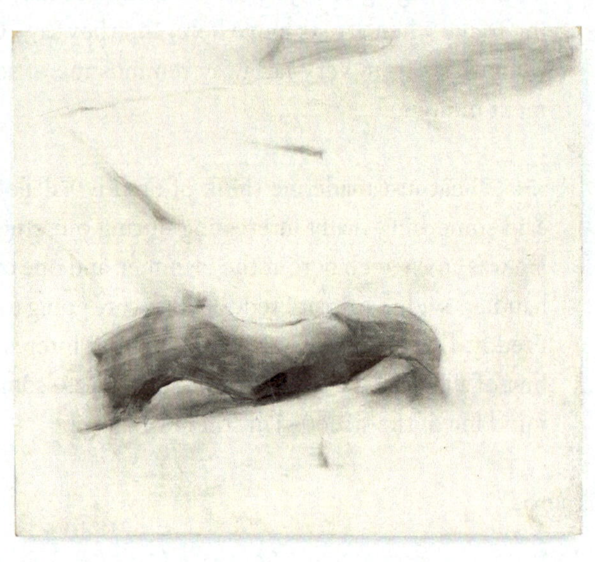

Beaux Mendes, Untitled, 2024. Charcoal on marble dust on panel. 12 × 14 in. (30.5 × 35.6 cm)

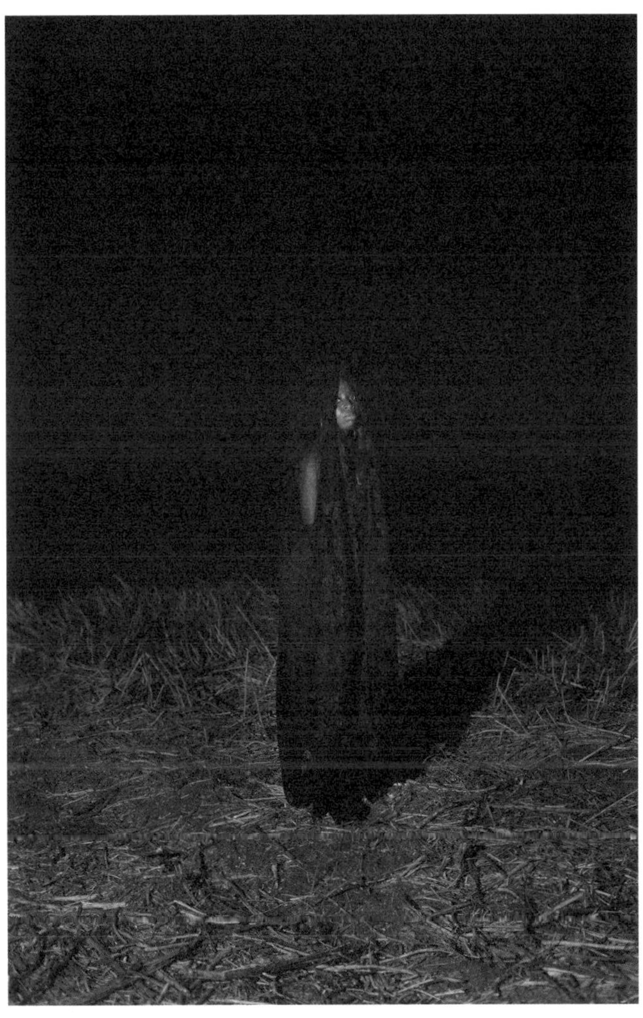

Widline Cadet, *Land of Plenty* #2, 2024. Archival inkjet print. 48 × 32 × 2 in. (121.9 × 81.3 × 5.1 cm)

49

E.H.   Precipitation.

P.P.   All of a sudden the building, the studio we were in, actually started falling apart and bits of light were shining through.

Freddy said to me that one of the biggest frustrations for him as an artist, and I think he's of Mexican descent, was that Black and brown artists, he felt, were limited in terms of self-representation to literal self-representation. The expectation is that you can't represent your identity using conceptual art. His stake here is talking about personal identity and history through the language of conceptualism.

E.H.   Jack Whitten talked about "Everyone wanted me to make Black figurative paintings," and that *he* wanted to paint whatever he wanted to paint. Coming out of Jackson Pollock and all that—he had a studio next to de Kooning (I think?) when he was a young guy in New York. He was really adamant about it.

P.P.   I wrote an essay on Suzanne Jackson for her forthcoming SFMOMA show. Same story.

But back to an earlier question you asked, how you find the people to even do studio visits with…With any exhibition, there are so many exceptional artists that are not in the show, right? You have to make decisions somewhere.

We really wanted to limit the number of artists. On the one hand, it's because there is a lot of moving image, which requires a particular amount of space. But also we

50

wanted to be generous with artists and not limit them to being represented by one or two things—unless that's what they wanted.

D.F.   What I appreciate about your process is your curatorial humility, because it's something I really find very important. You didn't set out with a grand narrative or try to find actors for your stage play. But of course that puts you out on a rope a little bit. You're not sure if something's going to emerge.

E.H.   Something seems to be emerging. We focused on who was going to be in the show, what elements of the work felt really important to us to represent in the exhibition, but have never pushed the idea of what this show is about, even though we've been asked many times.

P.P.   "What is the show about? What's the theme?" Our response: "It's a lot of themes."

E.H.   I went to UC Berkeley for a PhD in African diaspora studies. I thought I was going to be a Reconstructionist era historian when I entered undergrad, and look at me now, not talking about DuBois every day. Which is just to say that my understanding of art is really visual studies, and it comes out of Black studies.

When you were talking about humility, I don't know whether it is, but I have always tried to recede in any exhibition I do. Artist first.

51

P.P.   Artist first. Artwork first.

E.H.   Artwork first, audience second, curator third. Or in-stitution third, curator fourth?

P.P.   No one in twenty years, in ten years, next year—no one's going to care what I thought. You can probably name two or three curators that hold a place in history.

E.H.   We're going to trust the art object first, and anything we create together, rather than a particular narrative. We love artists; we like looking at art. That's going to help us navigate an exhibition where people are not siloed but interconnected.

P.P.   The less I understood something, the more intrigued I was. When I'm asking, "What is this person doing?" the more I'm drawn to it. I want to figure it out.

D.F.   You want to feel the subwoofer through your soul.

P.P.   I was thinking about Mike Stoltz too. He's really known in experimental film circles but not at all in the contemporary art world. We went to his studio, and the first thing he did was to show me a piece of film, "This is what film looks like." I'm like, "Yes, I know. I've seen film before." But it spoke to his deep engagement with the materiality of film, not only the images it can contain. He found slides of an experimental filmmaker from the 1970s who was almost

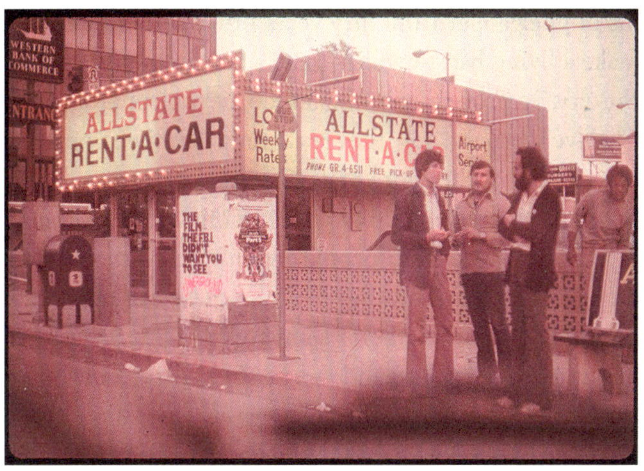

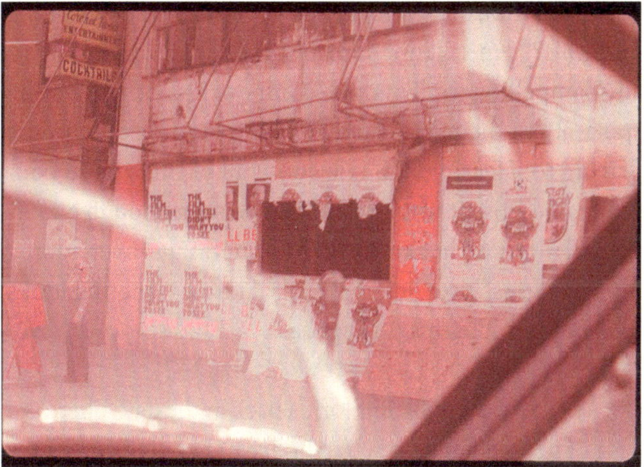

Slides from the archive of Peter Mays, found at the Echo Park Film Center's rummage sale and used as source material for Mike Stoltz's 16mm film with optical soundtrack, *Pinktoned*, 2025

his doppelganger from fifty years prior, who in order to make a living had to wheat-paste advertisements around the city. To prove that he did his job, he took photographs. They've aged, and now they're all pink. That becomes one component of this work that Mike's making.

And then he shot out of his studio window on film in East Hollywood, just people on the corner—their heads are out of frame—and they're doing these boring, everyday things. And then there's some weird digital image that he's transferred to film. And *then* he showed me some other work that he'd done, to give me a sense of where this project might go. It was just so nuts. The optical effects were dizzying and didn't really make sense. "Where are you going with this?" I'm still not sure, but there was something really compelling to all of these components and the way he spoke about them. He had a very clear location that he was driving to. Hearing him talk about all of this was so compelling because it was so foreign. I've seen enough experimental film, and he's really up to something—overlapping temporalities, histories, materials. I know what film looks like, but not like this, I suppose.

E.H.   Mike was a punk in Florida back in the day. There are a lot of people I'm drawn to who have these unusual entry points into art making.

P.P.   It's funny—I think there's just two ceramicists in the show. You can't move in Los Angeles without tripping over

54

a ceramic. Right? There's such a long history of ceramics, both in craft and as fine art—Ken Price, Ron Nagle…

E.H.   Long Beach. The history is huge here.

P.P.   And the two people who work in ceramics that are in the show, Bryan Rochefort and Alake Shilling—who does other things as well—really take that material and use it for the making of sculpture, allowing the grip of history to loosen and using it the same way you would use paper or found objects.

E.H.   It's one material out of many.

P.P.   Right. Whereas Bryan is a much more classical ceramicist.

E.H.   It's true. But you of all people know, having just done a Thomas Schütte exhibition that featured a lot of ceramics at MoMA—the definitions of media came out of your former institution in the early-mid-twentieth century. Everybody had to try to break the definitions down. Ed Ruscha, when asked about his use of photography early in his career, said, "It's like a paintbrush. I pick up a camera when I need to make something. I'm not a photographer." My guess is it's the same with many of these artists, including Alake.

P.P.   We didn't feel mandated to include ceramics, though maybe we should have, because of the vast amount of

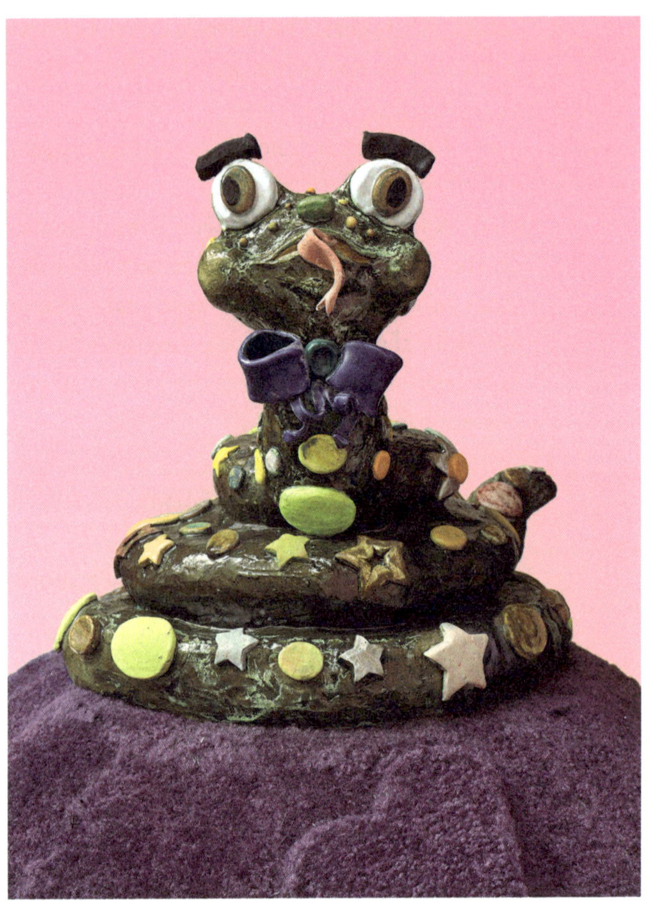

Alake Shilling, *Mister Spitz*, 2021. Glazed ceramic and enamel. 18 × 24 × 25 in. (45.7 × 61 × 63.5 cm)

ceramics that are being made in the city, and the long history of expert ceramicists.

E.H.   But this comes back to the no-methodology methodology.

P.P.   Right.

D.F.   You organically came to them, and I think an audience is going to feel that. It makes a lot of sense. You have
your ceramic section, your photo section, your painting
section, your strange archaeology of modernism section.

E.H.   It's two people's curatorial interests and perspectives
happening over a short period of time in this very long history of this place. It's a moment. It's a glimpse. We can't do
everything—it's not even 10 percent of what we saw—but
we did something.

D.F.   Do you know how many studio visits you did?

E.H.   Lots.

P.P.   My family wasn't living here. What else did I have
to do?

E.H.   It was like six or seven months of it. It felt bewilder-
ing at some point.

   Can I ask one question?

P.P.   Yeah.

G.N.   How would you like Made in L.A. 2025 to be re-membered?

E.H.   Remembered? Oh, fuck. As being a good show.

P.P.   That's a question I've never considered with any exhibition I've done. My curatorial approach: Put two works in a room. If they're good, that's all you need—or one work, for that matter. I want to create a situation for people to give art attention. People spend whatever, thirty seconds in front of an artwork? If they make it to forty-five, we succeeded.

David Alekhuogie

in conversation with Leigh Raiford

Through Photography

David Alekhuogie is an artist raised and based in Los Angeles whose practice begins with photography but quickly exceeds and expands the parameters of medium. In Alekhuogie's hands, photographic portraits of Black men's bodies become abstracted color fields and landscapes (his *Pull_UP* series, 2017); those color fields are joined with photographs of L.A. flora to become textiles (the series *To Live and Die in LA*, 2018); photographs of fabrics are collaged with found archival images to become architectural, suggesting the layering of memory and experience as complex structures (the series *Naïvete*, 2021, and a series intertwining photography and textiles). Experimenting with an array of printing techniques and materials, Alekhuogie presents a searching and wide-ranging body of work that poses questions about Black masculinity, radical aesthetics, and belonging. The following thoughts by Alekhougie, distilled from a conversation we had over Zoom, touch on the artist's relationship to photography, artistic freedom, and being in the world.

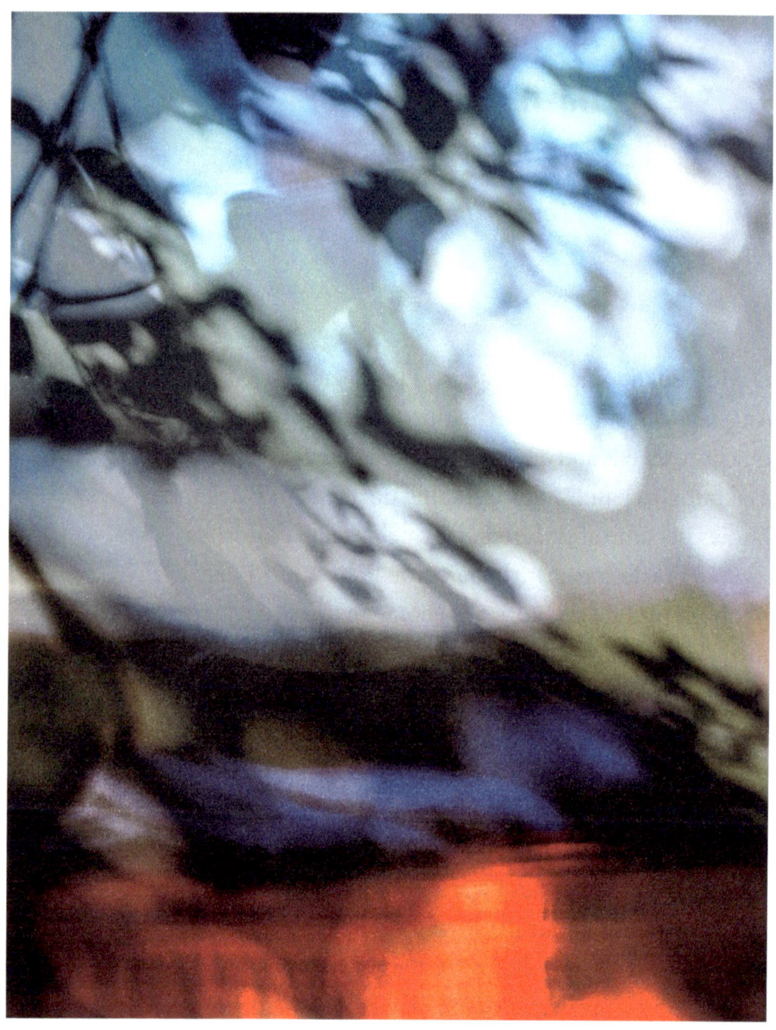

David Alekhuogie, *Firestation 30, Mom's garden (35.585620, -105.772740) (34.126420, -117.537730)*, 2021. Archival pigment print on canvas. 48 × 36 in. (121.9 × 91.4 cm)

60

I [David] started with photography through music and music writing. Studying ethnomusicology at UC Berkeley, my friends and I ended up doing a lot of music writing. And I started DJing quite a bit in undergrad. That was my entry point into photography: documenting parties. I've always related to being in any given environment where there's a kind of a social collaboration going on. I'm always finding that it's the situation where it's the easiest for me to be "on the job," whether that is playing music or doing documentation. It allows me to be in it and around it, in and out at the same time. You're a participating spectator. A DJ is very much that.

I think it would be worthwhile to ask a bunch of DJs what it means to be a good DJ. For me, something about it is this ability to view the landscape and allow people, a group of many people, to *feel*. I'm the most satisfied when people are thinking to themselves, "Oh, there's somebody here that recognizes me." That is so incredibly satisfying. I think it's more satisfying than having the coolest mash-up or remix or whatever. So much of it is like, "Oh, I too belong here."

FINDING A WAY THROUGH PHOTOGRAPHY

When I started shooting, it was mostly using film cameras— the nostalgia and the vibes that certain cameras have. I was really interested in Catherine Opie's work during this time.

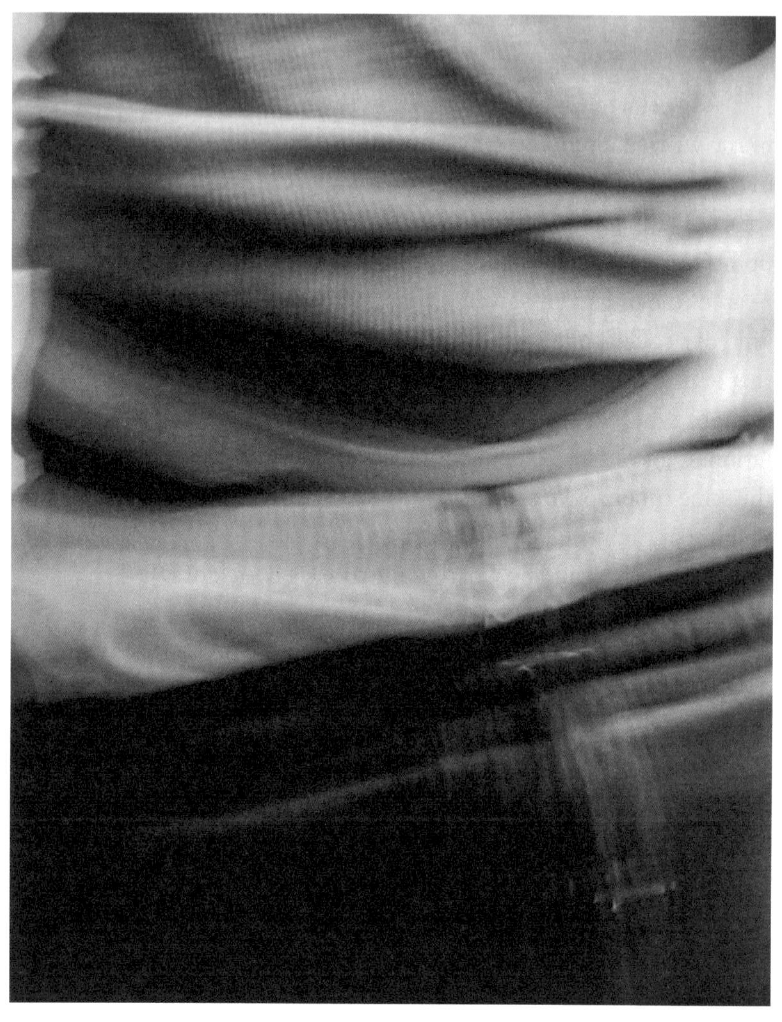

David Alekhuogie, *GRAVITY (Pull_Up g,g,g)*, 2018. Archival pigment print on canvas.
50 × 40 in. (127 × 101.6 cm)

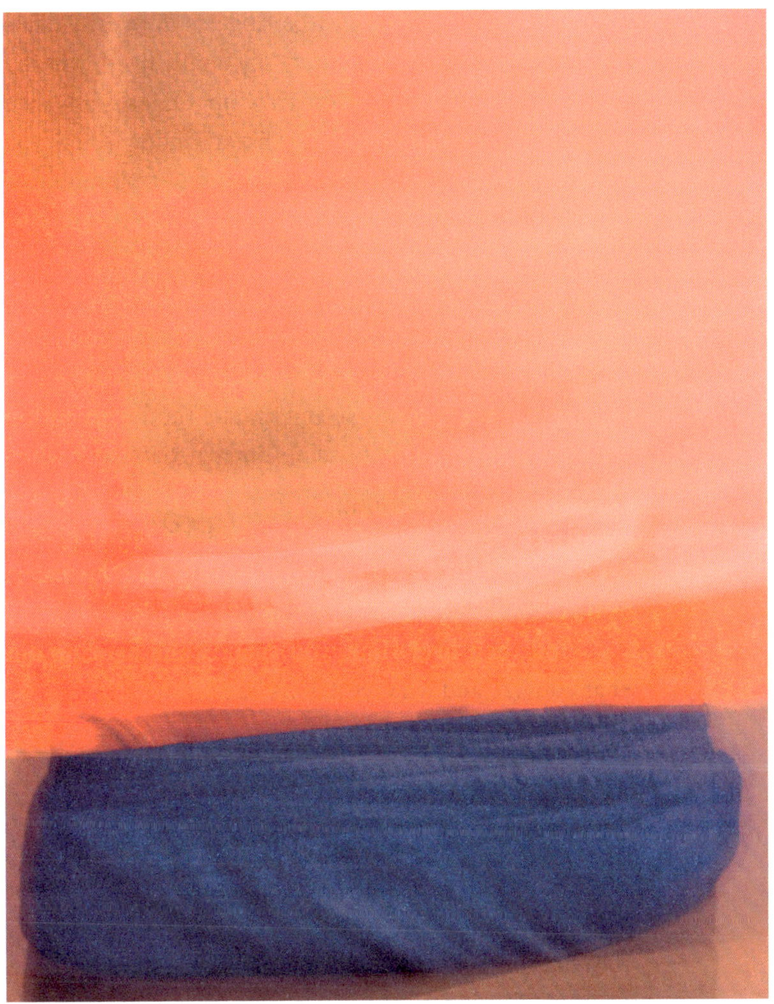

David Alekhuogie, *Pull_Up g,o,r*, 2017. Archival pigment print on canvas.
50 × 40 in. (127 × 101.6 cm)

63

She was photographing in Los Angeles in West Adams, which is not too far from where my family lived, where I grew up and where my mom grew up. Opie's work is super clean and transparent, almost like a window where you would want the picture to be. I really wanted pictures that were just the content and there was no stuff going on that distracted from that.

I also saw Robert Adams's book *Summer Nights, Walking* (2009). And I was like, "Oh, this is like poetry." It was really powerful because the palette, the tools he was using were super accessible and sparse. Yet the execution was virtuoso-like. I felt the same kind of excitement when I heard J Dilla's record *Jay Love Japan* (2007), an album of him working from a bunch of records he bought in Japan. These works are so much more interesting than the materials that the two artists were using.

And then over time, you spend time figuring out what you like and what you don't like.

FINDING A WAY BEYOND PHOTOGRAPHY

I see the photograph as an unstable object. But more than that, I see the working methods as unstable. What are the expectations of a photograph? What do people expect from photography? It's the feeling that photography is democratized or it has the capacity to allow people to access authenticity or legibility. The photograph has a fungibility. What makes a picture unstable is the fact that it can travel

64

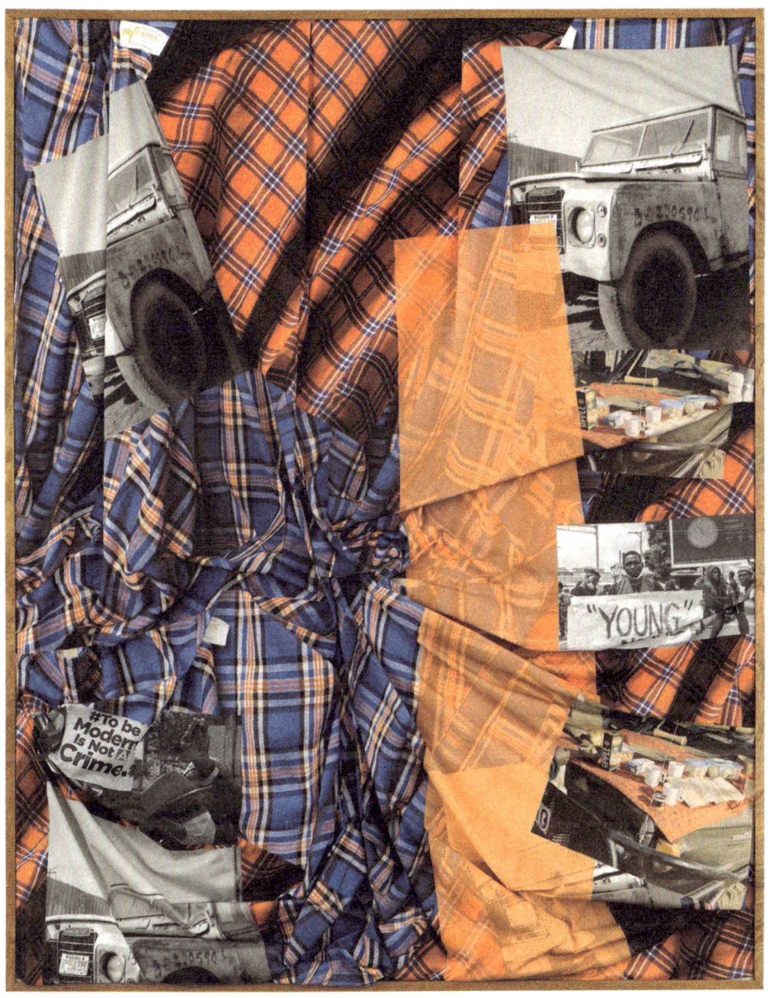

David Alekhuogie, *To be modern*, 2023. Archival pigment prints quilted to canvas, artist's frame. 70 × 60 × 2 in. (177.8 × 152.4 × 5.1 cm)

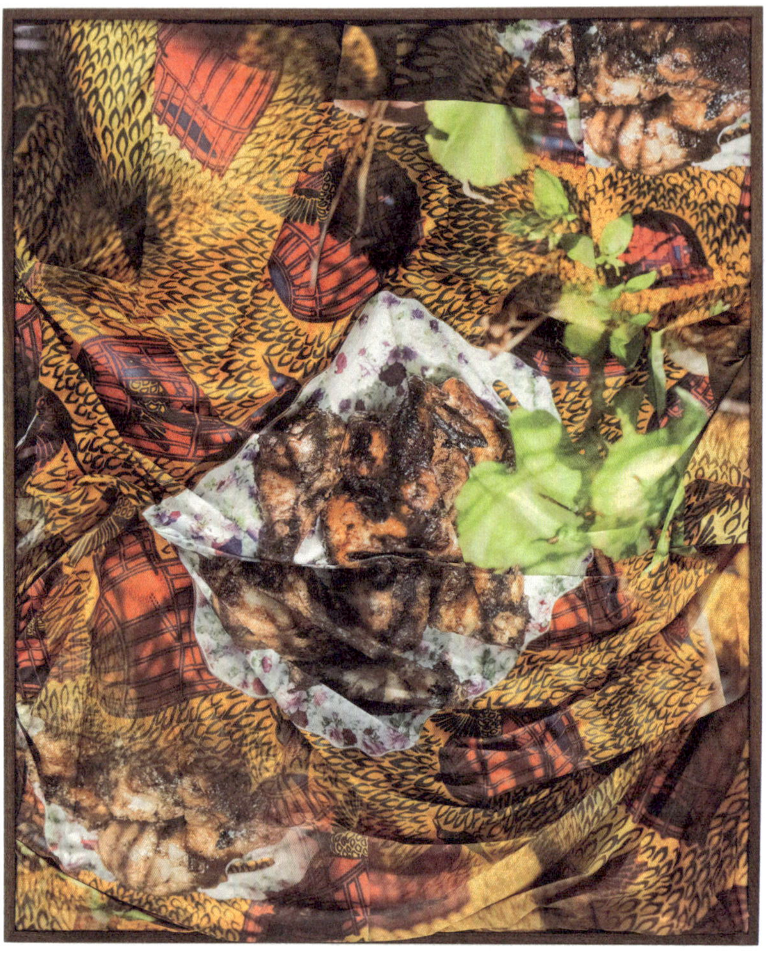

David Alekhuogie, *Still Life with Jerk Chicken*, 2023. Archival pigment prints quilted to canvas, artist's frame. 60 × 48 × 2 in. (152.4 × 121.9 × 5.1 cm)

all over the place. That's what makes the photograph a jumping-off point for all the other interdisciplinary things that I do. If I make a textile based off of a photograph, then the textile is trafficking off of that picture. The textile now has the credentials of that photograph.

The work that I'm doing about African sculpture is about the loss of access, looking for things that have not only been the spoils of war or the spoils of colonialism but also are culturally in the household. What's it like to feel as though somebody ran through your pockets? So, the photograph becomes a sort of performance of looking and finding and searching and rebirth, trying to perform the history of something that is really dispersed. There's something so rich and amazing that happens in this mispronunciation or mistranslation.

I would describe my work as belonging to the history of Black avant-garde performance, part of the legacy of the subversive reimagining of simply what is left over—what is left of my cultural inheritance, however broken it may be. This is a part of the Black avant-garde tradition. The performance and labor of collage, remix, repair, reprise, reordering are a through line, not just in Black music but in Black art globally and as a liberatory strategy historically.

This is the glue that I see in everything from sports to poetry and film. It's those moments of artistic flourish— of having the capacity to express yourself in the margins— that feel like their purpose is to mark a person's sense of autonomy, especially in situations that are oftentimes about

67

trying to turn you into a commodity, a mechanistic thing. You're just like, "No, you tried it, but I'm here"—you know what I mean?

Black House Radio/Michael Donte

in conversation with Henoch Moore

The Dance Floor Is a Procession

Genre is an institution, House music is a feeling. The dance floor is a procession—

Upon landing in Los Angeles, Michael Donte found himself in a stint working at and with YouTube, optimizing virality and commercial narratives for the digital giant. The experience was fruitful but predictable in what it offered—acute marketing and metrics-based learning, a nuanced connection to what "works" in that context, a deeper understanding of how communities interact online, alienation. When his time was up on that experience, Donte's connection to his personal history led him to pivot his life to Black House Radio.

The following conversation is about a platform made to celebrate Black artists and their contributions to the art form known as house music. It's centered in the concept of community and lives in the remains of the generational cyclone that house music stirred up.

What is the role of an identity-based music platform in an age of algorithmic dominance?

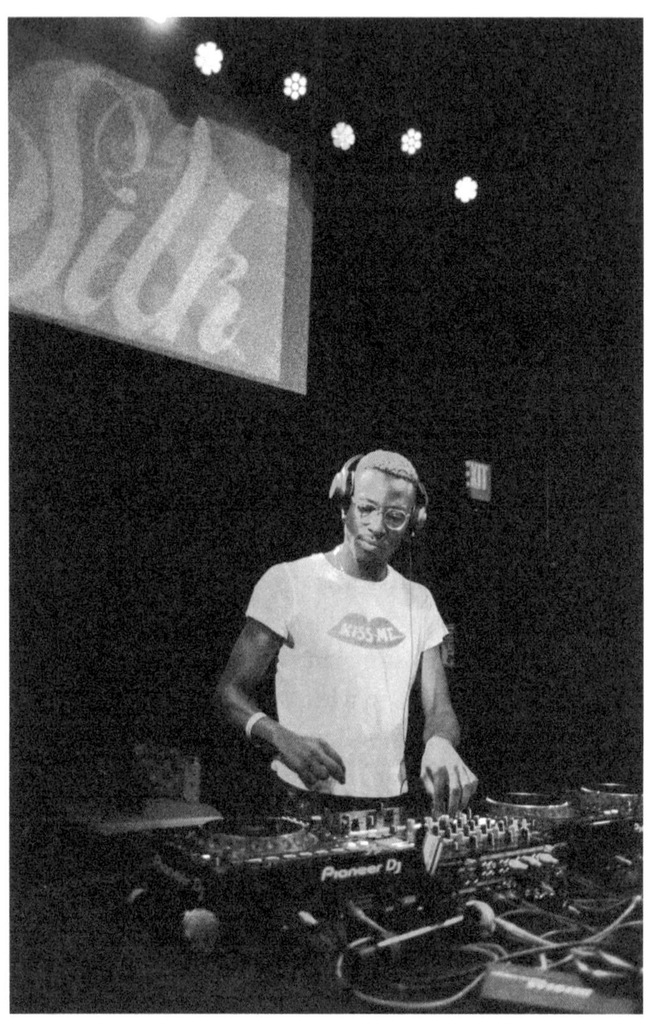

Michael Donte, 2025

What is Black House Radio?

Henoch Moore Let's start from the beginning. How did Black House Radio come to be?

Michael Donte I put together a deck—kind of a mood board but more intentional. Some slides just had words on them like, "Black House Radio feels like a warm hug from a grandmother." I could see the furniture, the tone, even where it might be in three years. It was similar to a business plan. I had the vision, but I didn't know how quickly people would get it.

So I focused on messaging—what's the mission—and then decided to go for it. I set up cameras and reached out to DJs I loved seeing around L.A. They didn't really know what they were walking into, but once we were in the room, it felt special. That feeling became the foundation. A few months later, we released the first episodes.

h.m. What was your personal entry point into house music?

m.d. I used to think house was just the fist-pumping, four-on-the-floor stuff—which didn't resonate with me. But then I realized I'd been a house fan since I was a kid. Gospel music was the bridge.

When I was twelve, I wanted to see Shirley Caesar for my birthday. Not even for religious reasons—I just loved choirs. The soul, the spiritual weight of it, the

71

melodies. Gospel pulled me in. And as I got older, that naturally led to soulful house.

A lot of the folks making gospel were the same ones making house. That spirit of joy and release carried over. Even now, most DJs on Black House Radio blend gospel into their sets without me asking. It just fits. That emotional and spiritual through line is what I'm always chasing.

H.M.   I love that. And that connection between gospel and house leads directly into questions around genre. Personally, I feel like genre often exists just to serve the industry—a way to commodify things. But house has always felt bigger than that. How do you think about genre?

M.D.   For me, house is more of a feeling than a genre. That's why it connects so strongly to gospel. What's a gospel song, really? It's something that moves you spiritually, emotionally.

When I'm curating music, I'm thinking about how the music makes me feel. Not what's popular, not what's trending. That freedom to follow feeling over category— that's what house is to me.

And that's why it allows for so much experimentation. Chopping up Lauryn Hill or speeding up Stevie Wonder—it all works if it feels right. The dance floor becomes a space for creative risk.

H.M.   That freedom feels core to Black House Radio's ethos too. Let's talk about curation. What's your approach?

72

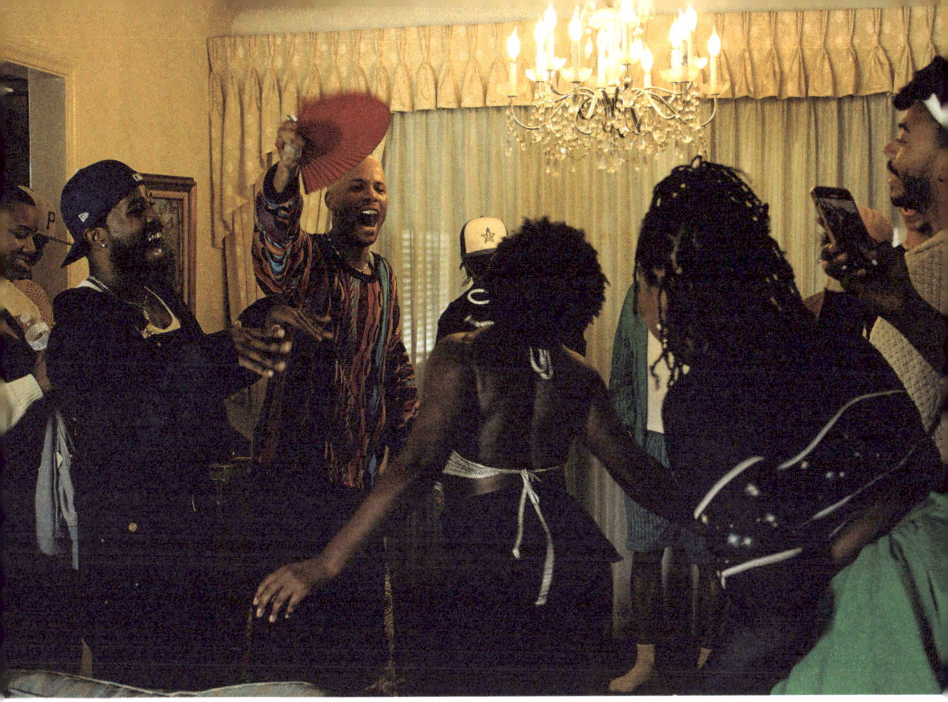

Black House Radio event, a.l.t. home, Los Angeles, March 2024

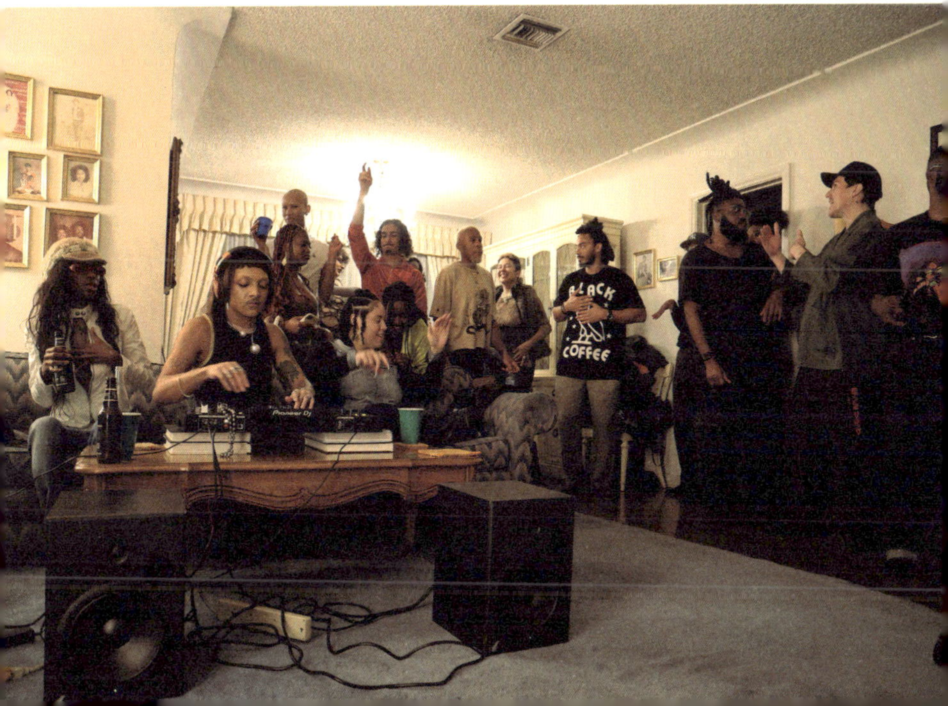

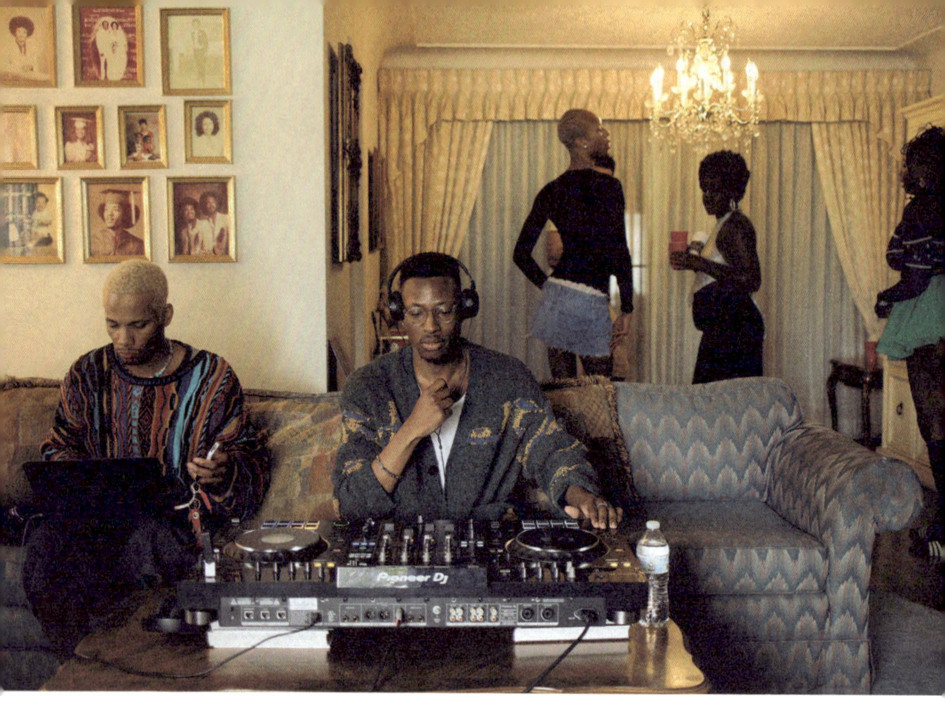

Black House Radio event, a.l.t. home, Los Angeles, March 2024

M.D.   It's always about what feels authentic to me. What belongs on the platform. Who deserves that moment. I could see Black House Radio evolving to include other curators in the future, which I'd love. Their lens might be different, but the foundation would be the same: honesty.

People ask how to get on the platform. Truthfully, it's not about submitting a set. You're better off inviting me to a party and letting me feel your energy in real life. Because it's not about transitions. It's about intention.

H.M.   And part of that intention shows up in the physical spaces you choose. Do you notice differences between throwing parties in L.A. versus New York?

M.D.   Definitely. Even in L.A., a small house party feels different than a warehouse event. Each city has its own energy. But what's consistent is the gratitude. People walk in and you can feel it—they've been waiting for this.

We've never had the kind of problems other parties deal with. No fights, no police, no chaos. I think that's because people know what they're stepping into. They've seen it online. They know the energy, and they bring that same care to the space.

H.M.   There's something sacred about that. Especially in a time when festival culture and mainstream dance spaces are dominating. Do you have thoughts on that shift?

75

m.d.   It's hard to say. I think what's mainstream really depends on who you ask. Some people might look at what we're doing and say that's mainstream too.

But if the essence of the culture was being lost, we wouldn't exist. The fact that we do—and that people respond to it the way they do—makes me hopeful.

h.m.   What about the digital side? You have a background with YouTube. How much of that experience informed Black House Radio?

m.d.   A lot. I used to help YouTube creators build shows and viral formats. Then I worked for YouTube itself. Eventually I burned out. Got laid off and realized I couldn't keep giving myself to companies that didn't value what I brought.

That's when I decided to put all my skills into something I cared about. That meant using what I knew about storytelling—thumbnails, titles, watch time, all of it. I knew I wanted full sets, at least an hour long. I knew longer videos would help with discovery. And I knew authenticity would always outperform gimmicks.

h.m.   That's so real. For folks just starting out, are there any digital tools you recommend?

m.d.   It's less about tools and more about paying attention. I watched Book Club Radio for a long time. They inspired me to embrace small gatherings and unique curation. And I learned from that.

76

One specific thing: thumbnails and titles matter. I test different ones to see what lands. I'm not trying to trick anyone—I just want people to find something real.

H.M.   Let's talk about your community. What kind of person shows up to a Black House Radio event?

M.D.   It's usually friends or friends of friends. You have to be invited. We tried an open RSVP once, but it didn't feel right. Now it's like a dinner party—you get invited because someone brought you in.

Throughout the day, we might have sixty people come through, but only twenty or so in the house at once. It keeps things intimate. And people always walk away with new friends. That's the magic.

H.M.   What challenges have you faced building this?

M.D.   Staying true. There's so much noise online. The temptation is always there to chase trends or numbers. But for us, it always comes back to intentionality.

And of course, there's money. This industry is complicated. But platforms like Apple Music are starting to pay DJs and producers, which helps. Still, the biggest challenge is staying organic and rooted in Black culture—Black DJs, Black dancers, Black curators. That's the core.

H.M.   Where do you see this going?

77

M.D.   It's scary to answer that. I had a list of dreams when I started, and a lot of them have already come true. We're doing a museum collaboration with the Hammer, which was on that list. That felt huge.

I want to keep growing digitally but also stay grounded in real-life communities. I hope we move away from screens a bit. Music is a connector, and I want to use it to build deeper relationships.

Eventually, I want to buy a house—a real physical space where we can host artists and gatherings. I want a record label. A management team. A structure that really supports Black artists. That's the long vision.

H.M.   That's beautiful. For people who want to connect with Black House Radio, what's the best way?

M.D.   Subscribe on YouTube. Follow us on TikTok and Twitter. We'll be sharing a P.O. box soon if folks want to send mail.

But honestly, the best way is to go see the DJs live. Go to their sets. They're a part of this too. You'll feel it when you're in the room.

Greg Breda

by Leigh Raiford

A Seed's a Star

Like his paintings, Greg Breda's South Bay Los Angeles home is filled with light and plants. A well-maintained lawn in front, a thriving garden surrounding a rectangle-shaped pool in the back, and flourishing plants on tables, floors, counters, and shelves inside, all reaching toward the light. Breda has lived most of his life in this single-level ranch home, which his parents purchased in the mid-1960s, about a decade after migrating from the segregated Jim Crow South. This is the house where Breda grew up with a sense of Southern California ease and community, among the first generation of Black folks to benefit from the gains of the civil rights movement. It is the house where, later in his adult life, he first took up painting, and whose formal dining room he would eventually turn into a studio. It is the house he shared with his mother—"my rock," as Breda refers to her—until she passed away in 2020. Breda maintains the home in much the same way his mother did for six decades: tidy, welcoming, calm yet full of vitality, abundant with an "appreciation of beautiful things."

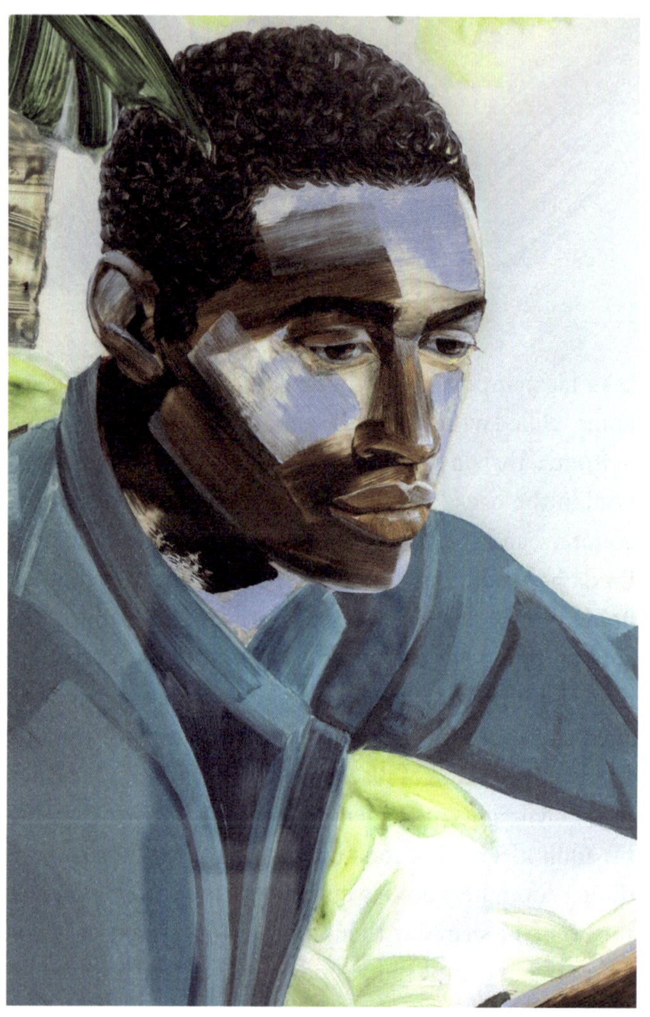

Greg Breda, *Erasing Shadows*, 2023. Acrylic on Mylar. 50 × 40 in.
(127 × 101.6 cm)

80

The plants in Breda's paintings, like those in his home, offer an invitation to "quiet ourselves, quiet our minds, take a breath," he says. The artist's canvases feature acrylic portraits of brown-skinned people enfolded in verdant surroundings and immersed in contemplation. Deep thinking is punctuated by a subject's hands perched gently on their chin, or held lightly to their heart, or clasping each other as if in prayer. These unnamed figures almost never look directly at us but rather to the light that comes from outside, or above, even through or from within the canvas. In turn, the light leaves its mark, periwinkle, cerulean, or lilac, across the figures' cheekbones and foreheads in wide brushstrokes. Like the plants with which they share the canvas, the people turn toward the sun.

Breda's paintings, like his home, create a tranquility that holds space for deeper conversation. The self-taught painter, who counts California artists William Pajaud and Raymond Saunders among his inspirations, says it was Kerry James Marshall's artistry "that showed me that the work needed to be about something … to have a conversation in the work." For those who choose to sit and stay awhile, Breda has developed across his paintings a "language of flowers," an architecture of light, and an orthography of color, enacting a soulful meditation that belies the paintings' lightness. Flowers are chosen for their historic and symbolic meanings—alliums for patience, dogwoods for rebirth, lilies of the valley for a return to happiness, birds of paradise for freedom. Allegorically, each figure's predominantly brown and blue palette contains a little red mark

81

on or near the mouth: "That is a reference to the words that we speak, how they empower us, how they can open a door," he says. "We create and destroy with our words."

Breda began painting on Mylar, a polyester-based surface that, in addition to being more affordable than linen or cotton, still allowed for large-scale work. He discovered that Mylar's materiality is full with symbolic possibilities. For Breda, the translucency of the Mylar prompted conversations about light, truth, and spirituality. His first solo show with Patron Gallery in Chicago, *Hei* (2018), was named for the fifth letter of the ancient Hebrew alphabet, the pictographic representation of which has variously been translated as "window" or "opening," a portal through which spirit moves. The exhibition elaborated this effect with works that included windows or mirrors alongside the paintings' central figures. In 2023, Breda began using polyester canvas, which makes visible the aluminum stretcher bars through the paintings' surface, to further elucidate the conversation with the *hei*. Now the painting is itself a window symbolic of the *hei*.

Breda's paintings, like a church or a garden, are a place to meditate on spiritual matters. With each work, the artist is searching, questioning: "I'm simply trying to understand what that relationship with the Most High means and trying to forge my way through that, however it comes. And really, the deeper you go into that, it's about how do you love people? How do you practice patience and extend compassion? How do you live by faith? How do you become a demonstration of grace?"

82

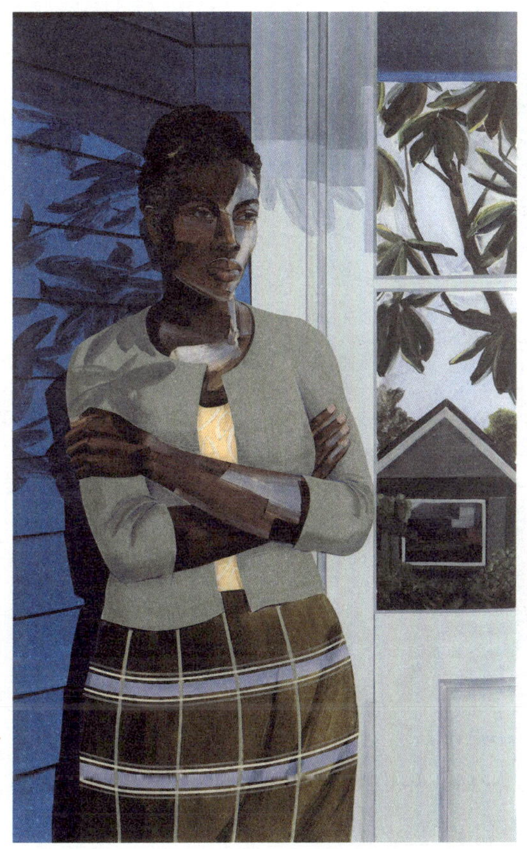

Greg Breda, *The Citadel*, 2018. Acrylic on Mylar. 63 × 40 in. (160 × 101.6 cm)

83

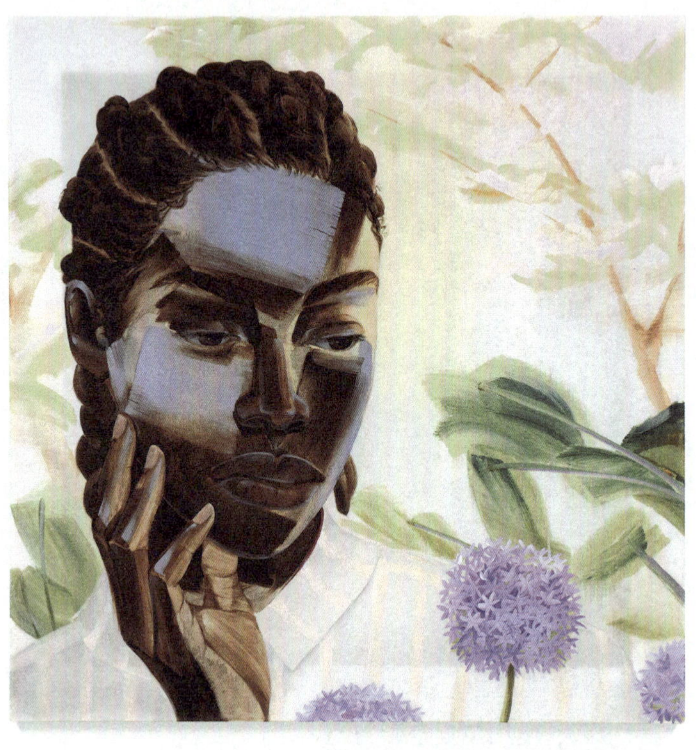

Greg Breda, *Arrival at knowing*, 2024. Acrylic on polyester canvas. 25 × 25 in. (63.5 × 63.5 cm)

84

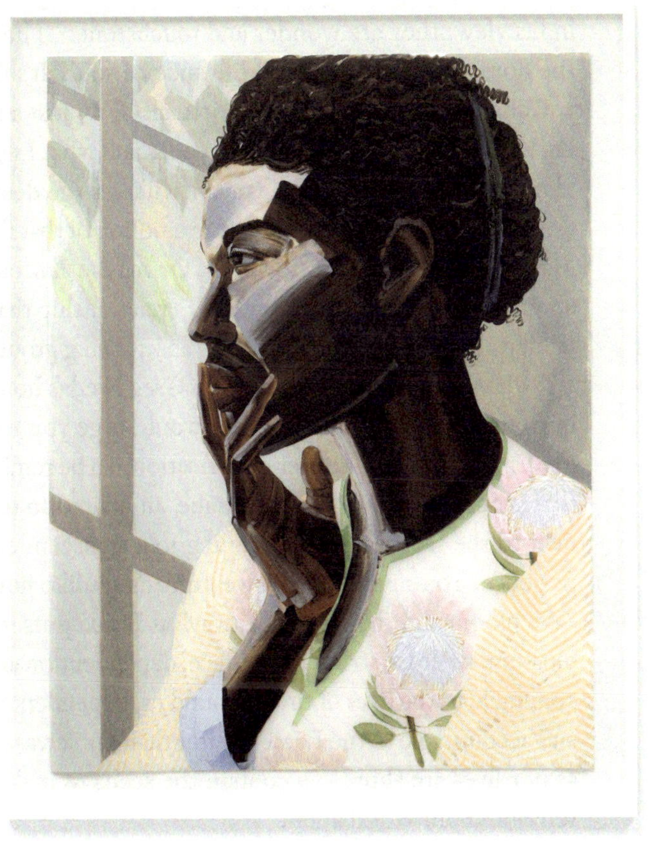

Greg Breda, *Morning Council*, 2018. Acrylic on vellum. 40 × 33 in. (101.6 × 83.8 cm)

85

In his paintings, as in his home and in many spiritual traditions, plants are key. They are catechism and paradigm in his view; they are wonder and touchstone: "The seed, the flora, plants are all about life and the soul." It's fine if you choose not to engage the spiritual. "If it's just a painting with a woman and a flower to you, that's what I want it to be to you," he says. "But if you are willing to go deeper, I want to talk to you about maybe the emotion of that flower. Maybe that's what that flower is. Or maybe I'm talking about the Most High. Or maybe it's a relationship that I'm talking about. Or maybe it's talking about being grounded."

If you ever do find yourself in Greg Breda's house or in front of one of his paintings, I would urge you to stay longer and have that deeper conversation. To be reminded that art can be a portal to the divine, an invitation to connect to the sacred, and an opening to a transcendent experience. To remember that we humans are like flowers: "We bloom and then we fade away," as Breda puts it. We blossom, we learn to live with grace, dependent on and accountable to the lives of those around us, dependent upon and accountable to the Force greater than ourselves. Even as our lives are short, we contain the seeds to make ourselves and our world anew.

Widline Cadet

by Esti Giordani

Imagined Archives

I met Widline Cadet at her studio in Los Angeles's Koreatown. She offered me donuts. I chose a plain glazed. She said she liked basic things too, then opted for the bright-yellow-frosted passion fruit variety.

In Haiti, where Cadet is from, passion fruit is as basic as an orange in Fresno. They grow all over. This reminded me that in Los Angeles, you wear where you're from—even if you've lived here for decades.

Born in Haiti, Cadet moved to New York City with her mother at age ten, eventually landing on the northernmost tip of Manhattan, Washington Heights, in an apartment where Cadet spent the rest of her childhood. It's the apartment her mother still lives in, the apartment to which Cadet returned after completing her MFA in upstate New York and during the pandemic, before moving across the country for a teaching engagement at the University of California, Los Angeles.

Wherever Cadet has lived, she has taken Haiti with her, in her interiority and in the work she makes. In Los Angeles, with its unlikely similarities to Haiti—the mixed

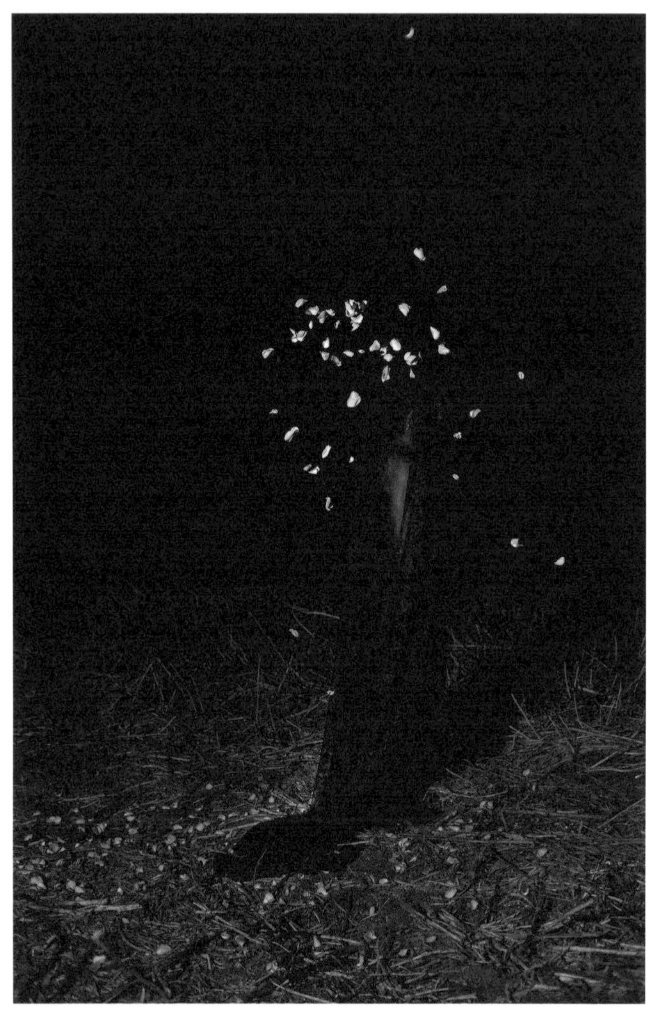

Widline Cadet, *Future Visions/Arive a*, 2024. Archival inkjet print.
48 × 32 × 2 in. (121.9 × 81.3 × 5.1 cm)

architecture (the breeze blocks), pacing, landscape, and weather—Cadet sees what she calls a "romanticized version" of where she grew up. Her work invokes mystery: the cosmic stuff, an implied narrative, nostalgia. She captures memories we've never had, disguised as the artist's or possibly our own, even when the subjects and landscapes bear no resemblance to our reality.

Cadet's photography, videos, and installations elicit a dreamlike world, navigating themes around migration, absence, identity, and diaspora. Through portraiture, staged scenes, and material from family archives, she blends personal and imagined histories, evoking a deep intimacy while keeping the spectator at a distance. Though specific, Cadet's sleight of hand compels viewers to fill in the story for ourselves. Who are these subjects? Who is the spectator? Whose eye constructs the image? The artist's work lives between definitive answers. In one recent photograph, *Future Visions/Arive a* (2024), a woman—a deity—emerges from a cracked sky fluttering with rose petals. She is someone from folklore, mythological. She is also the artist herself, unrecognizable behind a veil. It's the first self-portrait she's done in years.

While Cadet is a compelling subject for her own lens, she is most comfortable behind the camera, where she has more control. Where seeing is an act of being seen. Finding subjects for her photographs is organic; the artist often sources them from open calls on social media. In the beginning, she photographed friends, friends of friends, family members of friends—"Black women like to help other Black

89

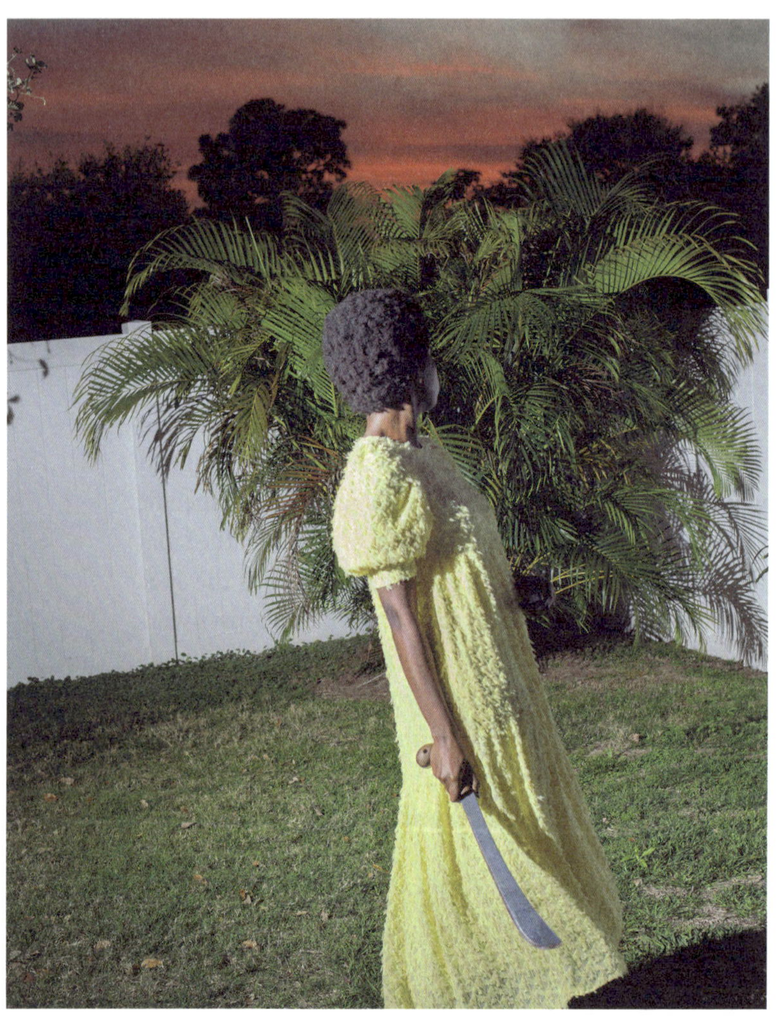

Widline Cadet, *Land of Plenty #1*, 2021. Archival inkjet print. 50 × 40 × 2 in. (127 × 101.6 × 5.1 cm)

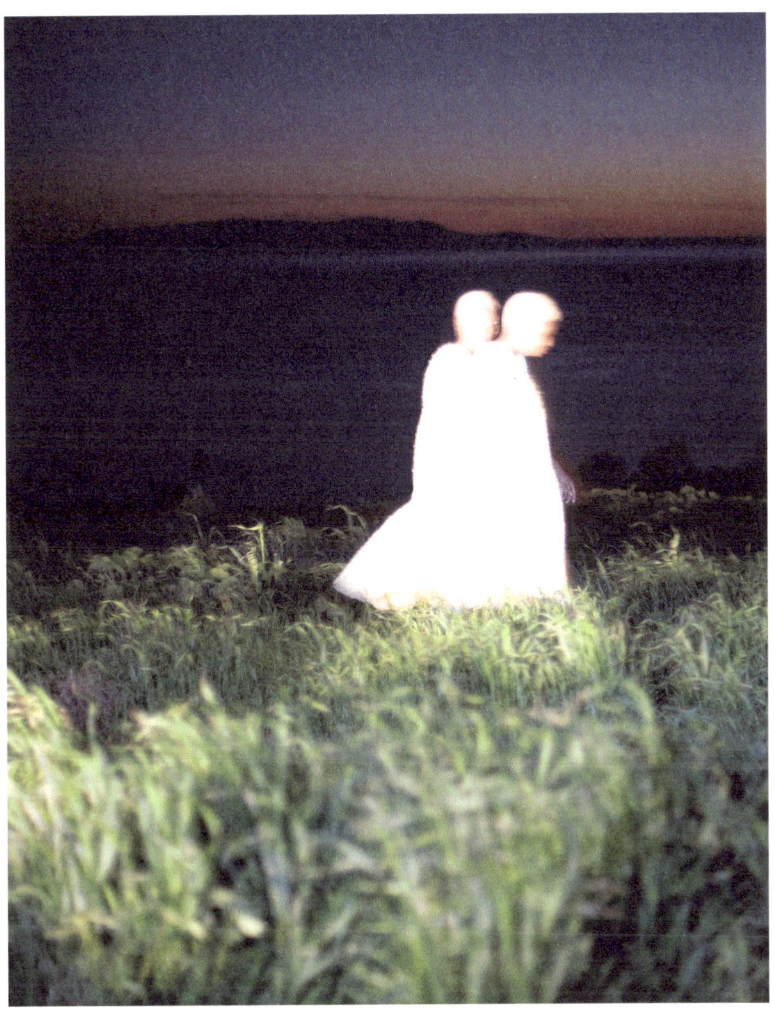

Widline Cadet, *Manyen distans (Touching Distance)*, 2023. Archival inkjet print.
50 × 40 × 2 in. (127 × 101.6 × 5.1 cm)

91

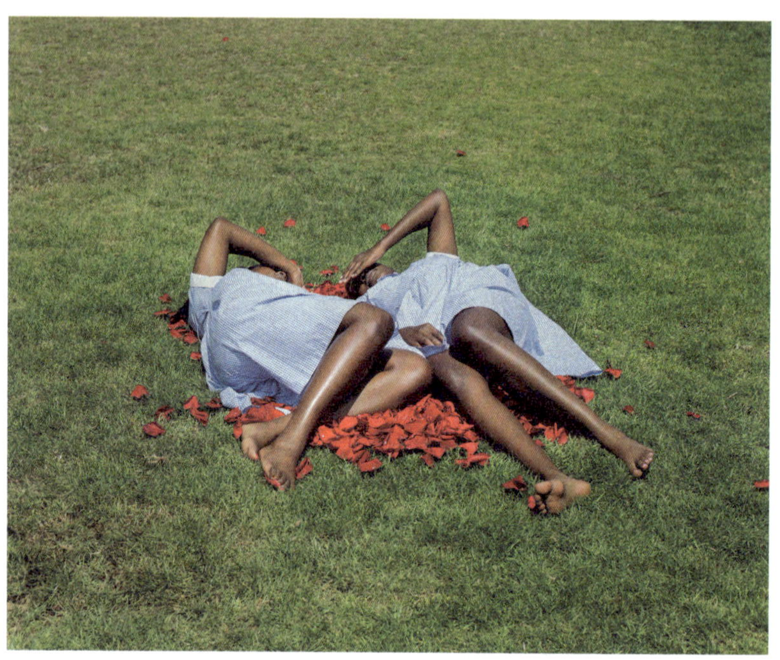

Widline Cadet, *Nan letènite (In Eternity)*, 2021. Archival inkjet print. 32 × 40 × 2 in. (81.3 × 101.6 × 5.1 cm)

women," she told me, a reciprocity birthing some of Cadet's most long-standing series. The relationships formed in the process of making the images are just as much a part of the work as the images that get shown. In *Nan Letènite (In Eternity)* (2021), two girls lie in a meadow. Who are they to each other? Friends on the verge of a breakup? Sisters reunited? Or strangers who responded to a post on social media?

"They're able to come and go as different characters throughout my work, and the characters shift," the artist says. "You can play my sister…or you can play this imagined version of someone in my family…or just a completely fictionalized character too."

When she meets her subjects, it's often for the first time at the location of the shoot. If there are multiple subjects, they sometimes know each other but often don't. "People are just so open," Cadet says. "It's amazing to see. Two strangers will meet. I'm like, 'Can you hold hands? Can you lock arms?' 'Yes,' they say. I appreciate it."

When I asked Cadet what she was working on next, she replied, "Letting go." She then showed me material for a new project: Laid neatly on the hardwood floor was a row of ceramic agave plants, some of them broken. Sprouting from the stalks were flowers that don't normally grow on agave—flowers from elsewhere, somewhere in Cadet's biography, a place that is still very much a piece of her even in its absence. These modulated forms are "a way of collecting, but also tracing these different places I've been," she says, forming "internal signifiers that have meaning for me." Cadet intends to use these ceramic cacti

93

in conjunction with photography, forming what she describes as a type of collage.

But glazes rebel. Clay cracks. "I anticipate a lot more breaking and I have to be okay with that," she says. Ceramics is an apt exercise for abandoning the perfectionist aspects of photography.

Cadet's practice is inspired by her mother (and "her thoughts on homemaking"), watching films and anime, doing nothing, cooking, and taking walks in Debs Park. "When people ask me what are my inspirations, it's not necessarily artists that I think of," she notes. "It's more so lived experience, and what I'm surrounded by that informs a lot of my work." Her ideas usually come from questions—ones she rarely answers. Sometimes images appear to her like visions, which she then transcribes in detail.

"There's this translation that happens between what I see in my mind and what I'm able to create with what I have available," Cadet says. The closer she gets to the finished piece, the more it drifts from what she had originally envisioned. Spontaneity and chance are fundamental: "What makes it into the image isn't even what I thought it would be at first.... What makes it in is what I'm excited about—what I don't understand, and a lot of accidents."

94

Carl Cheng

in conversation with Kate Nesin

Minerals, Conglomerated

The titles of Carl Cheng's recent survey exhibitions ring like maxims: *Nature is Everything, Everything is Nature. Nature Never Loses.*[1] For Cheng, such declarations are foundational. Yet across six decades the artist's work has insisted, too, on a meaningfully nondogmatic set of forms and practices: kits, devices, prototypes; kinetic, often interactive public projects; testing, tinkering, waiting, responding, changing.

In March 2025, I used a call recorder app to capture an ultimately 12,000-word phone conversation with Cheng. I asked questions about language and time; he provided answers about materials and making. What follows is a representation of and a reflection on our call together. It arrives here as an entirely partial, entirely "out-of-order" glossary.[2]

---

1   The surveys cited are those at Cherry and Martin (now Philip Martin Gallery), Los Angeles, in 2016, and at The Contemporary Austin; the ICA Philadelphia; Bonnefanten, Maastricht, Netherlands; and Museum Tinguely, Basel, Switzerland (2024, 2025, 2026).

In 1967, Cheng, at the advice of his accountant, formed the John Doe Company, a business entity that often displaces his own name. His account of the decision is streamlined: "As a company, I can deduct anything and everything I use for an artwork. And I've always liked the idea of an anonymous artist. You make work, but nobody knows who you are." Graciously, he adds: "People think about it now in a very serious way. The name really fills up"—with meaning, or meanings. I have found the name to be less vessel than rabbit hole. Mostly, people do not elect this anonymity; John Doe and Jane Doe are the placeholder names given to crime victims whose identity is unknown. Earliest on, from around the fourteenth century, John Doe was a fictional name applied in English court cases when a land title, rather than a person, was on trial. Thus it is a name that participates in the long Western history of corporate personhood, which Cheng's adoption disrupts, parodies, wields. The generically white moniker subsumes both Cheng's own Chinese name and his line of work such that other companies, and the Internal Revenue Service, would better respond to the artist's needs. "Much later I was in Austin, and the punk

2   I mean disorderly, but the sense of being out of service will resonate strongly throughout as well. In 1975, Cheng penned a text called "Out-of-Order Technology": "Breakdown, repair, breakdown, repair, !@#$%^&*@$@# / Whoops, I have to treat it like my loving relationship with my cats. / 'How are you feeling today, my purring machine?'" Quoted in *Carl Cheng: Nature Never Loses*, an exhibition brochure published by The Contemporary Austin, 2024.

rock musician John Doe happens to live there, so I met him. It was kind of funny: John Doe Company meets John Doe."

The John Doe Company developed primarily "nature products," some of which were containers within which nested "human rocks." In the *Erosion Machines* of 1969, for instance, Cheng shaped nuggets of plaster and set them on metal racks within a windowed, hot-yellow box. At right, internal nozzles spray one black-lit plaster mass with water, gradually weathering it; at left, other masses can dry and rest. "I was building machines that acted out natural phenomena—using natural processes as a basis for making artworks."

"Let's take a toaster. You buy a toaster, and it's supposed to work, right? You put bread in and toast it." (I notice, while listening, that both *rock* and *toast* can be noun and verb.) "Now, as soon as the toaster breaks down, it's useless." (It looks the same externally, it comprises the same materials, but it has ceased to perform.) "There's probably steel, plastics that make switches and buttons, a door hinge, a Nichrome wire, an electrical cord and plug. If they don't work together anymore, then how different is it from a rock—minerals conglomerated. So I consider them human rocks: anything made by humans that doesn't

97

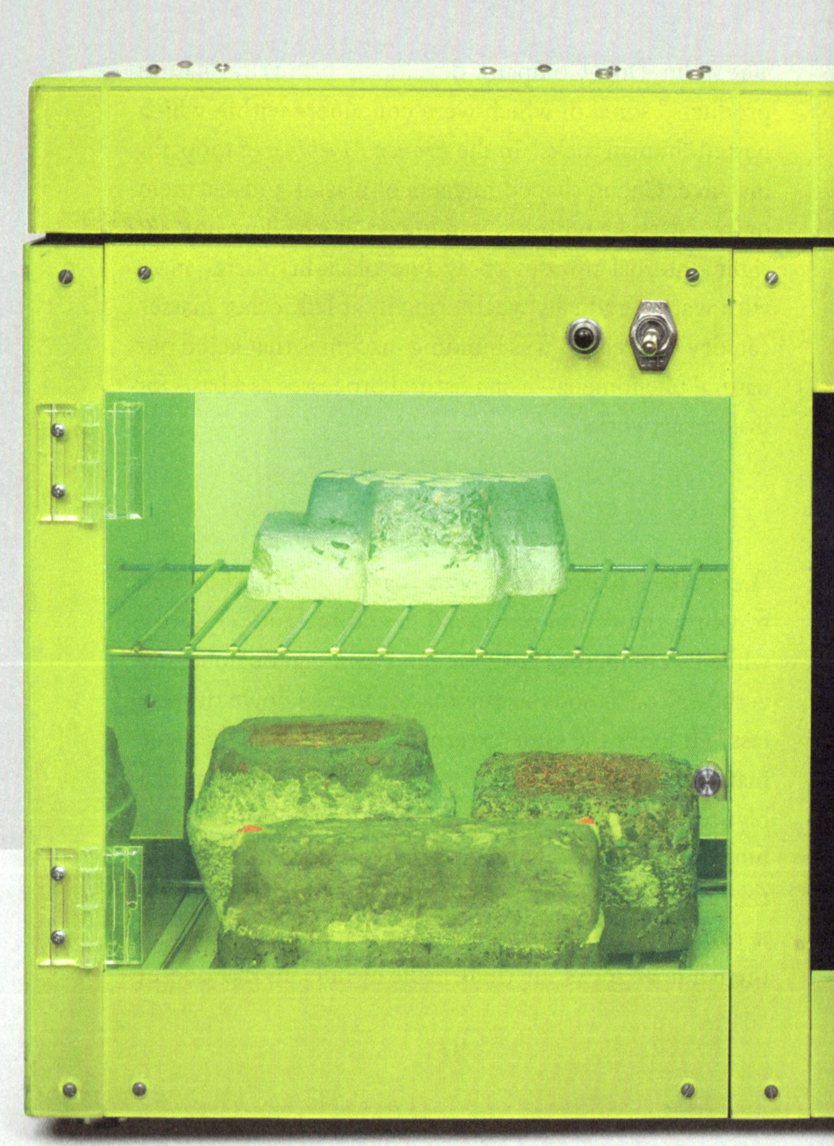

Carl Cheng, *Erosion Machine No. 4*, 1969. Plexiglass, metal racks and fittings, plastic, water pump, LED lights, black light, pebbles, four erosion rocks, wood base. 15 × 25 × 9 in. (38.1 × 63.5 × 22.9 cm)

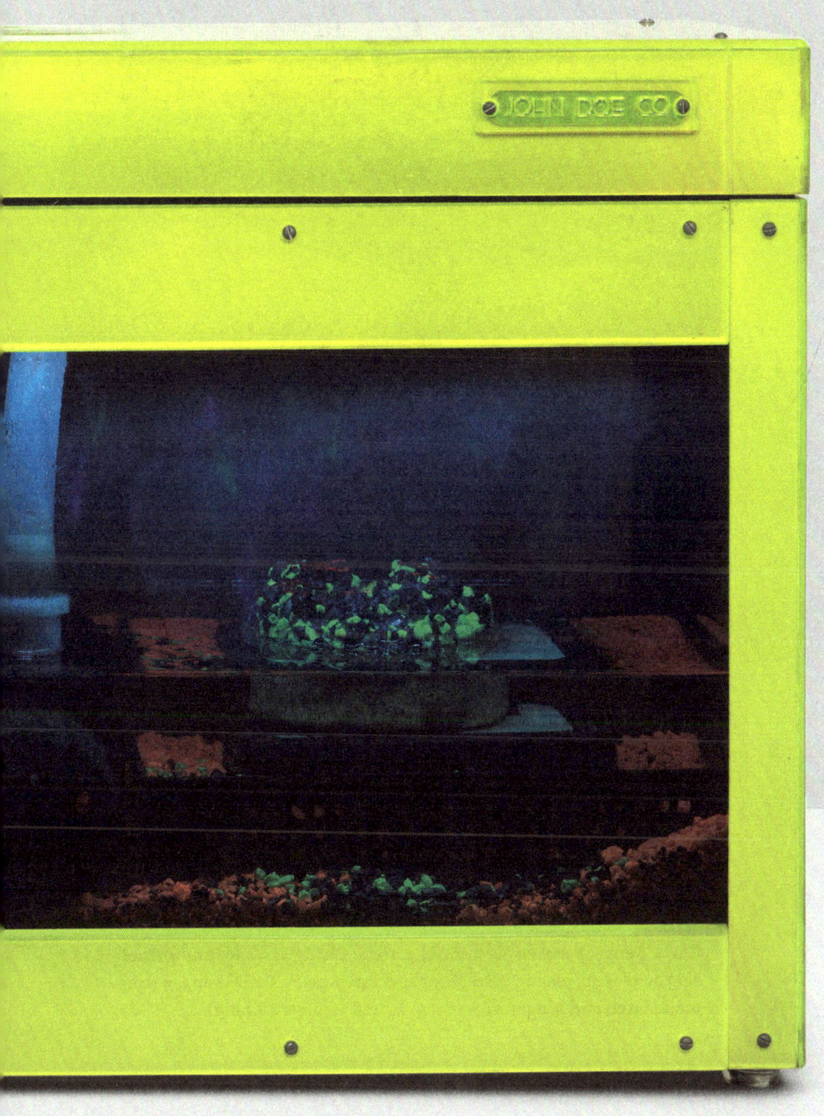

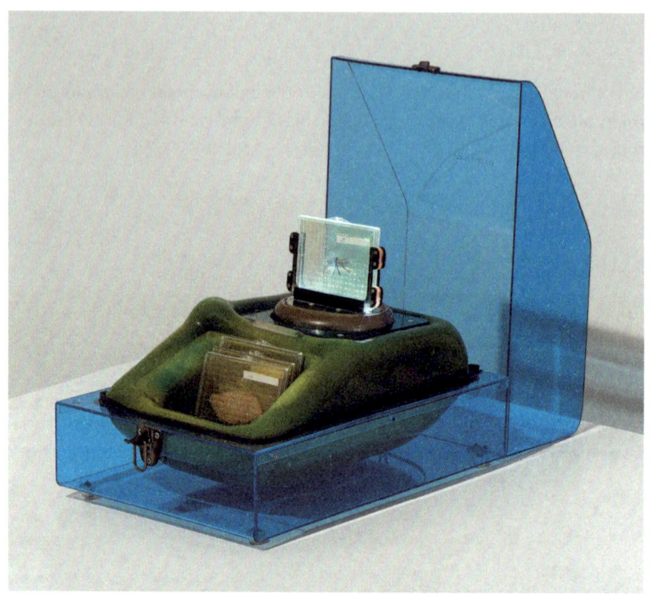

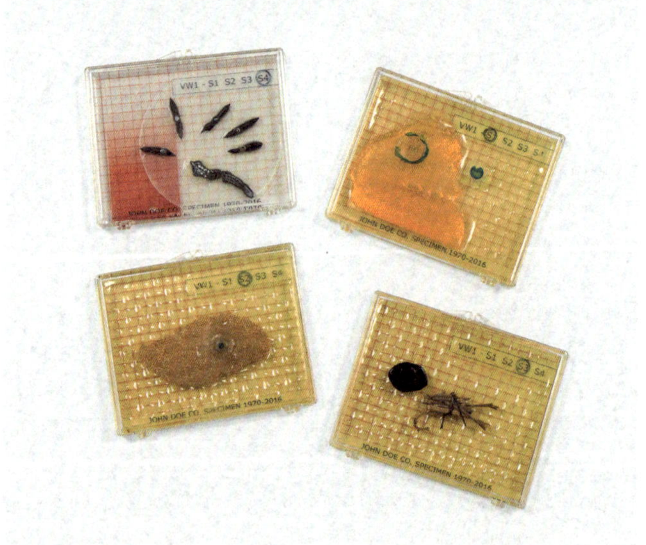

Carl Cheng, *Specimen Viewer No. 4*, 1970. Plexiglass, vacuum-formed acrylic plastic, plastic cases, four specimen cases, LED lights, wiring, metal latch and hinges. 11 × 12 × 19 in. (28 × 30.5 × 48.3 cm)

work…. Then it's just a lump of minerals and other materials. It'll end up in a dump somewhere."

I love the phrase *human rock*—funny sounding, wrong sounding. It means human-made and also implies, for me, at once a humanlike rock and a rocklike human. For Cheng, it has specifically meant the rocklike mounds he fashioned from plaster and the rocklike disposition of a broken machine. But then, in 1983, he made *Twin Rock Communication Indicator*, a black briefcase that, when opened, reveals rocks, a spectrometer, and wires for connecting the former to the latter. "It's a tool based on the idea that rocks can talk." And not just figuratively, as in rocks communicating their origin stories to a geologist, or the way we might say that an inscribed stone speaks. "It came out of the knowledge that trees and plants *can* talk to each other. I thought, well, the next case would be rocks and minerals talking to each other, because why not? In nature, everything is talking to everything.[3] How they're talking, we don't know, but I was projecting a tool—a projected or future tool, something that doesn't exist yet."

3   In her long poem attending to the behaviors and habits of crows, Cecily Nicholson offers a defining aim of communication among those that vocalize: "purposeful vocal control is the aim of communication / speech uses the tongue to count numbers and transmit // articulate quantities // seven caws just now, followed by two crrricks / seven again then two distant, singular notes from afar." Cecily Nicholson, *CROWD SOURCE: a poem* (Spiral Editions, 2024).

101

Another resonance for *projected* here is how readily humans project themselves onto the nonhuman (also how readily humans presume difference from the nonhuman). Given this, I found myself more inclined to talk with Cheng about anthropocentrism and anthropomorphism than about the Anthropocene. Many consider him among the first to make art about the Anthropocene, though he demurs. Demurral aside, one plausible synonym for *human rock* is surely *future fossil*, an umbrella term for imagining the traces of human impact on Earth as they will appear thousands of years hence. Not until my third pass did I recognize the oddity of the twinned rocks, the two largest stones that are an impossibly identical pair. At that point I confirmed: They are painted plastic, light to lift. Metaphors of heaviness and lightness are frequently conjoined in Cheng's works.

MAINTENANCE

Before speaking with Cheng, I thought about the Wardian case, a tool of empire devised to carry plant specimens across oceans; about the traveling salesman's suitcase; about Paul Thek's *Technological Reliquaries* (1964–67). In speaking with Cheng, I came to understand his sculptures' logic of encasement as keyed not only to portability and display but also to maintenance. After speaking

102

with the artist, I am haunted by the uneasy correlation between maintenance and impermanence.

CARL CHENG   My background [in industrial design] shapes my thinking about materials. Like with a toaster again, its Nichrome-wire heating filament—I'm aware of that piece of wire because that's the thing that usually breaks down first. I need to be aware of what's the part that's going to break.

KATE NESIN   If a work of yours breaks down, does its status change for you? Or does your work hold both positions—active whether on or off, functioning or broken?

C.C.   Right now I have to go to Philadelphia to fix something, a motor that's slipping a little bit. Really, that's a good problem to have. Because part of technology in itself is that nothing lasts forever. I don't think of my artwork as something that's permanent.

K.N.   Yet fixing what's broken, when you are able, remains important to you. I've been reading about the Cave Formation Repair Project, scientists who developed tools—like the Stalactijack, the Speleoclamp—to mend broken rock formations in the Lincoln National Forest in New Mexico. Geological, institutional, and studio time scales are wildly distinct, but one thing that's clear from looking at documentation of your installations is that most

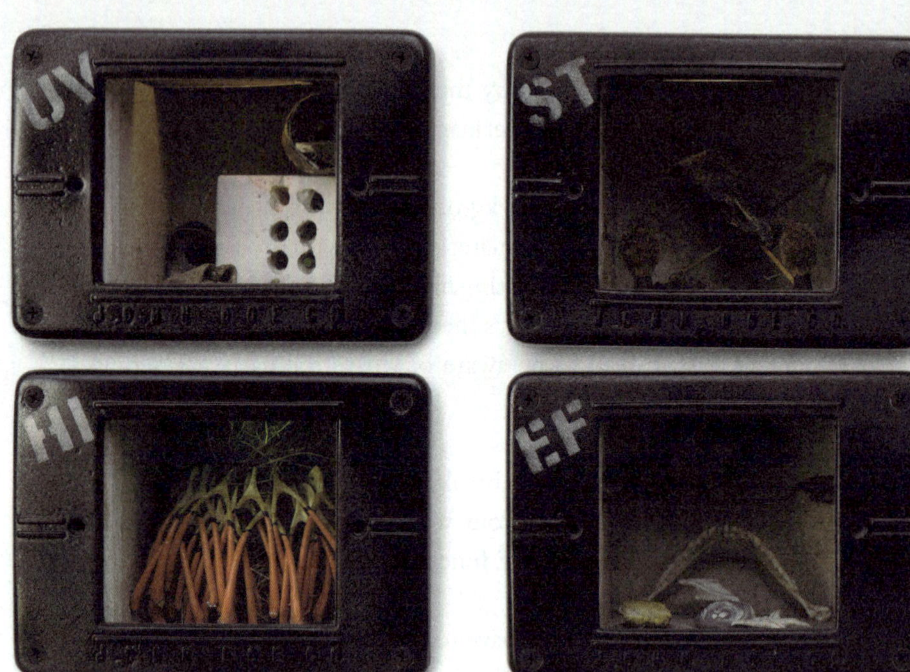

Carl Cheng, *Natural Museum of Modern Art*, 1979 (detail). Coin-operated console, two canopied windows, sand table. Overall: 144 × 240 in. (365.8 × 609.6 cm)

104

every artwork carries a date range spanning decades. Some titles are appended with 2.0, indicating an upgrade. I'm thinking of *Organic Visualizer/Assembler* (a motorized, internally lit vitrine of sorts, for observing materials gathered in the 1970s). The metal body of the vitrine is labeled 1976–88, and also 2016. Your work brings forward for me a curious association between natural processes of corrosion or decay, and something like technological obsolescence. The flip side of which is, I think, how progress gets defined, and by whom.

> c.c.   Many companies want their product to become obsolete so they can sell you an upgrade. But it's also true that there's always something, with technology, that can be added or changed out that would make it last longer or work better. I do upgrade my works, but that's a big point for me, because nothing I make is going to last forever.... You can also think about bronze or marble. Maybe it takes a thousand years instead of one year, but there's nothing that's permanent in nature, either.

k.n.   When a repair is needed, can someone other than you, the artist, also be the repair technician?

> c.c.   I don't make anything so quirky that it can't be repaired by somebody who's technical, with some engineering knowledge. I buy or make universal parts. And I have to make things with doors that open up, that come apart,

105

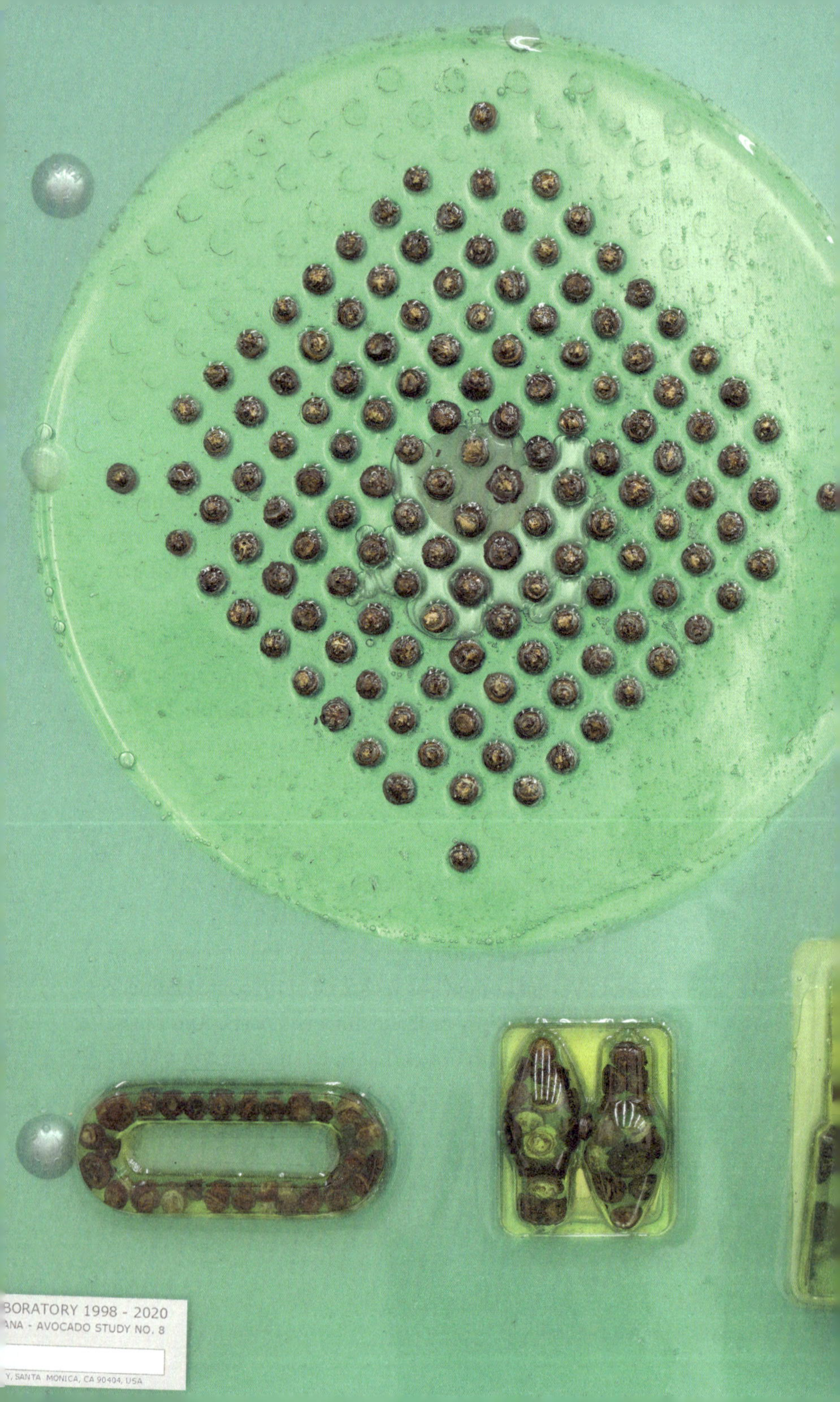

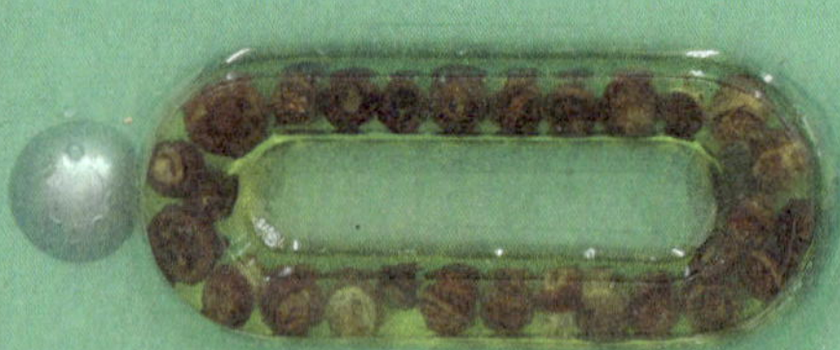

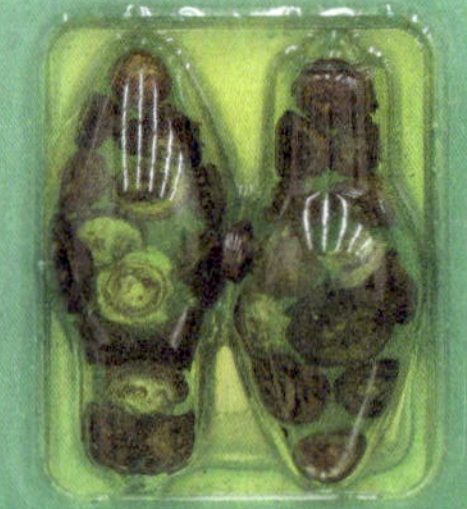

BORATORY 1998 - 2020
ANA - AVOCADO STUDY NO. 8
Y, SANTA MONICA, CA 90404, USA

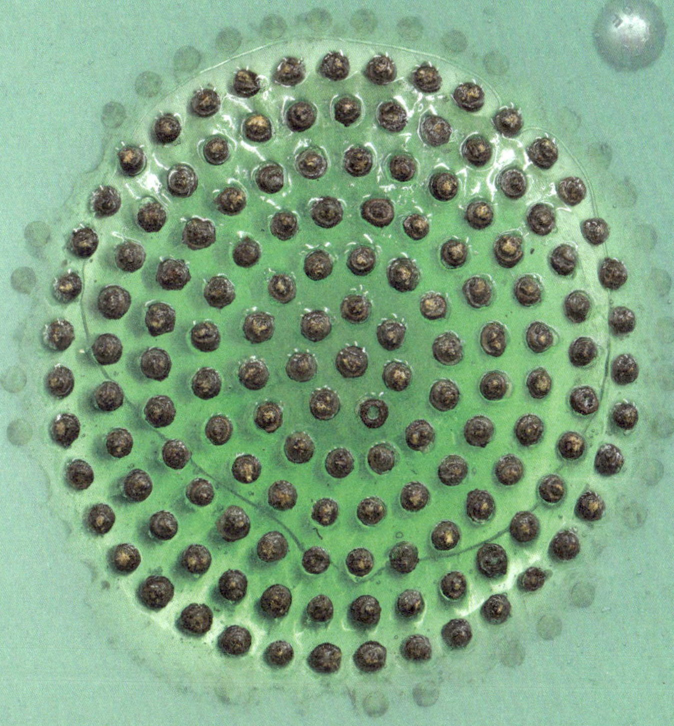

Carl Cheng, *Nature Laboratory Collection 3.0*, 1970–2022 (detail). Avocado skin sculptures, adhesive, cafeteria trays. Sixteen-part installation. Dimensions variable

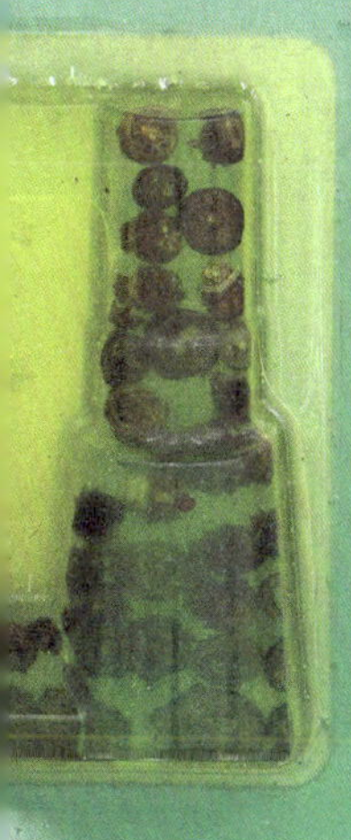

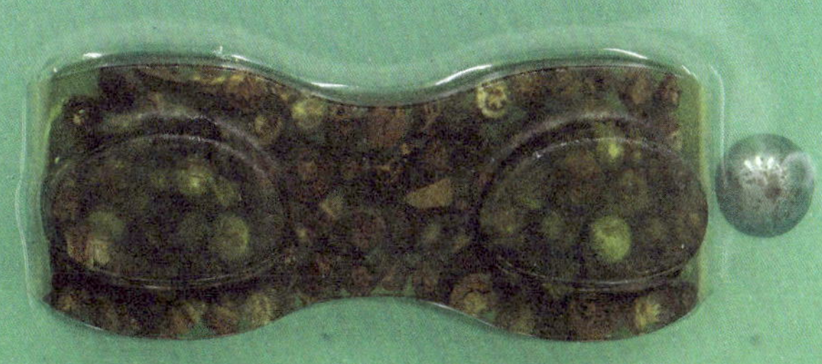

because you need to service it. So it's part of the language of making things, for me.

k.n. We *are* both talking about language!

c.c. There's no mystery in making it. That's the part that I think I'm trying to say. The mysteries are elsewhere.

108

Alonzo Davis

by Jennifer Buonocore-Nedrelow

Olympic Mural Project, 1984

*We [found] through [the Brockman Gallery] that there were
a lot of people who liked art, but we weren't reaching the
working class, certain segments of the middle class, and everyday people. They weren't coming in the doors. Whereas, with
murals and art in public places, they were confronted with
it in their everyday traffic patterns. So, we tended to…look
for public art sites where there was a lot of foot or automobile
traffic. [With] Los Angeles being an automobile city, it [made]
sense to put the art where there was the greatest circulation of
people. They tended to be in cars.*[1]—Alonzo Davis

In planning Made in L.A., the curators made hundreds of
studio visits across the greater Los Angeles area. Simply put,
navigating the city's ceaseless terrain by car is an integral
part of every iteration. For Made in L.A. 2025, the Hammer reimagines Alonzo Davis's *Eye on '84* (1984)—a mural
designed to be seen from a moving car—in the museum's

[1]   Alonzo Davis, "African American Arts of Los Angeles: Alonzo Davis,"
       (Los Angeles: The Oral History Program of the University of Cali-
       fornia, 1990–1991), 185.

lobby entrance visible from Wilshire Boulevard. As part of the Olympic Mural Project, conceptualized and spearheaded by Davis in advance of the Summer Olympic games in Los Angeles (July 28–August 12, 1984), *Eye on '84* originally manifested on a two-hundred-foot-long span of retaining wall along Interstate 110, also known as the Harbor Freeway. Many facets of the artist's career coalesce in this work of public art: his commitment to accessible art forms, his efforts as an indefatigable arts administrator, and his admiration for this city's diverse cultural communities.

Davis is prominently known as a cofounder, with his brother Dale Brockman Davis, of the legendary Brockman Gallery (1967–1990), the first major Black-owned art venue in Los Angeles; yet the gallery only represents a portion of an expansive practice rooted in community engagement. In 1973, Alonzo imagined transcending the boundaries of traditional objects and exhibition spaces to deliver art directly "to the people, not the elitists," insisting that artistic knowledge "should be available to all classes of people, crossing all races of man, becoming universal in its statement and direction."[2] In his visual work, Davis often used symbols like arrows to allude to a desire for personal and societal advancement. Also in 1973, the brothers established Brockman Productions, a community-oriented nonprofit that allowed them to seek public funding to realize cultural events and art throughout the city. Soon after, Alonzo began creating street murals, a practice intimately tied to his goal of making art available to a wider audience.

110

Like the Chicano mural movement of the 1960s and 1970s with which Davis's community muralism practice coincides, he radically employed the visibility and scale of public sites as a mode of social activism, reclaiming space for marginalized communities. According to the artist, he pinned his first work of public art—a temporary assemblage of wood, tin cans, bottle caps, leather, and paint—to the wall of a construction site related to the expansion of an episcopal church in 1970.[3] Soon after, Davis participated in the Crenshaw Wall (1973–75), a collaborative mural near Crenshaw Boulevard and 50th Street in Hyde Park that was repeatedly repainted. Throughout the 1970s, less documented and seemingly transitory objects and murals followed: an outdoor sculpture near Rogers Park in Inglewood, a painted retainer wall at La Brea Avenue and Veronica Street, and another painting on an underpass of the Santa Monica Freeway near La Brea Avenue, all made to expand the city's art-seeing public.[4] In 1980, Davis created a well-known mural at the Watts Towers Art Center. Originally commissioned by John Outterbridge while he was director, Davis later titled the mural *Homage to John Outterbridge* (1980; restored in 2021) in admiration for the artist's commitment to arts education.

After advocating for public art for over a decade, the 1984 Olympic Mural Project represents the culmination

2   Alonzo Davis, "Symbol Series: A Report of a Project Submitted in Partial Fulfillment of the Requirements for the Degree of Master of Fine Arts (Otis Art Institute, 1973).

3   Davis, "African American Arts," 184.

4   Alonzo Davis, "Recent Activities," artist's CV, ca. 1976.

111

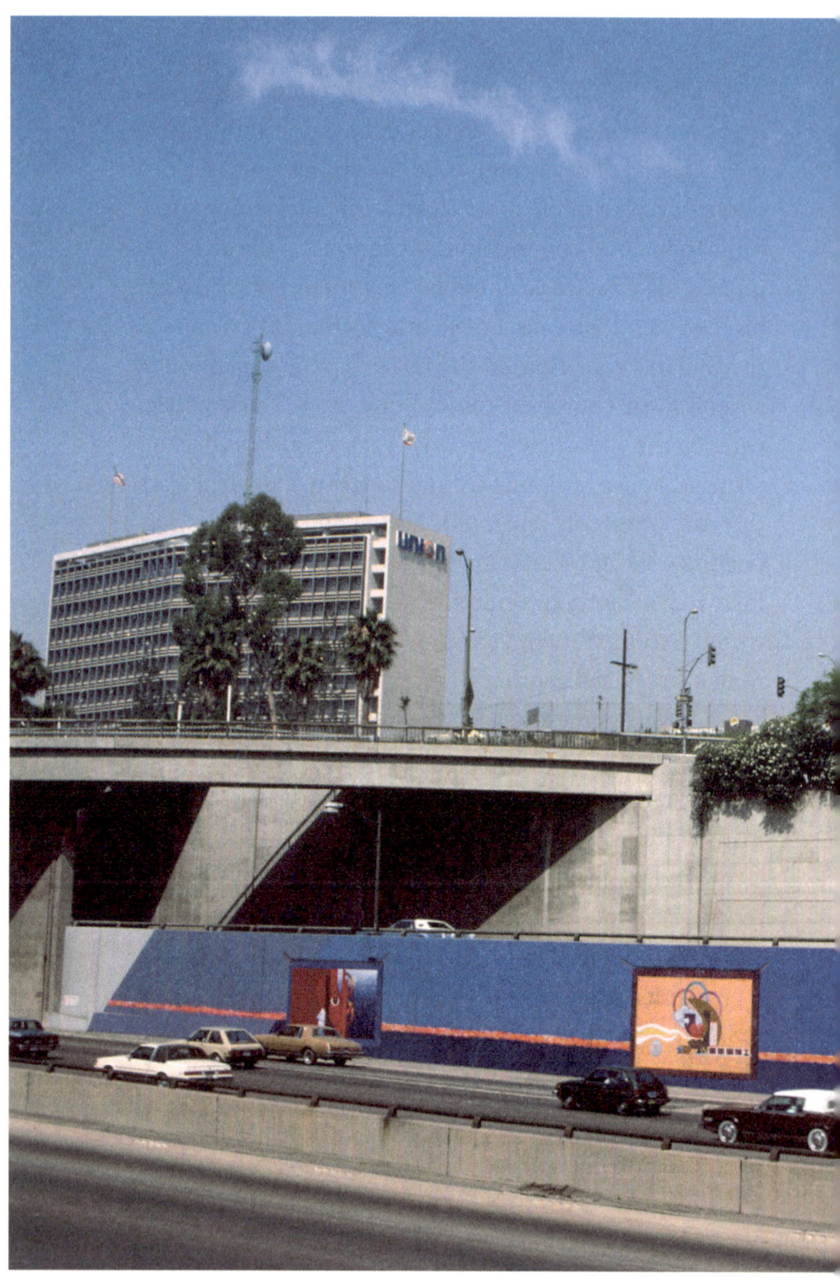

ALONZO DAVIS

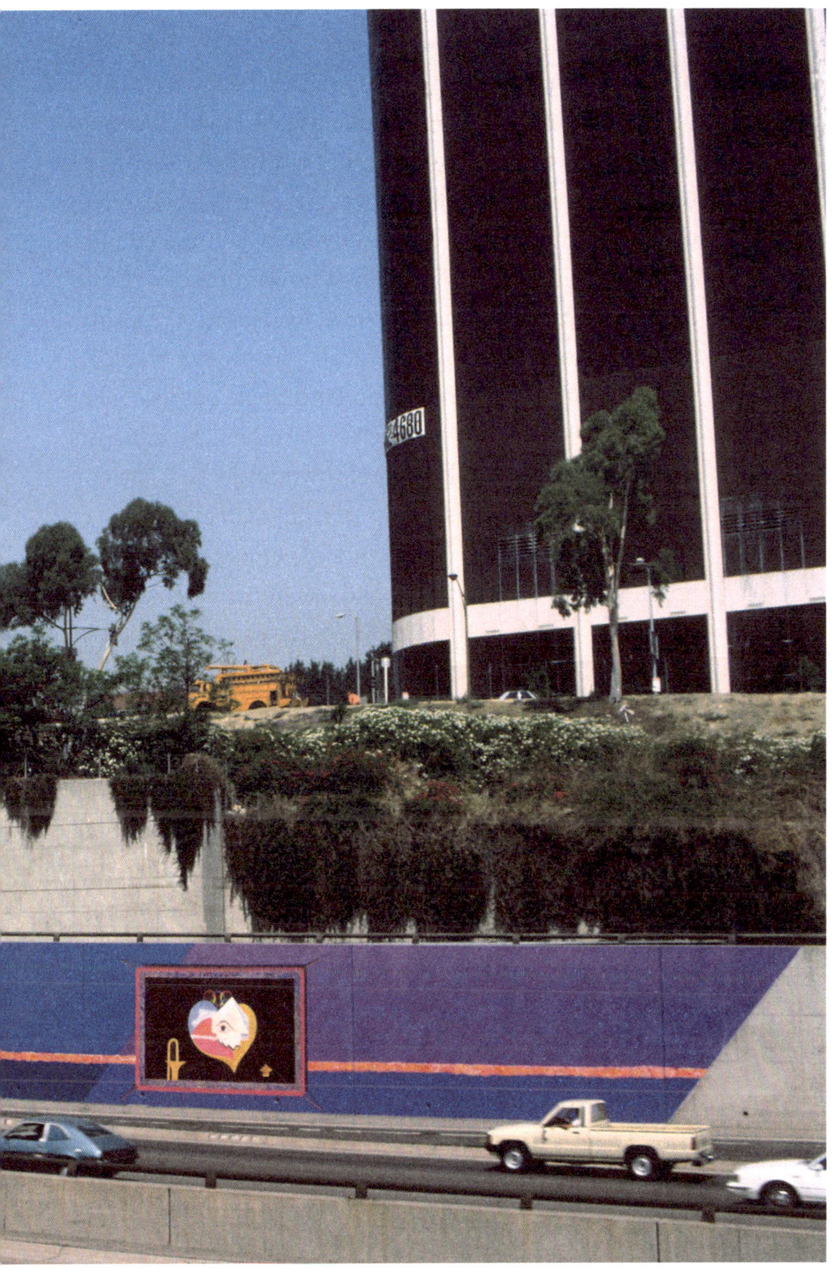

Alonzo Davis, *Eye on '84*, 1984. Acrylic on concrete. 20 x 200 ft. (6.1 x 61 m). Harbor Free-way South (I-110) at 3rd Street on-ramp, Los Angeles

of Davis's mural practice in Los Angeles. Following a failed proposal for the 1981 L.A. bicentennial, he saw the Summer Olympics as a pivotal opportunity to pitch another large-scale commission. In 1983, Robert Fitzpatrick, the director of the Olympic Arts Festival, a dynamic cultural counterpoint to the games, finally greenlit Davis's proposal thanks to the advocacy of Hope Tschopik, who joined the festival after working on the bicentennial. The project would involve the collaborative execution of a single outdoor painting by Davis, and his managing several other lead muralists working independently on their own projects. "The concept was to select artists who were good, had a high standard of excellence, who had done two or more murals in and around the Los Angeles area, and that hopefully that group of artists would be representative of the city and its various communities, ethnic and otherwise," Davis later said.[5]

With this in mind, Davis invited nine other established muralists to submit proposals: Judy Baca, Glenna Boltuch, Willy Heron, Frank Romero, Terry Schoonhoven, Roderick Sykes, Kent Twitchell, John Wehrle, and Richard Wyatt. As the intent was to create murals visible from the road, he negotiated with the California Department of Transportation to occupy four miles of the city's freeway system around downtown. "From my vantage point," Davis said, "[it was] the most visible place in the city, where the most amount of people travel. It was the gateway from the Hollywood Freeway and the Harbor Freeway into the [Los Angeles Memorial] Coliseum area where the games would…take place."[6] Though some Angelenos worried

114

the paintings would cause accidents, in Davis's words, they took the "monotonous quality of freeway driving in this slow, drudging, rush-hour section of downtown Los Angeles and [made] it a little more interesting."[7]

According to maps published in 1984, Angelenos could drive north on Interstate 110 from the Coliseum to encounter Richard Wyatt's *James* close to the Adams Boulevard overpass followed by the artist's *Spectators* at the Flower Street overpass.[8] Continuing north, they would then find Roderick Sykes's two-part *Unity* on the Flower Street on-ramp and adjacent wall. Kent Twitchell's *The 7th Street Altarpiece* was stationed on the east side of the 7th Street overpass while Terry Schoonhoven's *Cityscape* was on the Wilshire Boulevard off-ramp. Judy Baca's *Hitting the Wall* was seen on the 4th Street exit ramp of Interstate 110. Glenna Boltuch's *L.A. Freeway Kids* was on the south wall between Main and Los Angeles Streets opposite Willie Herron's *Luchas del Mundo* (*Struggles of the World*). South down the 101 Freeway, Frank Romero's *Going to the Olympics* appeared before John Wehrle's *Galileo/Jupiter/Apollo* on the opposite northbound side between Broadway and Spring Street. Spectators could then drive back south on Interstate 110 to find Davis's *Eye on '84* on the northwest wall of the 3rd Street on-ramp.

5   Davis, "African American Arts," 189.
6   Davis, 189.
7   Davis, 191.
8   Elenita Ravicz, "Sites of Freeway Murals," *Los Angeles Times*, June 23, 1984: 2, 8.

115

A trompe l'oeil succession of three quilt- or hide-like panels, *Eye on '84* appeared to be pinned to a banner suspended along the freeway's retaining wall. Like concurrent works in other media, the mural brought together universal symbols—Olympic rings, pointing arrows, eyes, and hearts—with cultural references from Davis's extensive travels. Along with *Homage to John Outterbridge*, the artist considered *Eye on '84* to be an extension of the *Blanket* series initiated in 1980, "cloth-like or suspended forms against a background," inspired by "images from the Southwest, Native American hides, Mexican blankets, clotheslines from the South, fabric and folk art…in Brazil and Haiti."[9] As the mural faced the sun head on, Davis layered colors less inclined to bleed, creating a fabric-like crosshatch pattern across the surface. *Eye on '84* included stamps of his own design signifying the transmission of ideas and foreshadowing prints such as *Act on It* (1985) from his *Voter* series that take the form of enlarged postage stamps. In 1990, Davis spoke of his hope to produce his own United States postage stamp. As "the ultimate public art form," such a stamp could exponentially broaden his reach to "millions of people."[10] While that project never came to be, the Hammer's 2025 reinterpretation of *Eye on '84*, however temporarily, makes Davis's mural visible from the street in Los Angeles once again.

9   Alonzo Davis, "Alonzo Davis: Artist," (Berkeley: University of California, 2021), 89; Davis, "African American Arts," 202.
10   Alonzo Davis, "African American Arts," 204.

116

Ali Eyal

by Sampada Aranke

Marked Living

Ali Eyal was born in Iraq in 1994, the same year as Operation Vigilant Warrior, one of many U.S. military actions the artist would live through in his country. Just nine years later, those events would intensify under Operation Iraqi Freedom, a cruel name for a violent effort that would brutalize Eyal's family and countless other Iraqi people. The artist lost many friends and family, the psychological and emotional impacts of which would alter the course of his life. My conversation with the artist took poetic turns: he generously shared his journey to art. I asked about his material choices. He took a turn into gesturing toward the unthinkable. I sat and listened, thinking of what I could possibly say. He patiently rerouted: a story, a place, a person, a thought, a feeling.

Eyal's practice spans mediums, as the artist works with painting, drawing, and video. Often taking place on large-scale canvases, his elaborate explorations of the intrapersonal negotiations and weight of violence vacillate between the representational and the abstract. The artist

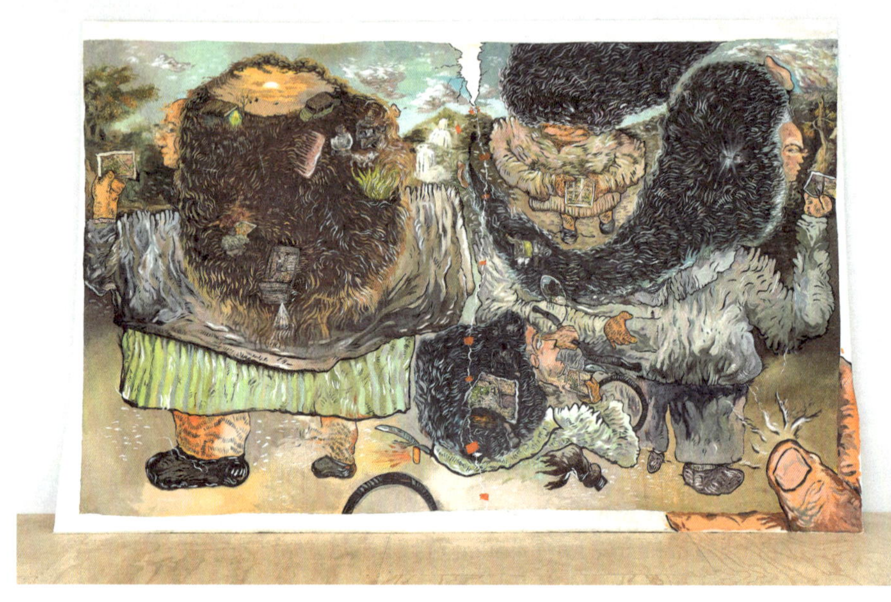

Ali Eyal, *Paper, pen, map in a pocket and*, 2023. Oil and Conté on canvas. 84 × 132 in. (213.4 × 335.3 cm)

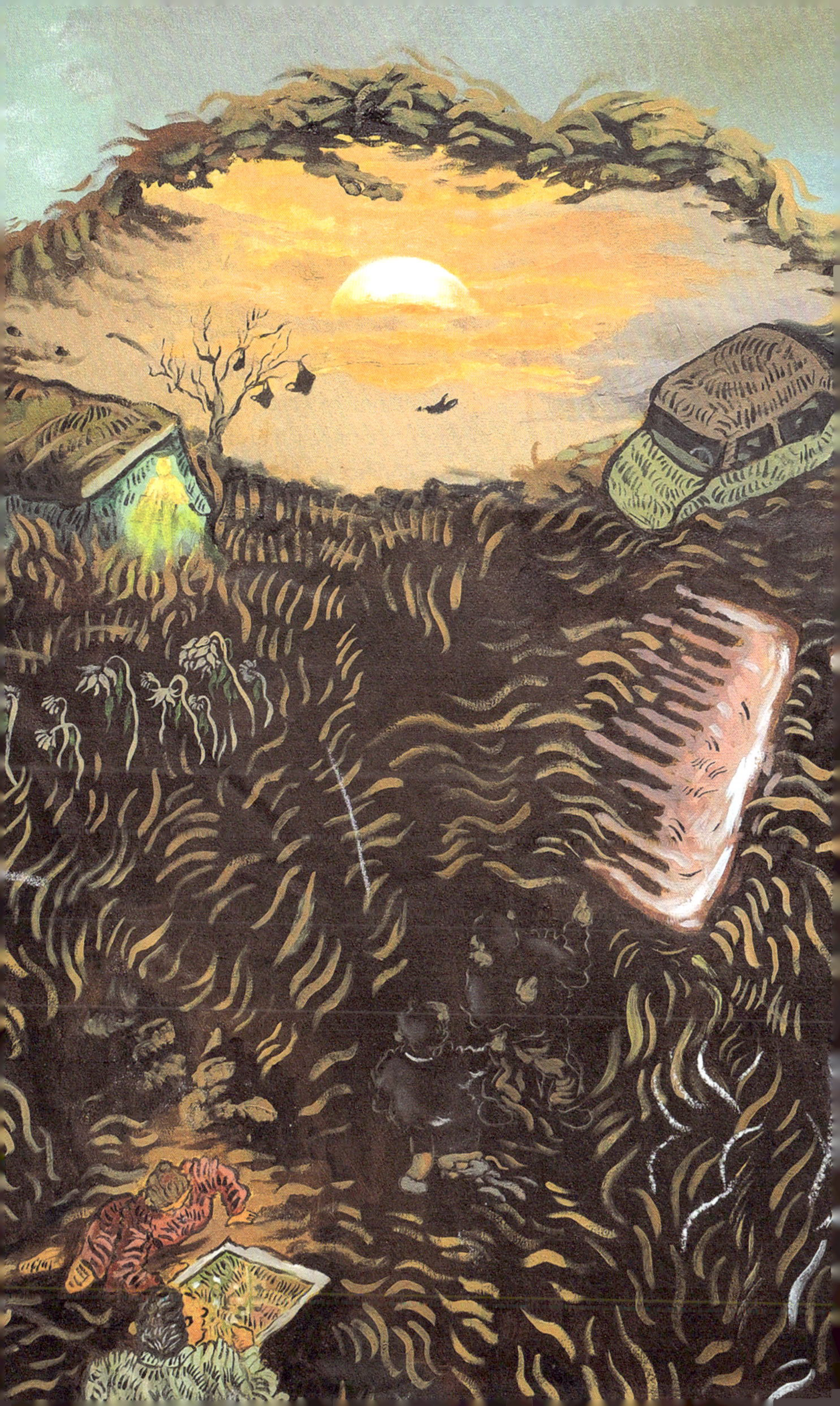

deploys color and line at a deliberately frenzied state, leaving the viewer to question the relationship between shapes, lines, and figures. Often these works resemble illustration, but that label escapes its definition as each work approaches the limit of that category. Most of Eyal's works dwarf the viewer, as they take up a space that approximates the stress and disorientation caused by memory.

In Eyal's work, we're given a visceral account of the psychological disorientation of what the artist calls "the after war." The after war is composed of all the seen and unseen repercussions of conflict, most notably those sensorial elements that simply cannot be repaired or accounted for in any just, material way. Eyal grounds the unseen in decidedly aesthetic practices that bring together mark-making with *marked living*, a distanced and complex relationship to the traumas of being in a body occupied by war. I am calling the artist's work a kind of marked living because of how the artist so movingly foregrounds life-giving and life-taking materials, poetics, and stories in his artistic choices. By deliberately balancing what can be seen and what will never be seen, Eyal attempts to offer a devastating and unflinching account of the permanent effects and affects of war on those who have endured it and those whose lives are protected by never having to face it.

Eyal and I had a phone conversation in early February. It was dreary in Columbus, Ohio, where I was calling from. As a born and raised Californian, I can never fully understand winter; my body doesn't really know what to do with it. Eyal and I found common ground in our collective need

120

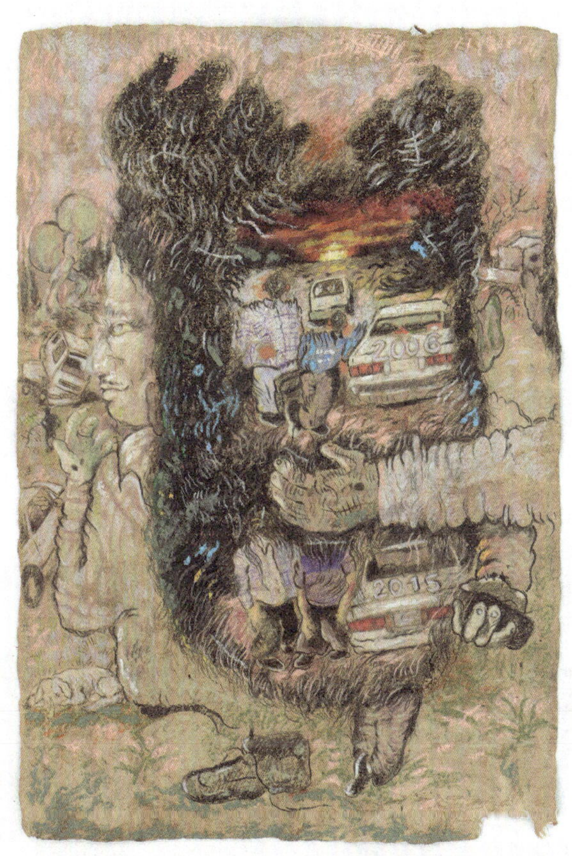

Ali Eyal, *I hope they will see this and*, 2024. Pastel on Bhutanese tsharsho paper. 23 × 16 in. (58.4 × 40.6 cm)

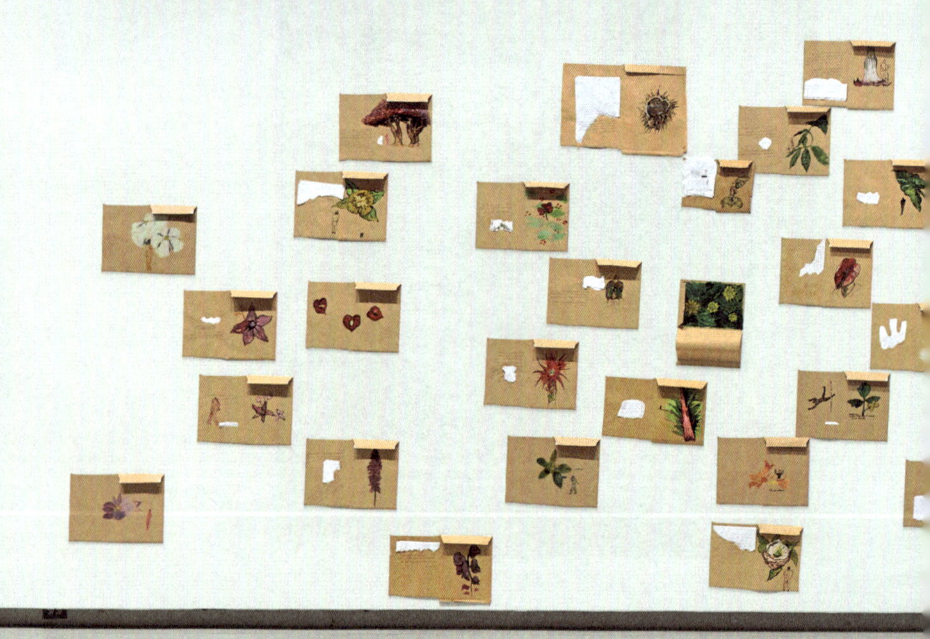

Ali Eyal, *Where Does a Thought Go When It's Forgotten?*, 2022. Oil, colored pencil, ink on envelopes, paper, and cardboard. Dimensions variable. Installation view, 58th Carnegie International, Carnegie Museum of Art, Pittsburgh, September 24, 2022–April 2, 2023

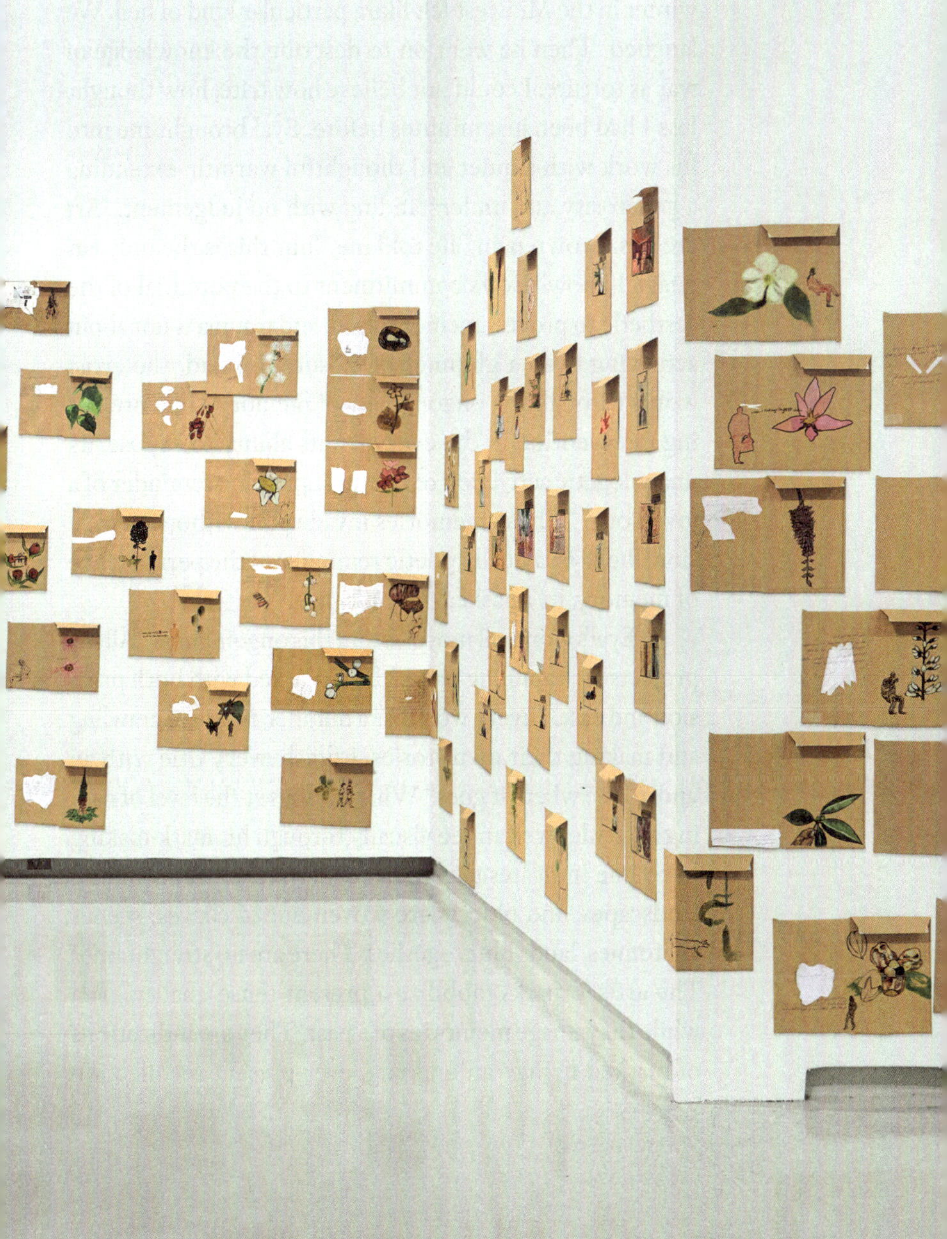

for the sun and its heat, especially in February. I told him winter in the Midwest felt like a particular kind of hell. We laughed. Then he went on to describe the knowledge of war as torture. I could not believe how trite, how thoughtless I had been just minutes before. Eyal brought me into his work with a quiet and thoughtful warmth, extending a generosity and understanding with no judgement. "Art creates its own pain," he told me, "but this is the only language I know." Eyal's commitment to the potential of the aesthetic to process memory, grief, and trauma is not about achieving even a glimmer of closure. Instead, the artist works through the ongoingness of memory—its unrelenting intervention in the everyday, its ability to expose, its unapologetic activation of the most piercing reminder of a loved one. "Those memories invade you without permission," he says: a dually poetic reminder of the permanence of memory, its unasked-for presence.

Eyal's works all move within this ongoingness. "All my projects are rambling pages," he remarked with both precision and ease. "Every work has a number, titles are crawling and making their own stories. I finish every title with an 'and' to see where it goes." What he does at the level of naming and titles we can see visually through his mark-making. Each line indicates a frenetic, energized motion. Bodies, landscapes, and objects are woven out of curves; scenes, anatomies, lands blur together. There are no straight lines. The artist's marks mobilize a present-tense quality, even while they image memories of a past. They are indications of marked living—an ongoing, ever-present recollection

124

of terror and intimacy, chaos and the permanence of anxiety. Each mark annotates a kind of psychological excava-
tion. Eyal's practice is one of living alongside, with, and
through the violences we endure. Indeed, his work is a
model of what scholar Ronak Kapadia calls "insurgent aesthetics" in his book of that title, a practice that centers the
"intimacy, affect, and sensation" that forms "the sensorial
life of empire" in an effort to offer "open-ended and sensu-
ous models of subjectivity, collectivity, and power." Eyal's
commitment to the painful language of art, and his ongoing
and unrelenting manifestation of memory, models a kind of
marked living that extends out from the unimaginable to
the relational.

Hood Century/Jerald Cooper

in conversation with Todd Lerew

Know Where You At: Archiving the Hood

Jerald "Coop" Cooper was raised in the West End of Cincinnati and worked in the music industry before expanding into other creative spheres. In 2019, he started @hoodmidcenturymodern on Instagram to share his observations of the interface between twentieth-century architectural and urban design movements and Black communities and culture, with the tagline "Yes! There is 'modernism' in the hood!" Having since built an informal global network of preservationists, Hood Century is now taking on broader subjects, including community archiving and urban planning as activism. Coop's L.A. studio overlooks the San Gabriel Valley, including the historically Black section of Altadena that was devastated by the Eaton Fire, which was not yet fully contained when this conversation took place on January 18, 2025.

TODD LEREW How do you define this project, Hood Century?

  It's a view of the city with the language from us. It's architecture, it's design, spoken and shown in our language. And that language to me is a derivative of hip-hop culture.

T.L.   You were just saying the "art thing" is new to you.

J.C.   It's kind of crazy, because I was a talent manager in my past life. I was managing Young Guru, who is Jay-Z's audio engineer and DJ. And I was really kind of obsessed with getting people to understand that there's such a thing as an audio engineer. I found myself doing a bunch of creative things and introducing him to the world.

T.L.   I feel like there's a through line between what you're describing and the Hood Century work. People are absorbing this content, this media, this art that's part of their life. But they might not think about what goes into it or who all is involved in making it happen. What's the history and context behind it? You're kind of doing the same thing now with architecture and urban communities through your platform.

J.C.   I'm glad you caught that. It's about accessibility through language. Like the idea of "edutainment," where if I want to educate you, I could use shit that you already know. If we wanna teach, kids are on Minecraft at the library in the hood right now. I'm often in the hood at libraries, and these kids are actually building worlds. I'm like, yo! That's great. Let's actually then give them an assignment about their hood, and they can build their own spaces.

T.L.   You often talk about Hood Century as a translation project, picking up a conversation about architecture and design that's typically happening in an academic sphere or in white spaces. Do you imagine that it could serve as a model for other kinds of translation projects, for other communities or cultures that you're not part of?

J.C.   Hell yeah. And I hope it does. And not only that, but also as a proactive model for communities. I have been asked to do consulting work utilizing the language that I have developed from the Instagram page: "Could you help us think about creative ways to engage with Black people that historically have been in this community, but maybe don't feel like they can?" I mean, that's the point. This shit can't just sit online. It really has to start to be active.

T.L.   Alongside this kind of activation that you're describing, there's a strong archival impulse in your work. How are you looking at knowledge transmission intergenerationally?

J.C.   God bless that my family archive is just so rich. I got briefcases from my dad—he was a DJ. He threw parties and shit. My mom is like a hood archivist because she basically just keeps everything. I have over forty thousand

129

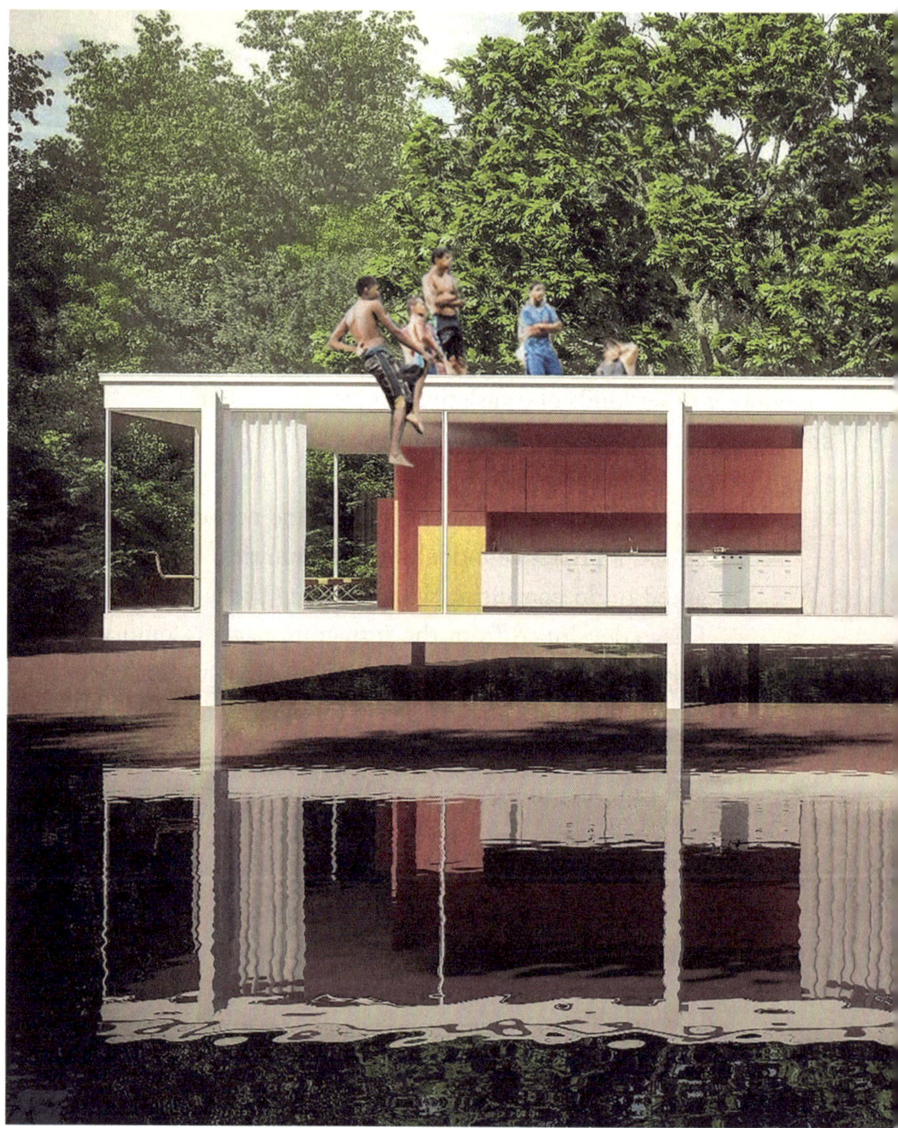

Jerald Cooper, *Summertime, No AC*, 2022. Photo collage. 10 × 18 in. (25.4 × 45.7 cm)

130

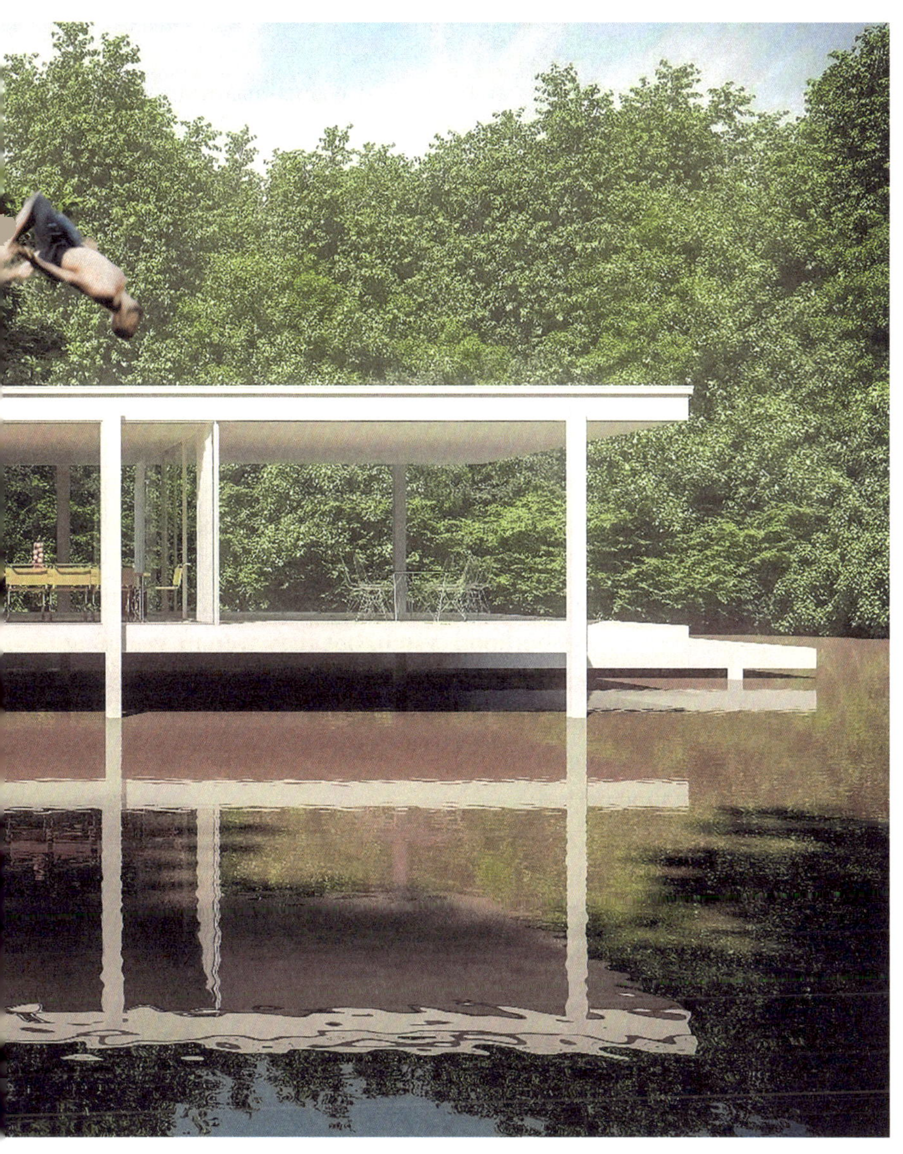

131

images. And I'm archiving it. I wanna make sure that we got it. Pops, he kept it for a reason. I want to challenge people to archive their family.

T.L.   That hits harder right now. As we speak, Altadena is still smoldering, and the toll of what was lost keeps rising. I see the preservation work you've been doing as a kind of response to that. Whether or not we have these disasters and the mass erasure that we've seen, we need these memory projects.

J.C.   There you go. And it is crazy, I was literally just researching Altadena the day before and I was so blown away by the neighborhood organization S.E.N.C.H. They were a neighborhood watch, but they weren't watching for the break-in criminals that you think a neighborhood watch is for. They were there for the white folks who were trying to sabotage their living situation during this redline period.

The Altadena thing is just gonna be so impactful for so many years with folks looking and saying, "You know what? I really need to make sure that I shore up my grandma's house, or our archive." Scan the pictures or do something. I think it's gonna be the silver lining of it, this awareness. I got this feeling that a lot of my friends in Atlanta and Cincinnati who are viewing these fires from the outside are kind of like, "Yo, I gotta make sure my people's shit is straight."

132

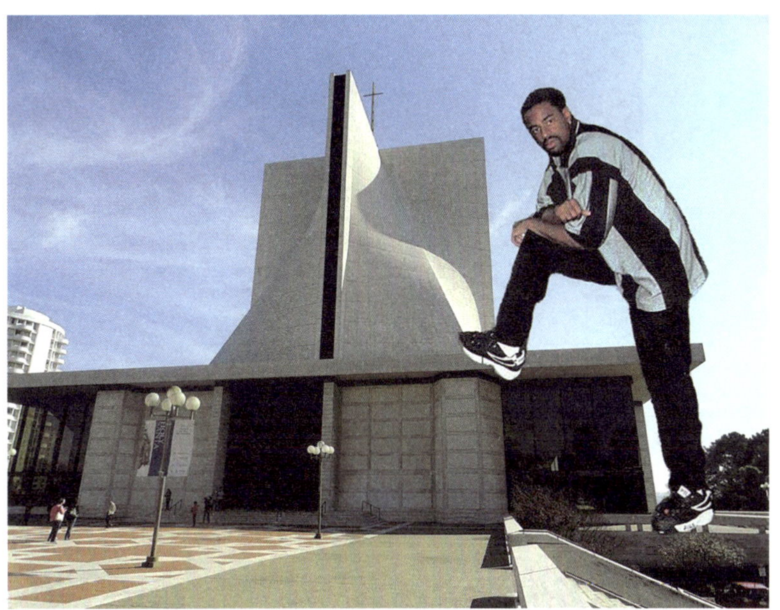

Jerald Cooper, Untitled, 2022. Photo collage. 17 × 24 in. (43.2 × 61 cm)

133

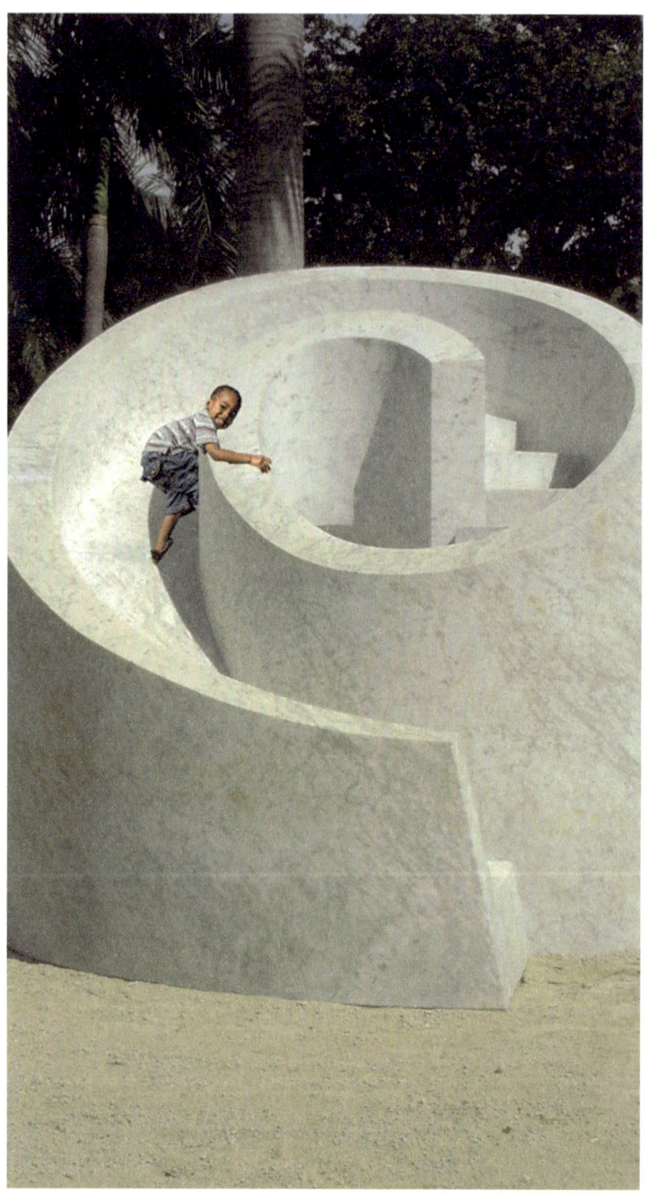

Jerald Cooper, Untitled, 2023. Photo collage. 11 × 7 in. (27.9 × 17.8 cm)

T.L.   A lot of cultural institutions have or are actively
building community-level Black history archives. What do
you think are the possibilities and/or limitations of a pro-
fessionalized approach?

> J.C.   First of all: yes. Let's do that. But I'm terrified of
> where our archives end up. Right now our culture is most-
> ly kept by white institutions or government-based institu-
> tions. And that's terrifying, because they don't fuck with
> us like that. But then I visit the library. I got a chip on my
> shoulder, but I'm at all of these archives too, pulling them
> out and utilizing them and being thankful that they exist.
> So you see the duality there.

T.L.   You talk a lot about knowing your hood or knowing
where you're at…

> J.C.   Know where the fuck you at, bro!

T.L.   What does it mean to you to know a place?

> J.C.   It's that vibrational energy of familiarity. You know
> how it is when you go back to a café and they say, "Oh,
> you were here yesterday." That feels so good. But then on
> the other hand, I have asthma because of where I'm from.
> Where I'm from has led to me having almost the lowest
> life expectancy in this country. And now things like these
> fires, I can't even really be outside, because of where I was
> at. And so that's what the "know where you at" is.

135

I look at Ladera Heights or some of these places that were white people's cribs. When white flight hit, they jetted. Can you imagine motherfuckers intentionally building a crib and then leaving in less than a decade because you don't want to be around the people? And guess what? They coming back. It is so cyclical. They named it. They designed it. Crenshaw, Baldwin Hills. Crenshaw was a white-only area originally. There's a bit of a liberation just in the knowing.

T.L.   How is L.A. as a place important to you and to the Hood Century work?

J.C.   I have this crazy connection with L.A. because of the culture. It's the Ohio culture, it's the Louisiana culture. Black L.A. is not from L.A. Black L.A. is from the South, where I'm from.

The first time I came here was when I was sixteen. I played basketball around the country. We played all these L.A. high schools, like Dominguez…So I knew about places here and the cultures here. L.A. culture is just such a part of my experience. And now being able to navigate it, being able to get in a car and not use my GPS to go to West Adams or South Central. Learning about cultures is one of my favorite things. When I started to open myself up to different experiences in Southern California, it became such a wealth of culture and knowledge. L.A. to me is one of the most beautiful and insane places in America. It's a city that I'm just so enamored with. And I'm still in that discovery phase.

136

Hanna Hur

by Suzanne Hudson

For Hanna Hur

In July 2024, Hurricane Beryl, a Category 5 storm in the
Atlantic Basin, made landfall on the Texas Gulf Coast. Beyond the loss of human life, widespread flooding damaged
critical infrastructure and buildings, including the Rothko
Chapel in Houston. Funded by John and Dominique de
Menil, it opened in 1971 as a nondenominational place of
congregation; its spare, light-suffused interior is encircled
by fourteen large, site-intended paintings. Mark Rothko
made the paintings shortly before his death and did not live
to see them installed. The pieces are near monochromes in
various admixtures of soft black. They disambiguate from
each other via the viewer's process of attunement to texture,
to nuance, to the nonselfsame unit of the painted mark that
finally cedes individuation for a surface. Panels are singular or abutting. Facing across the space are two distinctive
triptychs, each composed with a middle section raised in-
crementally above the others, recalling a typology of medi-
eval and early modern altarpieces with outstretched wings
flanking the center. In these historical precedents, con-
spicuously elevated segments—physically redoubling the

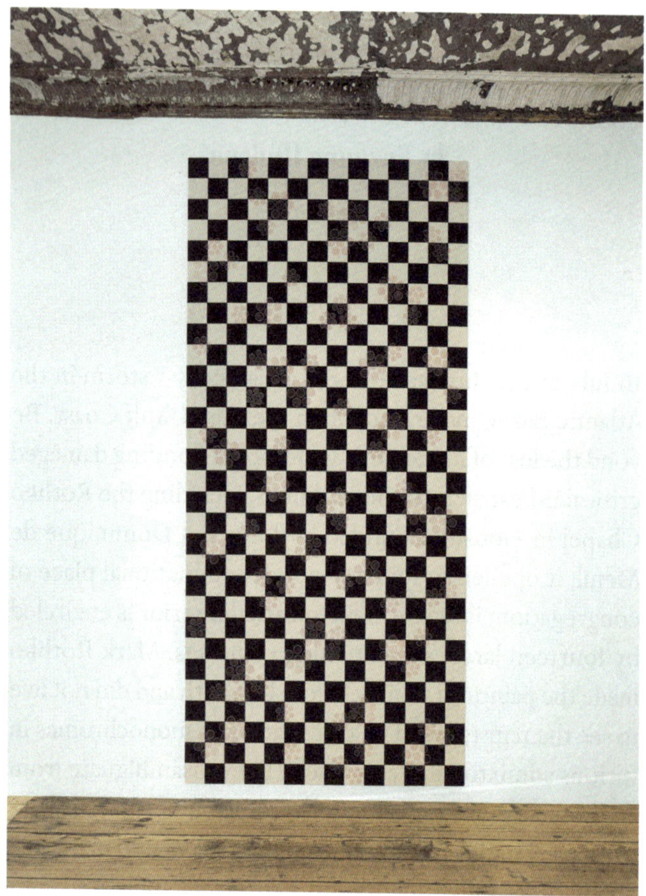

Hanna Hur, *Sun ix* and *Sun x*, 2024. Colored pencil, Flashe, and pigment on canvas over panel. 60 × 56 in. (152.4 × 142.2 cm) each. Installation view, *lost Thing*, Dracula's Revenge, New York, March 8–April 14, 2024

138

implicit liturgical hierarchy they picture—are further suggestive of souls bound for heaven. In Rothko's ecumenical, nonnarrative abstraction, by turns leaden and lambent, the possibility of ascent nonetheless remains.

Rothko's structuring device of the off-kilter canvas separating two others physicalizes suspension relative to a horizon. Suspension can imply something arrested or brought to temporary abeyance, like the whole of the chapel as it awaited restoration and compensatory images of its once and future state-saturated media feeds. (It has since reopened but remains, perhaps even more than before, palpably present in such expressions of collective mourning for what was presumed to have been lost.) As a noun, it also names the "action of suspending or condition of being suspended," as from an armature. The *Oxford English Dictionary* adds to these meanings by reminding us that suspension is also agentive; in the word, there is a kind of reciprocity of being between "something hanging from a support" and "a support on which something is hung," or between "the condition of being suspended, as particles, in a medium" and "a collection of suspended particles." Paintings hang on the wall as matters of course, sometimes in skied installations. Many likewise have conjured weightlessness within the frame, as though figures that appear to be floating in space, in cloud-streaked celestial scenes of angels unbothered by gravity.

As I write this, Hanna Hur is beginning to work on the largest canvases she has painted to date. As with the Rothko paintings that lift their central panel, these are

139

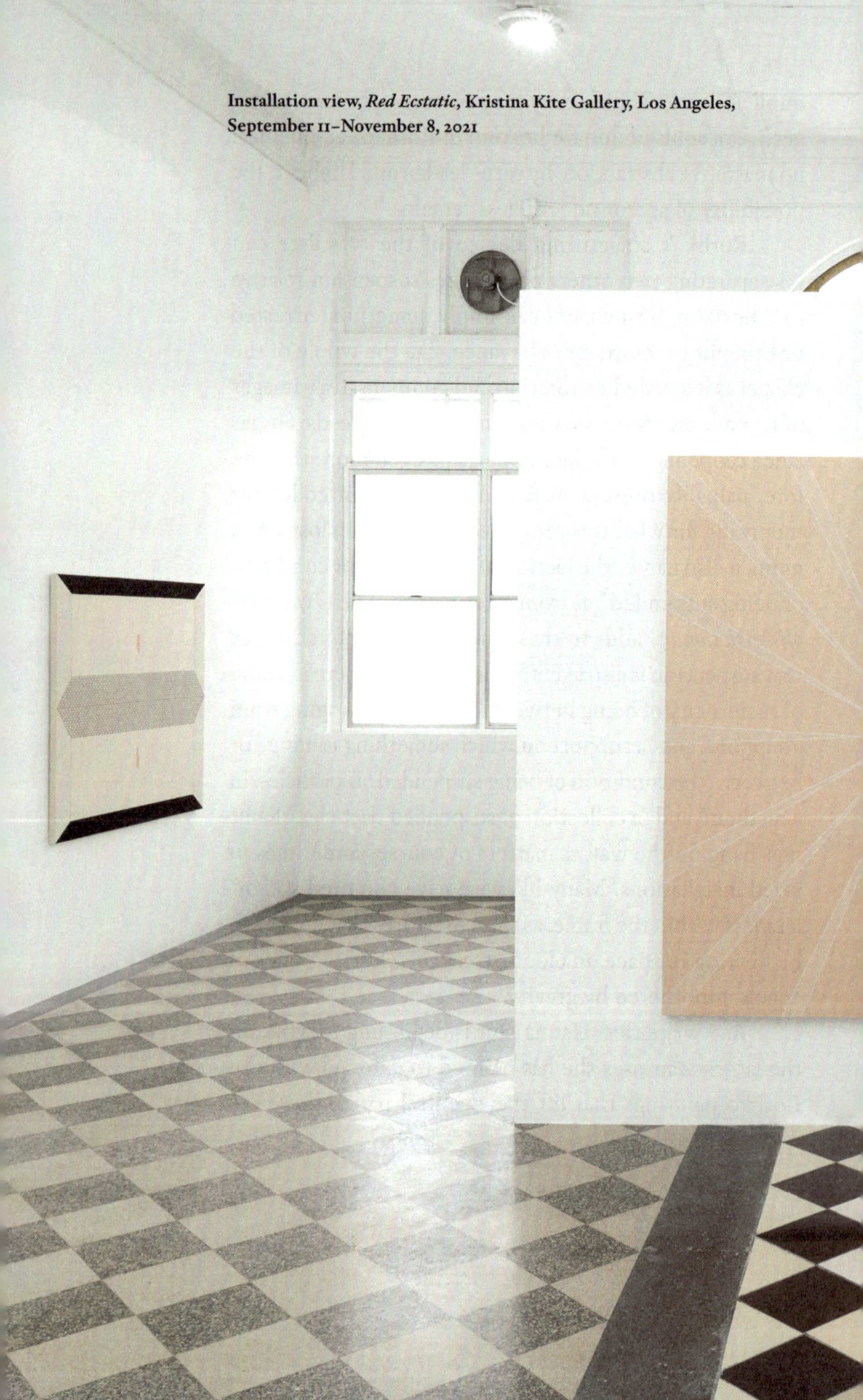

Installation view, *Red Ecstatic*, Kristina Kite Gallery, Los Angeles, September 11–November 8, 2021

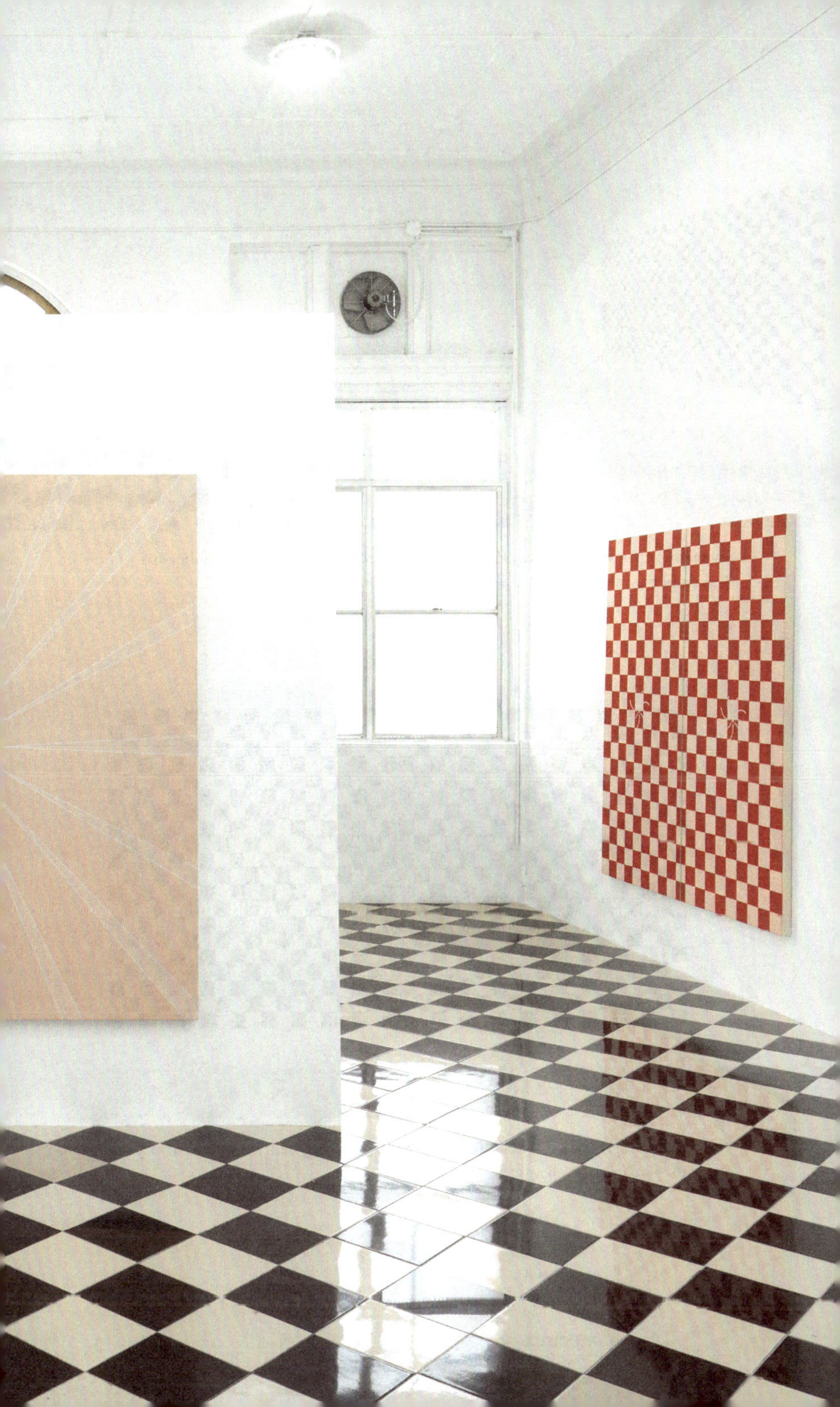

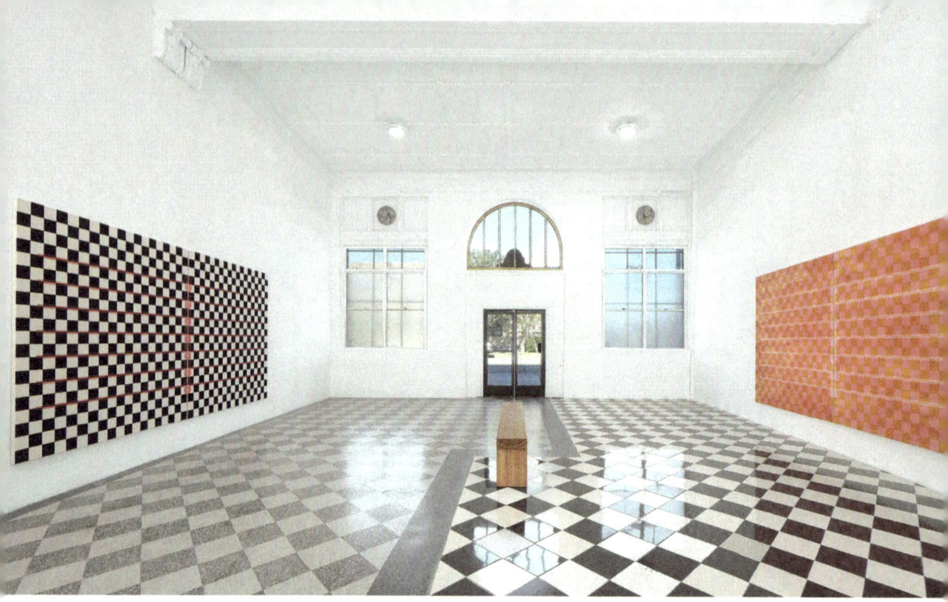

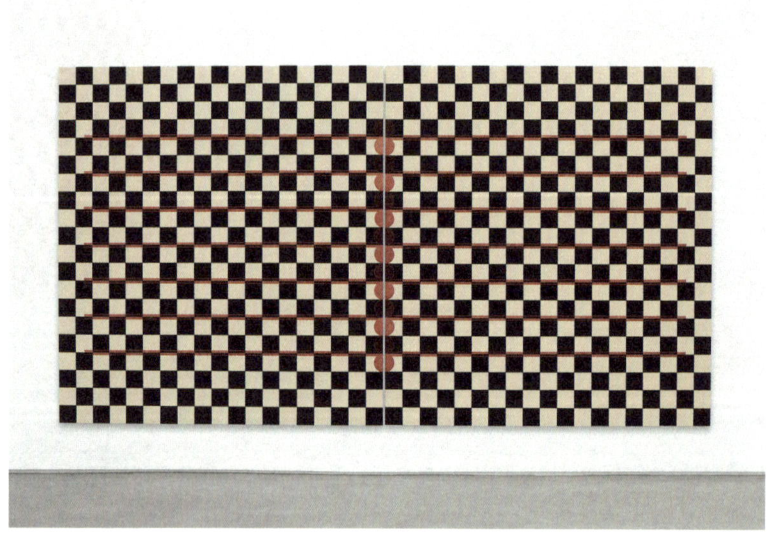

Installation view, *Two Angels*, Kristina Kite Gallery, Los Angeles, November 11–
December 23, 2023

Hanna Hur, *Angel ii*, 2023. Flashe, colored pencil, and pigment on canvas over panel.
80 × 156 ½ in. (203.2 × 397.5 cm)

framed by ascension. In their overwhelming size, they will exploit the vulnerability of a body that wishes to see them: neck exposed, arcing back…eyes straining to see the elevations, and also the patterned geometry configured on vastly scaled fields of white on white on white, the visual analogue of snow dampening sound. There will be five of these paintings in the Hammer's so-dubbed vault gallery, a long room at the museum that is not unlike an apse lacking an altar. A Hur painting can anyhow be made a focal terminus, as did the vertical *Sun vii* (2023) at Dracula's Revenge, New York, in 2024. Or it can envelop a body, alone or in unison, and make one exquisitely aware of the limits of apprehension. For her 2023 show at Kristina Kite, Los Angeles, Hur set twinned paintings, *Angel* and *Angel ii* (both 2023) on opposing walls, forcing the matter of choice. I described it like this at the time: "Whichever one picked, the other exerted an ineffable presence—an experience of inexorability characterized by being attended by something that exists irrespective of your regard, even as it solicits it."[1]

Differently enfolding was a recent installation at Doosan Art Center, Seoul, that Hur titled *8*. It revolved around four freestanding walls angled inward to carve out a chamber within the otherwise starkly empty gallery. To see the four paintings on the interior walls was, however, to miss those Hur had installed outside them. The whole plan extended the swirling imagery of Hur's *Threshold* (2024) to

[1]   Suzanne Hudson, "Hanna Hur: Two Angels," *The Brooklyn Rail*, December–January 2023/24, https://brooklynrail.org/2023/12/artseen/Hanna-Hur-Two-Angels/.

143

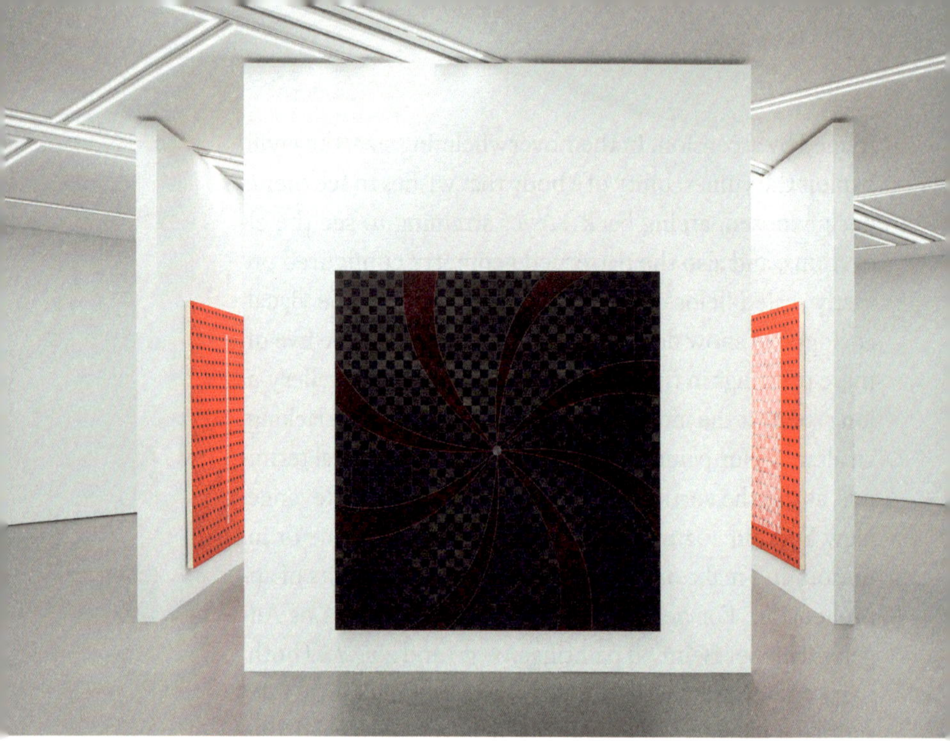

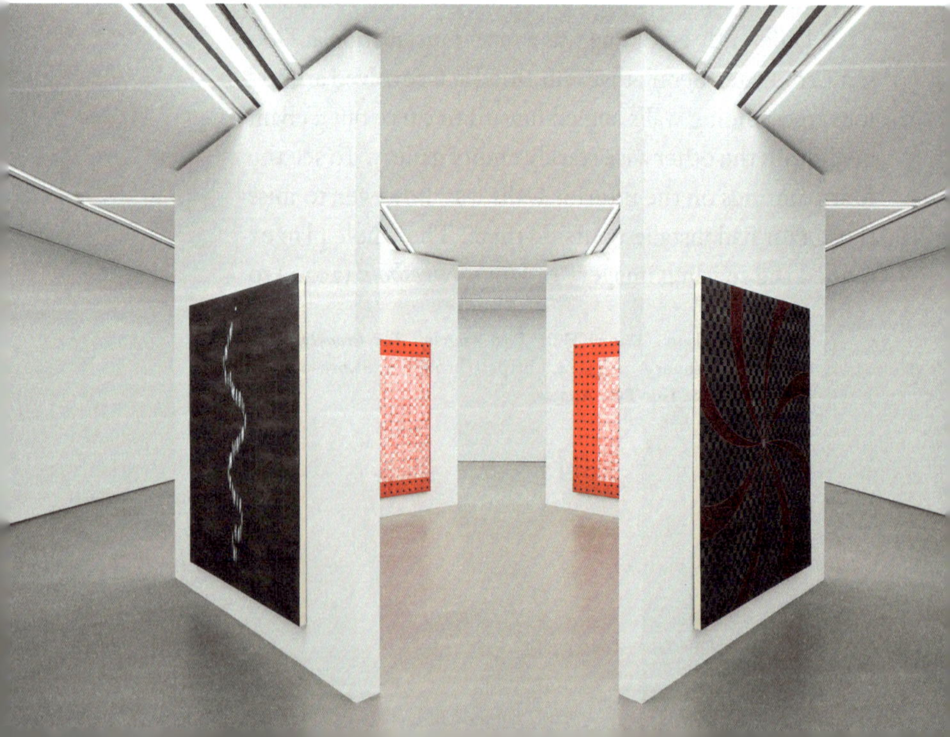

Installation views, *8*, Doosan Art Center, Seoul, November 13–December 21, 2024

effect a pinwheel around which a circumnavigating body might move. The title *8* was illustrative, specifying the number of pieces in the show; it was also diagrammatic, a schema for infinity and the endless looping that the architecture set up. Therein Hur radicalized the ceremonial dimension of viewing as a complement to that form of meditation through repetition experienced as a precondition for—and then function of—disciplined making. Hur has understood earlier works as portals: *Gate* (2019), for one, but so many others, including vital floor works made of chain mail. She has discussed these in relation to a trip to Korea, where she consulted a shaman with whom she performed a seven-hour ritual to appease her ancestors.[2] These new pieces likewise are conduits. Temporal dissonance of past and future—both chronic shifters—profoundly unmoors.

Suspension recast as lightness is a posture. Its enactment amid everything conspiring otherwise is something like a privilege.

2   Sharon Mizota, "Review: Art as a Portal to Korean Ancestors? The Mesmerizing Work of Hanna Hur," *Los Angeles Times*, July 1, 2019, https://www.latimes.com/entertainment/arts/la-et-cm-hanna-hur-bel-ami-review-20190701-story.html

145

146

147

Kristy Luck

by Esti Giordani

Forms of Potential

The painter Kristy Luck is introspective, curious, and un-afraid of uncertainty. The same could be said of their work, which they describe as "intuitive, slow, bittersweet, and somewhat surreal." (Not without clarifying, "I don't identify as a surrealist, but I see it.") Luck's paintings are spontaneous, loose, and expressionistic. Vibrant shapes and forms offer mythology to some spectators and abstract play to others. Whether representing infinite landscapes or aching body parts, the paintings are intimate. Though Luck's brushwork is controlled and intentional, there is nevertheless a sense of the unpredictable—something feral lurking just out of view, maybe from the natural world or perhaps from the shadows of Luck's imagination.

Though Luck has a desire to specify their intentions or identify narrative threads, they aim to "set up a situation where I'm finding it instead of directing it," as they put it. Potential is a potent theme both in their process and the finished work. For both artist and spectator, potential is the act of searching—the act of identifying something unseen as it unfolds in real time. "When I'm making images or getting closer to finishing a painting…I'm trying to see potential in things, or put things together to see new potential…I'm thinking of how that relates to the potential of the images for multiple people to see potential and to try to name what that potential is."

This way of seeing is a guiding principle shaped by resilience. When Luck first moved to L.A., resources were tight. They had to make do with whatever materials they could find, all while figuring out how to make images that could not only hold an entire wall but also contend with the more resourced work dominating the art market. Over time, resourcefulness—scrappiness—led the artist to view obstacles as sources of inspiration. "I think it comes from limitations," they said, "interacting with them as if they're creative rather than binding or negative."

Luck grew up isolated in rural northern Illinois. A shy and quiet child, they were an avid journaler at the prompting of their mother and grandmother. When their sister read their journals without permission—a cruel rite of passage—Luck adapted: "I started putting images in them instead—something that wasn't easily discernible." They would later on attempt to write and illustrate their own books, "but then the writing never came."

Luck's images would eventually evolve into a practice centered around painting. After finishing an MFA at the School of the Art Institute of Chicago, Luck came to Los Angeles. "There's a history and a nerdiness with painting that I inherited from being in Chicago. But in L.A., the light and the sexiness of things, my work couldn't not be

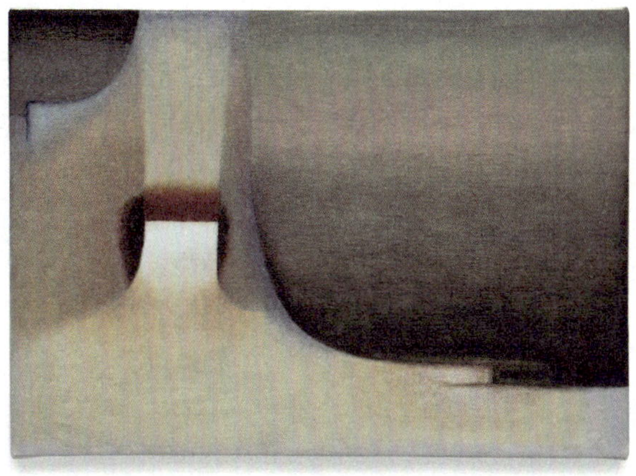

Kristy Luck, *The Cruelty of Flatness*, 2025. Oil on linen. 9 × 13 × 1 in.
(22.9 × 33 × 2.5 cm)

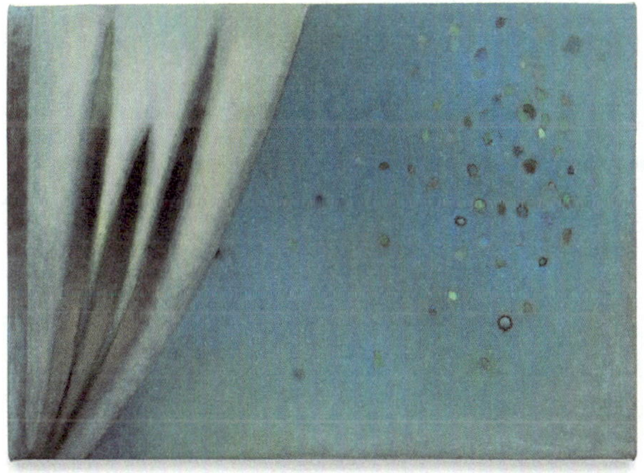

Kristy Luck, Untitled, 2024. Oil on linen. 9 × 13 × 1 in. (22.9 × 33 × 2.5 cm)

151

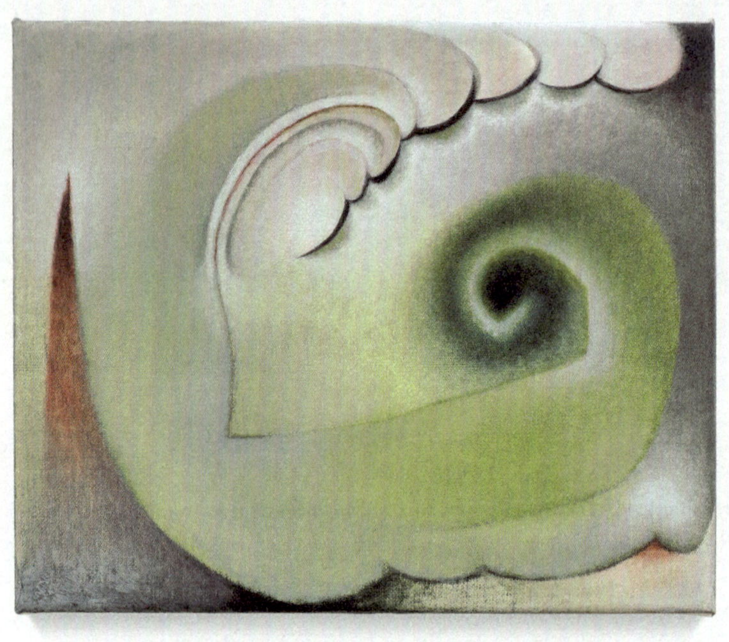

Kristy Luck, Untitled, 2024. Oil on linen. 9 × 13 × 1 in. (22.9 × 33 × 2.5 cm)

influenced by the city." You can see it in their use of light and color. An untitled painting from Luck's 2024 series *One time, one time, one time…* draws from the dusty pink hues of a smoggy sunrise over the San Gabriel Mountains.

Like many artists (particularly in Los Angeles), Luck is deeply inspired by films. Movies are often on in the background as they paint—ones that they've seen over and over, ones they know by heart. The artist is fascinated by how films "create a sense of mystery…how something can end unresolved," applying this aspect of cinema to their own work. Luck's practice is also highly physical, guided by instinct. "I trust my body—my eyes, my hands—to know more than I do," they say. Preferring an asystematic approach, they often go into a project "not really knowing what will happen or what it'll be." This uncertainty acts as a kind of engine, even when the stakes are high and a show is fast approaching. The artist trusts that with time and the sheer repetition of their practice, it will all work out.

When I spoke with Luck in the months leading up to Made in L.A., they were unsure what they were going to present in the exhibition. "I'm on the fence…whether I work larger or keep it really small." The artist has long wanted to work on a smaller scale, but they found that smaller works didn't command the same attention. In a 2024 show of the *One time, one time, one time…* series, however, Luck got the opportunity to work exclusively at a smaller scale and "deliver on that impulse I'd had for a while," finding a rhythm and new directions that have yet to be explored.

153

At the end of our conversation, Luck shared an anecdote about the time they saw a wildcat in South Pasadena, an urban vision that is distinctly Los Angeles: "It stopped me. I haven't seen something like that anywhere else. It was as big as a medium-to-small-sized dog.... We looked at each other and then it just disappeared." Much like Luck's paintings, the wildcat—an unexpected image, maybe even an illusion—appeared for a moment, then was gone, leaving only the trace of something untamed and mysterious, something fleeting yet indelible.

154

Patrick Martinez

in conversation with Robeson Taj Frazier

Beneath the Surface: A Ride-Along through East L.A.

Patrick Martinez's broad-ranging practice includes "cake paintings" that depict various leaders and thinkers, neon-sign installations that mirror street-level commercial signage, and mixed-media landscape paintings composed of materials associated with Los Angeles's physical and architectural terrain. Martinez plays with genre and remixes iconography in a manner that (re)maps Los Angeles's cultural traditions while offering alternative visual landscapes and landmarks that encompass the entire city. On an early Saturday morning, we took a drive down Cesar Chavez Avenue.

ROBESON TAJ FRAZIER   What are you working on for Made in L.A.?

PATRICK MARTINEZ   I'm creating an installation. It is composed of wood panels that are fabricated to look like cinderblock ruins. I think one will be placed outside the exhibition space and another inside. *Make a right.* The outside panels will look like ruins, but contemporary ruins, of suburban and urban neighborhoods. The inside panels will be similar but different in shape. Like it was once concealed and then got exposed. Similar to the Indigenous ruins that the Spaniards built churches on top of. *Yeah, we can go straight.*

Part of it is about acknowledging the subtleties of L.A. and how residents traverse its landscape. Some people perceive L.A.'s different neighborhoods as disconnected. Like, "This is the urban area, and this is the suburban area." But I'm interested in considering the connections between these places and the understated features of these connections. *You can make a left.* I'm also thinking about what connects Indigenous ruins to here. Borders and barriers don't disconnect the soil. They don't stop birds and snakes from passing through. And that's my thing, that analogous idea. Breaking down those walls to reconsider the past and think about how the L.A.nd connects. *Make a right here. Keep going straight.*

R.F.   I feel you. Right now, we see people sitting outside houses. Children playing in front of public housing. People sharing land. Sharing soil, as you put it. None of this is what popular culture or media presents as "L.A." or as "city life."

P.M.   Right. That mixture and that balance. Mom-and-pop commerce. Community graffiti. Murals. The quiet moments. Not just the city as "dramatic" and "sprawl." I'm always thinking about the people and energy that shape L.A.'s different surfaces. When I drive or ride my bike, I pay attention to the day-to-day progression of a wall and the buildings that are knocked down and rebuilt. All of this represents movement and labor. Even if you don't see people doing the work, you see the traces of it. Let's say a mural gets tagged up with gang graffiti and then gets painted out by the building owner. All the activity has an additive effect. It's not someone adding and then someone subtracting. No, they are all making a mark. And sometimes it's a mark that conceals what's underneath.

R.F.   That's a unique way of thinking about the city's surfaces and the layers that exist within them. What's also deep is that when you add layer on top of layer of paint like this, it's more likely to crack and peel and reveal the conditions of its own existence. And that's what your work does, to some degree. You take the layering to its natural conclusion. You also frequently gesture toward the materials that these surfaces are composed of. Distressed stucco, neon and LED signs, spray paint, window-security bars, vinyl signage, and other recognizable materials—all of these have been used or referenced in your work.

P.M.   I want to elevate those materials to a certain level of attention and use them as a vocabulary to speak about the times. To represent now. I'm also interested in the surfaces that people associate with their neighborhoods, the surfaces that they understand as community. And how these surfaces come to comprise the landscape of L.A. I guess that's why I imagine myself being a landscape

157

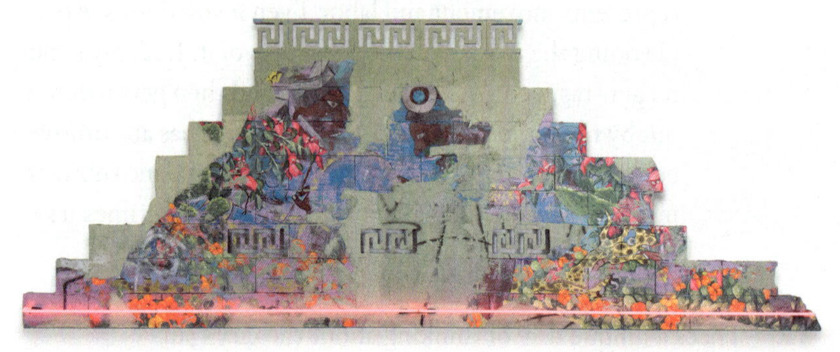

Patrick Martinez, *Warrior Garden*, 2024. Acrylic, stucco, grout, adhesive, neon, spray paint, and latex house paint on panel. 72 × 192 in. (182.9 × 487.7 cm)

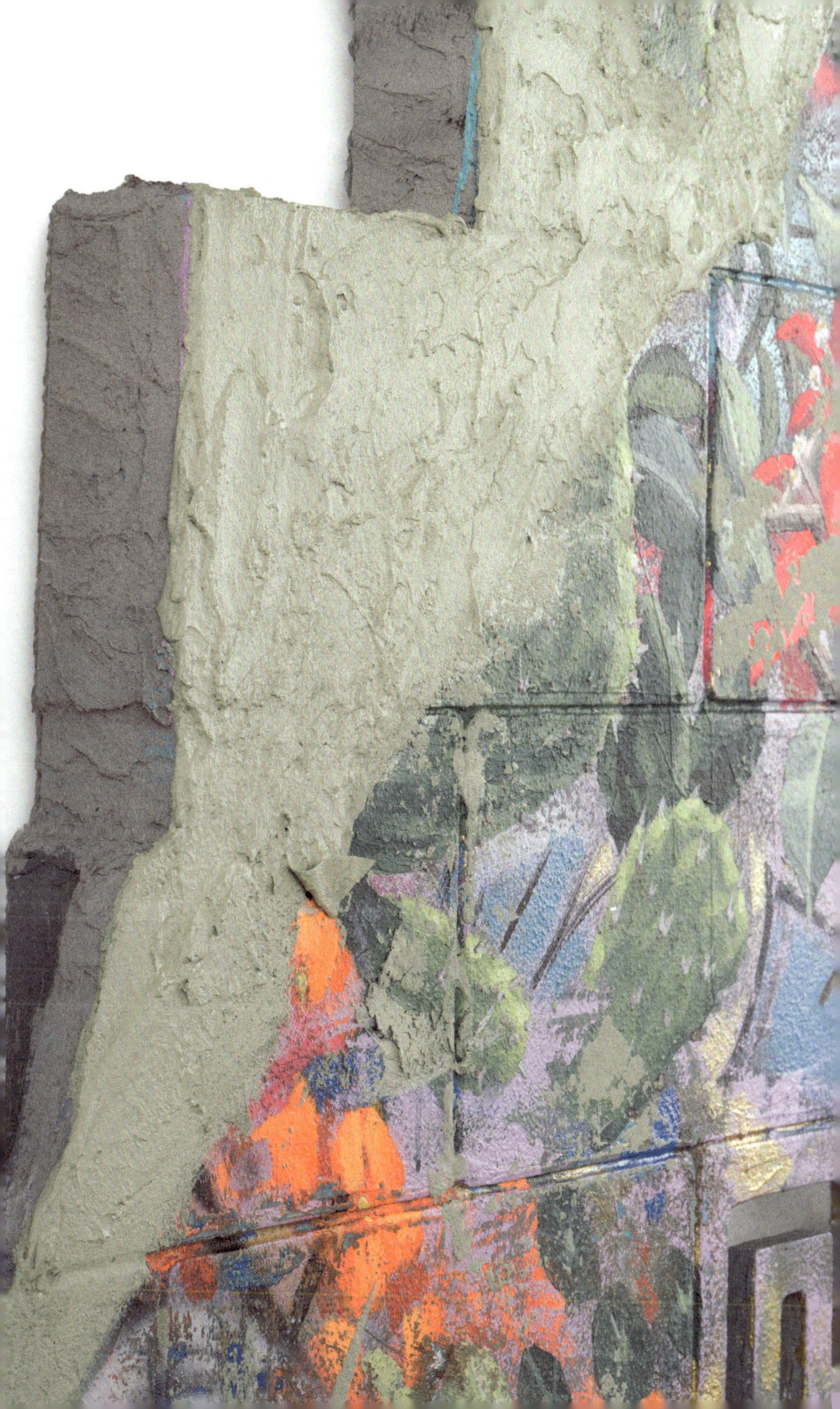

painter. Like a Winslow Homer but searching for new ways to communicate while also reaching back to the past. For instance, look at that building. [*Points to what used to be the Self Help Graphics & Art Building, located on the 3800 block of Cesar Chavez Avenue.*] See how the tile and ceramic is embedded into the walls? I'm incorporating that into the work I'm creating now.

R.F.   When did you start developing your interest in the city's surfaces? What sparked your observations of L.A.'s terrain?

P.M.   When I was eleven years old, I saw spray-can art and thought, "That's amazing!" I didn't even consider that they were using materials that we weren't supposed to use to make art and transform surfaces. After that I was hooked. I got more heavily involved in graffiti with my older brother. We would take the bus everywhere, trailblazing the city. We were always observing the L.A.nd, like, "Check out that rooftop!" Graffiti's renegade culture is still part of my practice. Even with the formal training and technical skills that I've developed, that attitude of transgression and its practice of observing and reacting to your surroundings and making art with nontraditional means informs the work that I'm doing now. It was the spark that pushed me to locate the layers of the city and then add to these layers. And today, I'm adding layers to the issues that I think are important.

160

R.F.   *Should I loop back here? Cool.* Several of your works explore gentrification and the displacement that it caus- es. Theft of land, the redefining of land, and changes in the quality of life are central to settler colonialism. But it not always explicitly named. Especially who is gaining.

> P.M.   And who is losing. It tends to be people we know. That's what informs me. The people who are struggling who have been priced out. Economic violence is a slow burn. Neighborhoods I've visited my whole life are chang- ing. Certain aesthetics and materials from these commu- nities are disappearing. As an artist, and as an archivist, I want to represent those fleeting materials and use them as a vocabulary to say, "This is what's happening." I want to treat them as having value. As a way of telling people to look around and pay attention to their surroundings. Be- cause if you're not paying attention to this, you're not pay- ing attention in life.

R.F.   Facts. We've been driving through L.A.'s Eastside. How do these neighborhoods influence your work?

> P.M.   I've spent much of my life on the Eastside. I grew up in Pasadena, and then I moved to Montebello. Since then, I've lived in Lincoln Heights, Northeast L.A., Highland Park, Eagle Rock, Monterey Park. The Eastside taught me that what creates L.A. are these neighborhoods that blend into one another, that exist neck to neck. You can see this diversity in the food, the language, and the people. My

161

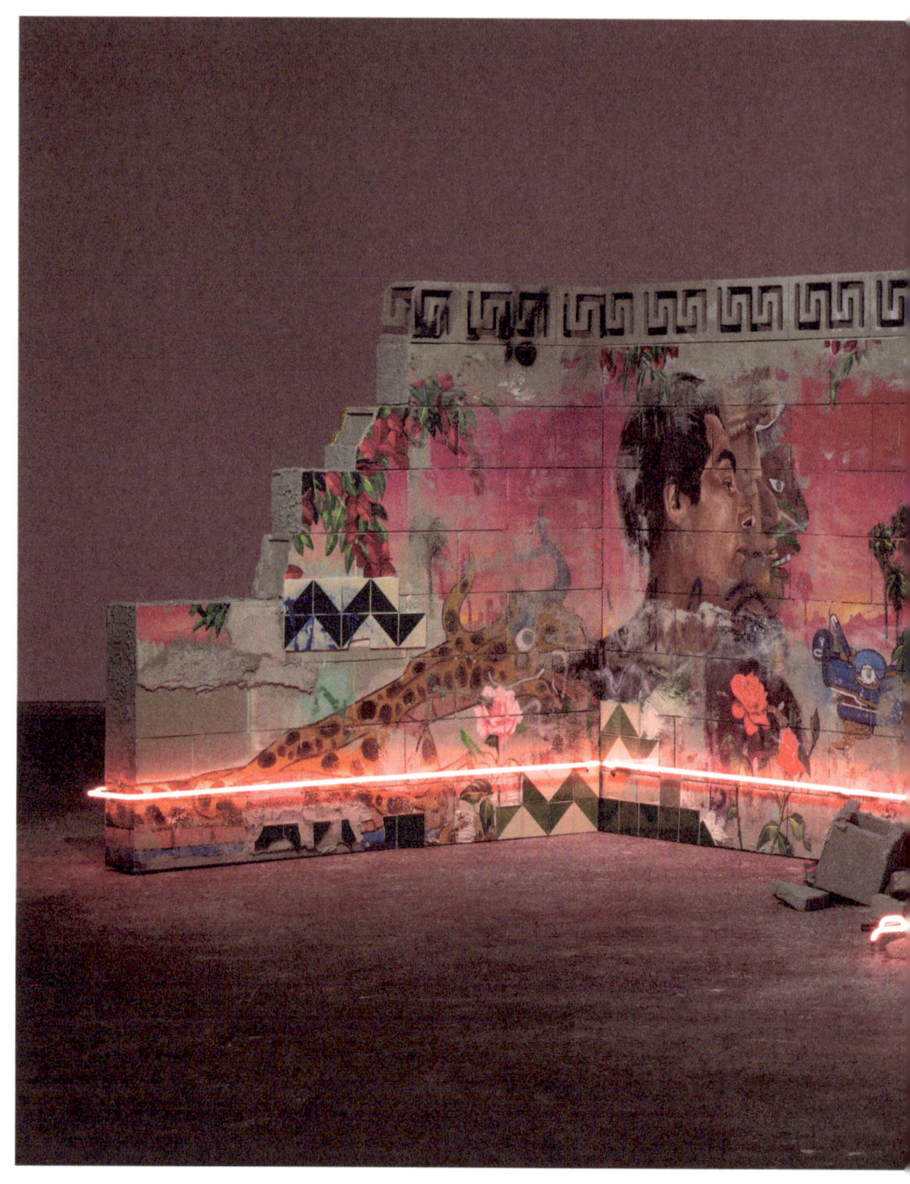

162

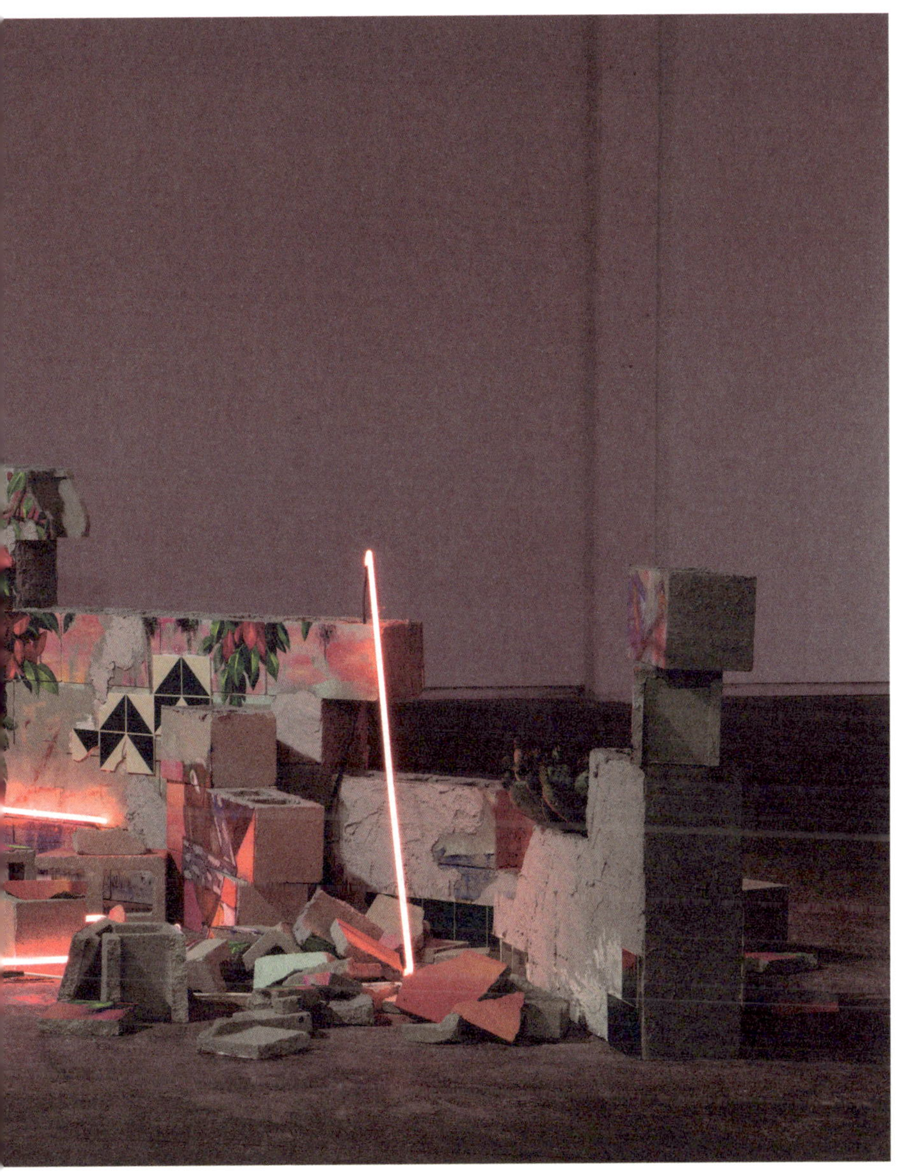

Patrick Martinez, *Ghostland*, 2023. Stucco, ceramic tile, neon, cinder blocks, acrylic, Mean Streak, bougainvillea plant, spray paint, and latex house paint on panel. 72 × 222 × 126 in. (182.9 × 563.9 × 320 cm)

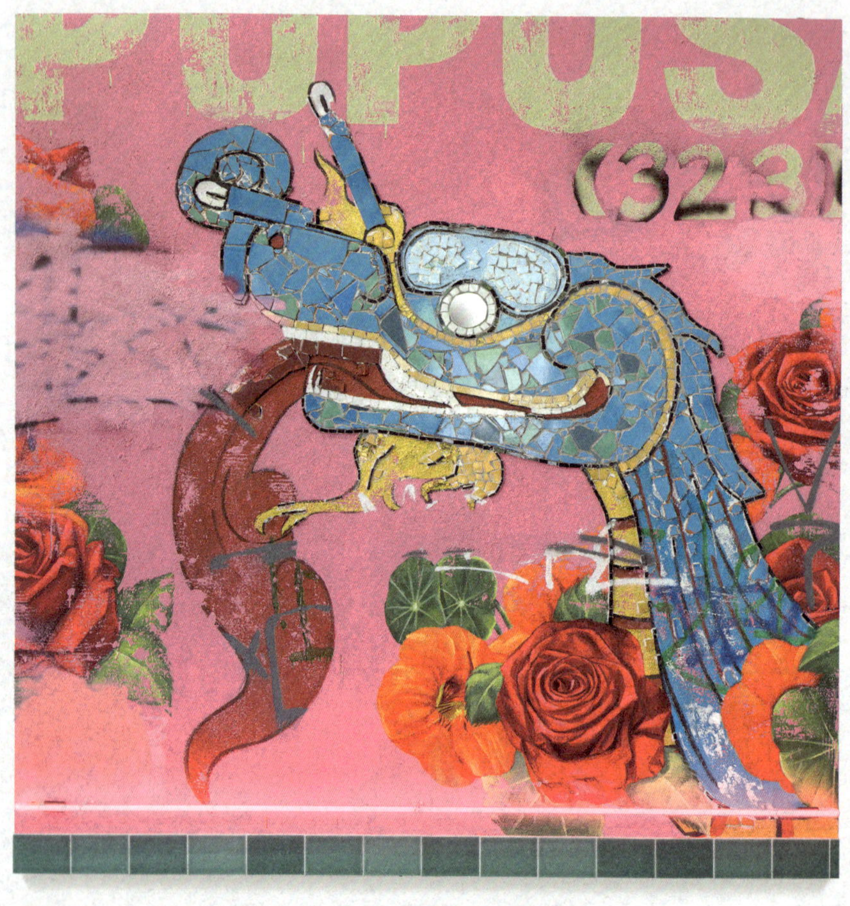

Patrick Martinez, *Feathered Serpent Immersed in Flowers*, 2024. Stucco, neon, shattered tile, broken dish tile, grout, acrylic, spray paint, latex house paint, mirror, ceramic tile, and tile adhesive on panel. 84 × 84 in. (213.4 × 213.4 cm)

work is informed by this mixture. The mixing of all those things together and the incompleteness, the never-ending nature of this mixture. For some people, a successful painting is a finished production of art. But several of my works are not resolved. There are certain sections where a person might think, "What's going on? Is it painted out, or is this painting not finished?" And that's because there is still more to be learned. There's still area to fill in. There are still questions to be answered. I think about that when I reflect on these neighborhoods. How they blend and how they change. There's a lot of that history on the Eastside. If you connect with that and try to understand it, you can feel L.A.'s charisma.

R.F.   *Turn left here? Got it.* How has being a parent impacted your work?

P.M.   I used to think life is all about art. Me at the center making work. That's no longer the case. My family gives me clarity. And everything is more amplified because of them. The love within the work is now realer and bigger. My daughter is always drawing. It's crazy because my father was a photographer and made jewelry. His brothers and his father painted, drew, and carved. They weren't in the art world. But they made art because they felt that there was this *thing* that needed to happen. And that's how I approach it. This is something innate. It's a real calling. As I've gotten older, though, I've become more aware that how I deliver it is also a product of my parents. Of growing

165

up with them and seeing how they went about things. When I was a kid, my mom frequently went to swap meets to buy ceramics and paintings that she would decorate our home with. And my dad would give me books to read about Indigenous cultures. So just as much as the city's different surfaces show up in my work, so too do my parents' aesthetics. They're really the foundation, the base.

R.F.   We're almost back at your place. You get nice views of the city from up there, huh?

P.M.   Oh yeah! From the back you can see Long Beach. When I have get-togethers, people ask, "What am I looking at now?" I tell them, "Oh you're looking at Montebello. Wilmington." Movies and shit make you think that L.A. is just the Westside. But from up here, you can see a lot more. I love it. The way the city looks at night. Twinkling. *Yeah, make a right.*

Beaux Mendes

in conversation with David J. Getsy

A fixed point for the world to orbit around

Beaux Mendes's paintings result from a commitment to spend time in place. Engaged in a slow process of observing and imagining, Mendes transforms the natural forms they encounter, such as branches and bones, into associative new forms that hint at the bodily, the erotic, and the personal. The resulting works, begun on-site and finished in the studio, often focus on twisted branches of trees as if they were limbs wrapped around each other. Mendes adds images and associations from their past and memories, and none of the resulting paintings offer a straightforward capturing of the observed. Abstracting from the forest and projecting imaginatively onto it, the resulting works tenuously present partial images that seem to struggle to take shape on the canvases.

Mendes has found analogous anthropomorphisms elsewhere in nature, and for Made in L.A., they are creating a sculpture based on a fossilized mammoth tusk. Like the trees that they have painted, this tusk's surface suggested the human body in its resemblance to limbs, folds of flesh, and skin. The artist interpreted this mammalian

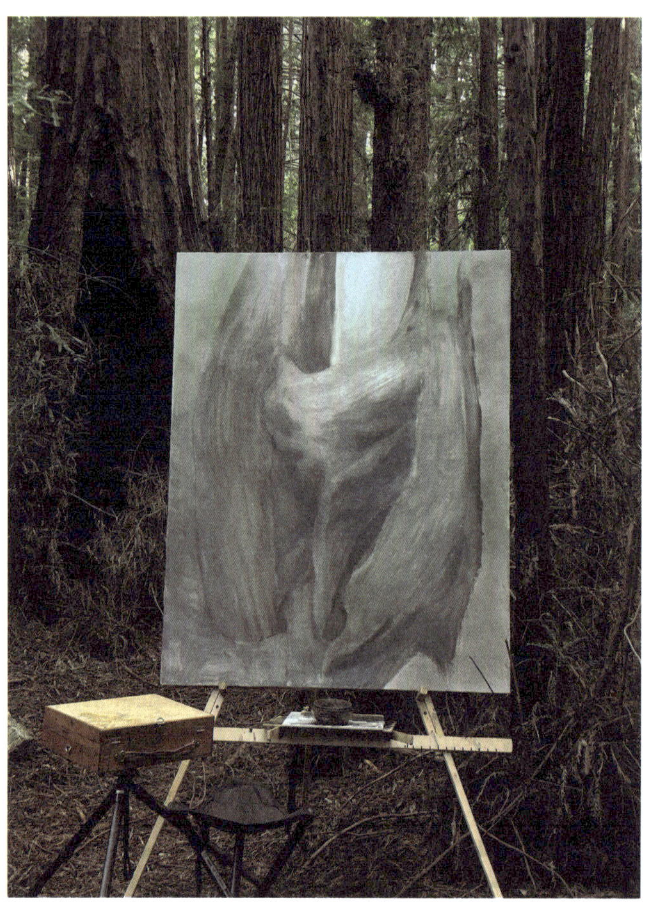

Beaux Mendes, *Ribcage Tree*, 2025. Oil, charcoal, and grease pencil on half-chalk ground on linen. 54 × 43 ½ × ¾ in. (137.2× 110.5 × 2 cm). Big Sur, CA, March 2025

168

tool as a cantilevered sculpture, then wrapped it in parchment made in the traditional manner—from horse skin, decades old, found crumpled in a warehouse. The result, in one more suggestion of metamorphosis, resembles veined stone. Mendes's practice captures the analogic possibilities of taking the found or the observed as the occasion for seeing what else that form (be it a tree or a tusk) can or might be. It is this search for potential that motivates the artist's rapt looking at the forest and the trees.

DAVID GETSY   In looking at your previous work, I returned again and again to the scene of you intently observing in the forest, looking at objects like trees and roots in order to find new forms that might emerge from them. What's the relationship for you between finding and imagining?

BEAUX MENDES   That's an interesting question, because I take on but also break with some of the typical associations with plein air painting. My paintings based on observation intentionally distance themselves from the Romantic landscape tradition. I take it on—like a kind of drag—so I can question its terms. These are not the grand vistas of traditional landscape painting, which have historically visualized empire and expansion. Instead, my imagery is more intimate and tentative, like throwing smoke on an invisible thing to see that it is there. I want to make paintings of land that do not function as windows but rather appear as if they might be looking back at you.

169

D.G.   But you do still make your process arduous by immersing yourself in these sites, sometimes for days on end,
in order to see how they look back at you.

B.M.   Yes, that's why it's hard to answer your question.
Making the work in this way is the vehicle that I use to
move through the world. It's the part of my life that I
feel has the most stability for me. I want to be with the
trees—to just sit and wait for nothing in particular. It's
only through painting that I can allow that for myself. And
yet it's a lot of effort to set up these studios at these sites.
Maybe I'm going partially because I don't know if phone
service will work up there, and I can focus in a different
way. Up there in the woods, I am suddenly extremely far
away—even if I haven't traveled all that far. I bring all these
materials and equipment. It's a whole endeavor to set up
in these places. Sometimes I'm airbrushing and so I have
to bring a portable air compressor. I use a lot of materials
that you wouldn't necessarily associate with plein air painting, the cliché of which is a French easel and just some
paints. I'm incorporating wood stains, stenciling, and other things that are actually a lot harder to do with wind and
dust around.

D.G.   Do you feel you need to find something interesting
once you're there? That puts a lot of pressure on you. Also,
you're not really painting the landscape but rather extract-
ing elements from it.

170

B.M.   It's a slow process, and I think there's something more mystical or spiritual that takes place. I try to become sensitive to the cues and the traces in the space. What else is there that is being communicated to me? What is more than the immediately observable? It's not that I think I'm uniquely privileged to be able to see these things. They are potentially always there, and one can tune into them. For example, there might be a stain on the ground, and I might see a face in it. I could paint the ground or I can paint this constellation of stains. Then suddenly something else entirely emerges. There's such an infinity of that in the woods or up in the mountains. I learn a lot from being around these trees. I start to feel like I have a relationship to them.

D.G.   What is that relationship?

B.M.   For a while now, I've had the feeling of being called to make paintings of trees that are not really paintings *of* trees but a collaboration with them. I'm afraid it seems incredibly grandiose to suggest that I am somehow able to speak for such tremendous entities. I think what I mean is that this aspect of my work requires an opening up of myself to become a channel for another consciousness to move through me. This past week, I traveled to Big Sur to paint a redwood root system I had seen some months before. It resembled a splayed rib cage. As I worked, a ghostly ancient being with a trunk like an elephant kept assembling on the surface of the canvas. When I tried to

171

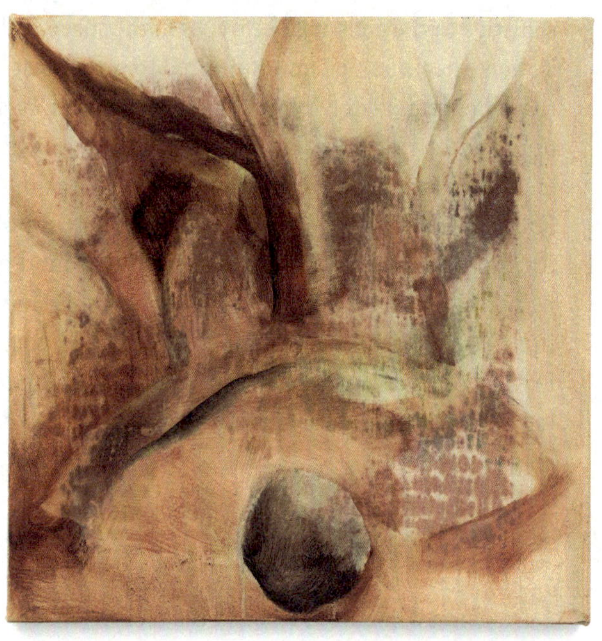

Beaux Mendes, Untitled, 2024, Oil on sheepskin parchment. 12 × 12 in. (30.5 × 30.5 cm)

172

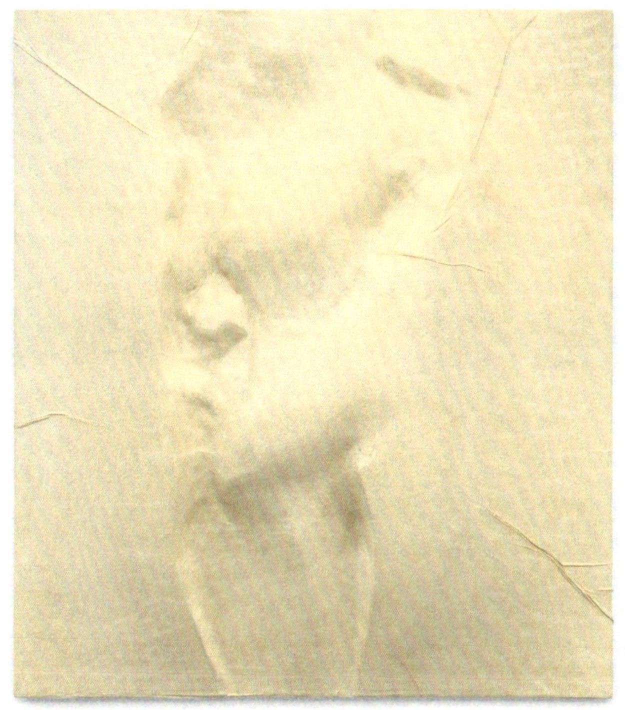

Beaux Mendes, Untitled, 2024. Sheepskin parchment on CNC-routed MDF. 22 × 20 × 2 ¾ in. (55.9 × 50.8 × 6.8 cm)

173

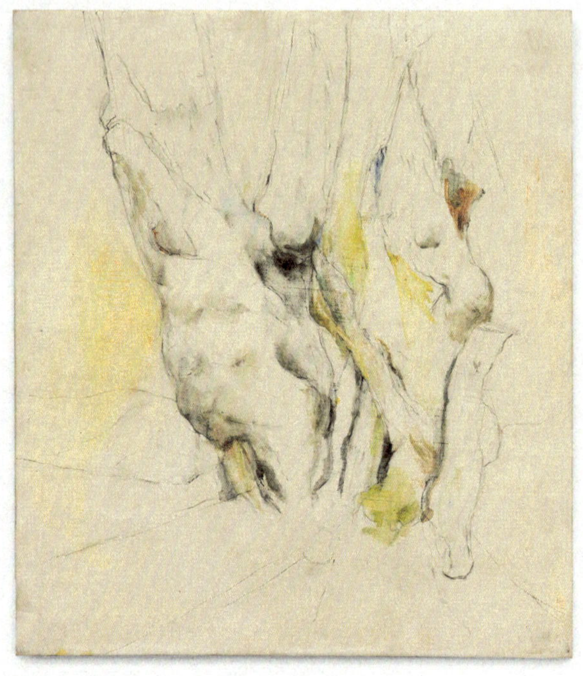

Beaux Mendes, Untitled, 2024. Oil, charcoal, and grease pencil on half-chalk ground on panel. 15 ½ × 14 in. (39.4 × 35.6 cm)

174

force what I had intended to see—the rib cage—back onto the painting, it resisted. A party of Steller's jays descended on the root system to screech at me. I came to feel that I was expressing something that didn't belong to me; instead, I had given myself to the tree. The painting that emerged does not feel exactly mine, and this is a relief.

D.G.   Can that relational attitude toward observing and finding be understood as a way of approaching the world? After all, most things are not just more than they seem at first. There are also many ways in which those things have potential to be transformed, to be seen differently, or to become something else. In some of my writing, I've used the term *capacity* to think about how the potential for variation and multiplicity—about people, bodies, genders, and relations—can be held in an object or form, even if it wasn't originally planned to do so. What strikes me is that your associative engagement with (and receptivity to) the woods also demands that we take the time to see the potential in the unplanned—that is, the trees, their limbs, and the forest floor that surrounds them. From these natural elements, you conjure bodily forms and erotic couplings.

B.M.   One of the reasons I love trees as subjects is because I feel they have so much space or capacity for projection and association. Maybe this is because they have a kind of intelligence or wisdom that can support complexity without the need to define it. They live in a different time and scale. You start to see connections everywhere; in a way,

175

you could start with anything. For the work, you just need a fixed point for the world to orbit around.

d.g.   What a beautiful way to say it: "You just need a fixed point for the world to orbit around." The choice of one thing, at one time, as creating a world and evoking possibilities. For the time you spend with them, those branches are just such a center point.

b.m.   It is similar to how I learned to draw. You just have to decide that one line is a stable point, and then you can triangulate everything off of that. It really doesn't matter what it is. It's a kind of world-building that starts to take on its own engine. When that happens, that's when I feel a painting actually becomes an artwork, because a kind of consciousness takes root—a consciousness that feels like it has started directing itself or me. It gains its own momentum, which I think is beautiful.

Na Mira

(how to jump through the sky?) SEMI TRANSLUCENT
STATE (corporeal or nation?) CENSURE (empty the signifi-
er to multiply the signal?) CALCIFY (permanent twilight?)
CENTRIFUGAL FORCE CADUCEUS CROSS (the dragon eats
its tail?) SYMBOLIC RUPTURE (dragon hill military base in
united states?) CONCENTRIC TOURNIQUET (can the military imaging regime be corrupted?) STAR POWER CELES-
TIAL INCANTERE (what is the song?) HER HEART TERROR
EXOSKELETON (western princess?) CORRELATE (aban-
doned princess?) CARNAL HUNGER (theater of war?)
PROVOCAT (cut?) 짤라 (vengeance?)

New Theater Hollywood/ Calla Henkel and Max Pitegoff
by Heidi Schrek

Performing Paradise

I spoke with Calla Henkel and Max Pitegoff about their latest work, *Theater*, from my home in Brooklyn, while my twin four-year-olds staged their own play—about a flying horse and her pet frog—in the next room. It was a gray hopeless sort of day in January 2025, and I'd just spent weeks immersed in their series *Paradise* (2020–22). Set in TV Bar, an actual bar Calla and Max once owned in Schöneberg, Berlin, the series centers around a group of artists struggling to keep their bar afloat amid financial and personal disintegration. Filmed on lush, grainy 16mm film and featuring mostly nonactors, it weaves scripted narratives together with the spontaneous encounters of bar regulars, skillfully confusing reality and performance. Like my daughters—unselfconscious about what was real and what was imagined—*Paradise* delights in how people perform themselves. Deeply moving, uncanny, and often hilarious, the show occupies the elusive space where life and art intertwine, capturing with tenderness our human desire to find meaning within the theater of everyday existence.

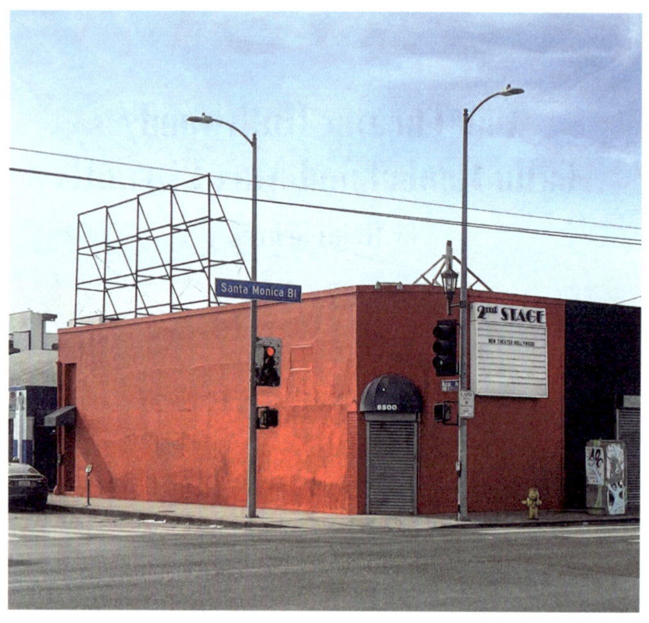

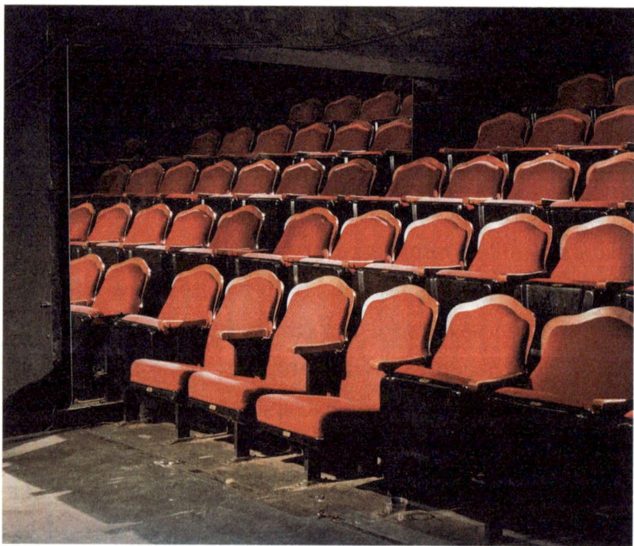

New Theater Hollywood

For over a decade, Max and Calla—who first met as art students and "photography nerds" at Cooper Union—have been making vital, community-based work in Berlin, where theater is the beating heart of public life. "In Berlin, the dentist and mechanic go to the theater," Calla says. "It's the political and emotional vernacular of the town." Now they've moved to L.A., where they have revived an old theater on Santa Monica Boulevard and are producing plays and performances by other artists while at the same time making their own film in the space—a documentary fiction in the vein of *Paradise*, which is not coincidentally called *Theater*.

As a lover of independent L.A. theater since the 1990s (The Actors' Gang, Circle X Theatre Co., Justin Tanner), I wondered how Max and Calla came to the beautiful, crazy idea of managing a theater in Los Angeles in 2025—a town in which theater is definitely not at the center of civic life. They confessed that they weren't quite sure how they ended up in this predicament themselves. After being part of the artist takeover of the legendary Volksbühne theater in Berlin in 2017—where they staged new shows every weekend for months and months—they said they had vowed to take a break from theater, maybe forever.

And then they were walking down Santa Monica Boulevard, near Cahuenga, when they saw the sign on an old black-box theater space: *Available*. "We had an immediate gut recognition—an 'Oh fuck' moment," Calla says. "We wanted to get back into theater, but we weren't ready to say that. So we had to construct this mythological door—a film about theater—to get us there."

181

The duo's storefront theater in Berlin had been called New Theater, and so they decided this new space, a decade later, would be called New Theater Hollywood. The name made them laugh. "I think it's because humor, when it works, it strikes raw pain," Calla says. "And there's something about theater in Los Angeles that's very funny but also completely tragic. In L.A., theater feels disconnected from the collective dream; it's always an audition for something else." "In L.A., theater is a liminal space," Max says, which is sad but also a kind of gift. "It means we get to make it all up."

The hunger for meaning, for experiences that transcend the grind of transaction and capitalist ambition, is an almost desperate through line in Max and Calla's work. An intense longing for connection and community suffuses the work they are creating in their new theater space, which, they let me know, happens to have a resident ghost. Is it the specter of revolution, I wonder, or the ghost of theater itself—nudging us toward more intimate, vulnerable forms of gathering? "We think it's a stage manager," Calla tells me, laughing. Max agrees. "It's very efficient." Calla adds, "If someone makes fun of theater, or things get a little less serious, or say, there's a fashion shoot, shit doesn't work out that well. But if it's theater, the energy is on." Max offers that the space is haunted in another way: "People are always stopping by the theater to say they performed here years ago. Bit by bit we're starting to piece together the history of this place."

182

Meanwhile, Max and Calla are writing a new history inside the New Theater Hollywood, layering their film *Theater* delicately over past performances—a kind of emotional palimpsest that honors what came before. They lovingly attend to the grunt work of running a theater (toilet cleaning, marketing, producing the work of fellow artists), and their careful attention to the essential tasks reflects a broader truth: The act of maintaining something worthwhile—whether it's a theater or a country—requires consistent, collective care. I tell them there is something particularly beautiful to me right now in the patient dedication they bring to their work, fostering a space by simply showing up, nurturing it, and creating art from whatever resources are available. They say they're actually being "greedy"; they feel galvanized by the artists they're producing. "We're learning so much from these artists, and we're working with people who have so much to teach us," Max says.

In *Theater*, Leilah Weinraub plays Kennedy, an Uber driver who gets a payout from the city after being hit by a bus and uses the money to buy a theater on Santa Monica Boulevard. Kennedy's cash quickly runs out, and she has to live in the space. Because she's broke, she starts renting it out. "All the rentals that happen in Kennedy's theater in the film are the actual shows we're producing here," Calla explains. The duo captures moments of real rehearsals, backstage interactions, and other fragments of reality and fold them into the narrative. Sometimes

183

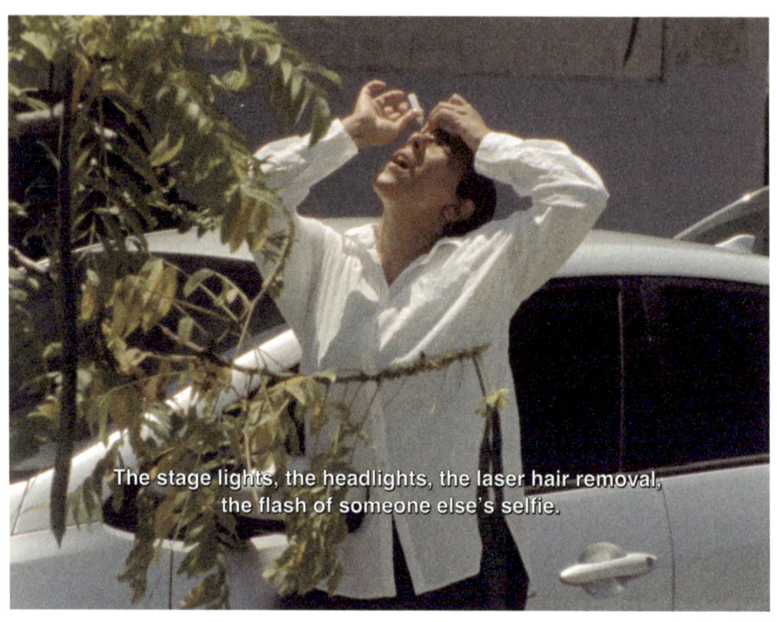

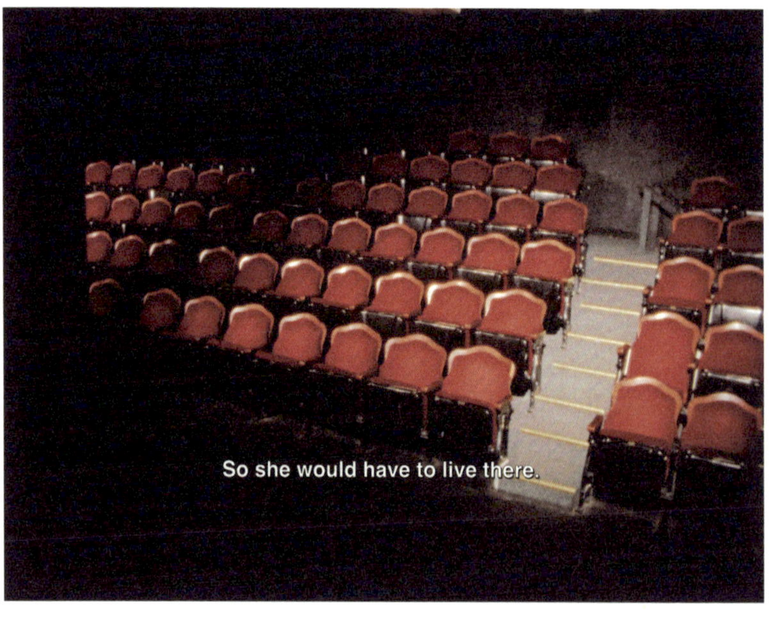

NEW THEATER HOLLYWOOD

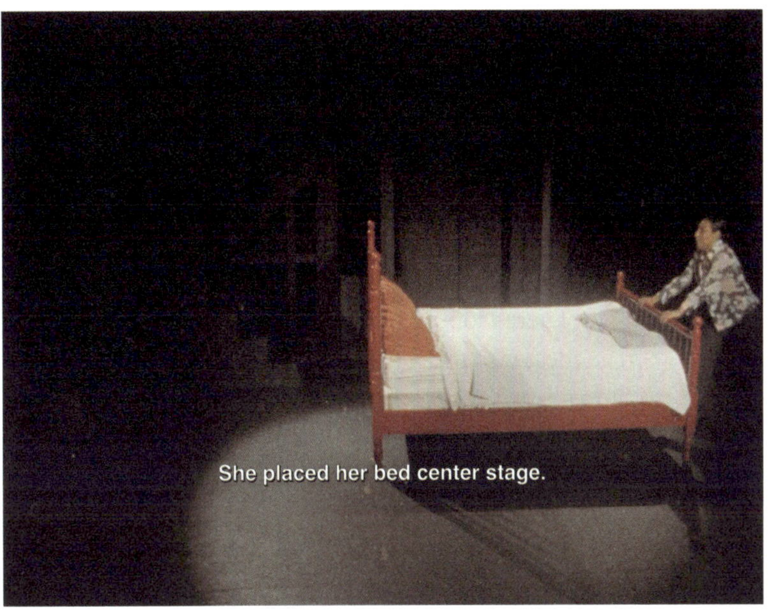

Stills from episodes one and two of Calla Henkel and Max Pitegoff's *THEATER*, 2024

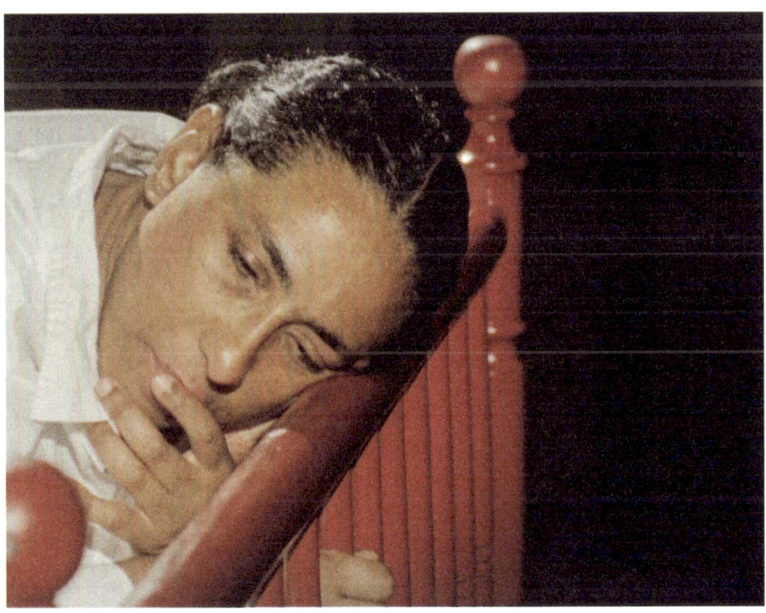

Weinraub interacts with the real-life performers, absorbing them into the fiction. Recently, a famous actor walked into the space for a fashion shoot, took one look around, and freaked out. "I don't want to do anything *surreal*," he said before storming out. Henkel and Pitegoff immediately knew: "That's going in."

There's something about that moment that feels like true theater to me. The actor's panic, his desire to control the narrative. A person stepping into a space, unsure of the rules, afraid of looking foolish.

Toward the end of our conversation, Max mentions that his teenage stepdaughter recently came to see a play at New Theater Hollywood. Her review? "This is so awkward. The theater's awkward. The play was awkward." I thought about my daughters in the next room, performing for no one, completely unselfconscious—for now. At some point, performance stops being instinctual and starts feeling embarrassing, until maybe you find your way home to it again, to letting yourself feel awkward and connected instead of disconnected and safe.

Max and Calla are building a space for that: a home where theater, in all its strangeness and hesitation, its failures and small miracles, can unfold. A space where life can be messy and awkward and perpetually in rehearsal.

186

Pat O'Neill
by Giampaolo Bianconi

Plastic Poet

Pat O'Neill is a key figure in West Coast experimental cinema, renowned for his pioneering use of optical printing and surreal visual collages in film. Beyond these innovations, O'Neill has also sustained a remarkable second career in the plastic arts, particularly sculpture. These two bodies of work have rarely been exhibited in tandem, however. This separation reflects the broader institutional and cultural divide between avant-garde cinema and sculptural production in postwar Los Angeles. The infrastructure for experimental film was often informal and ephemeral—limited to artist-run screenings, university departments, and underground venues—whereas sculpture was integrated more directly into the gallery and museum system. As a result, O'Neill's contributions to the two fields developed along parallel but rarely intersecting tracks. Yet despite their distinct visual languages and exhibition contexts, his works in film and sculpture share a deep and consistent investment in industrial materials and technologies.

O'Neill's films *7362* (1967) and *Water and Power* (1989) are known for their innovative use of the optical printer. Developed in the 1930s, optical printing became a key tool in experimental filmmaking, enabling precise layering, compositing, and the creation of complex visual effects. O'Neill's mastery of this technology placed him at the forefront of a movement that treated film not simply as a narrative medium but also as a site of material and perceptual inquiry. These works deftly combined scenes shot by the artist with found footage, creating startling juxtapositions of space and time. O'Neill's montages often examine the interplay between natural landscapes and urban development in California, reflecting his abiding interest in the connections and clashes between the environment and human civilization.

At the same time, optical printing played a crucial role in the evolution of Hollywood special effects, contributing to the rise of blockbuster cinema in the 1970s and 1980s. In this sense, the artist's work exists in critical dialogue with both experimental and commercial film histories. Beyond avant-garde circles, his technical prowess also found its way into Hollywood: he contributed optical effects to films as diverse as Melvin Van Peebles's *Sweet Sweetback's Baadasssss Song* (1971) and *The Empire Strikes Back* (1980). Nevertheless, his independent film works remained distinctly personal, marked by unconventional structures and a sly sense of humor. This distinctive blend of technical innovation and whimsy in O'Neill's films provides a crucial context for understanding his work in other mediums.

O'Neill's sculptural practice is marked by an embrace of synthetic and industrial materials, particularly fiberglass,

188

which gained popularity in the mid-twentieth century for its versatility, lightness, and durability. Initially developed for military and industrial use, fiberglass became increasingly accessible to artists, appearing in the work of figures associated with sculpture in Southern California. O'Neill's use of fiberglass aligns with this context, but he often pushed the material toward more eccentric and ambiguous forms. Like celluloid film, fiberglass is a plastic—a product of petrochemical processes and a hallmark of twentieth-century mass production. Both materials are intimately tied to systems of transportation, spectacle, and technological mediation.

Parallel to his filmmaking, O'Neill pursued sculpture from the early days of his career, exhibiting sculptures and photographic works in galleries beginning in the 1960s. His initial efforts were assemblages crafted from wood and metal, often with libidinal or darkly humorous undertones. By the late 1960s, his approach evolved toward more polished constructions in contemporary materials. The artist became known for creating highly finished fiberglass and plexiglass forms with playful shapes—incorporating elements like horns, fur-lined curves, and even oversize pickles—in place of traditional sculptural motifs. These objects exemplified his taste for absurdity and tactile experimentation.

Safer Than Springtime (1964) is one of O'Neill's early sculptural pieces, created just a few years after he completed graduate school. This fiberglass, aluminum, and steel work consists of a bright green, pickle-like form

189

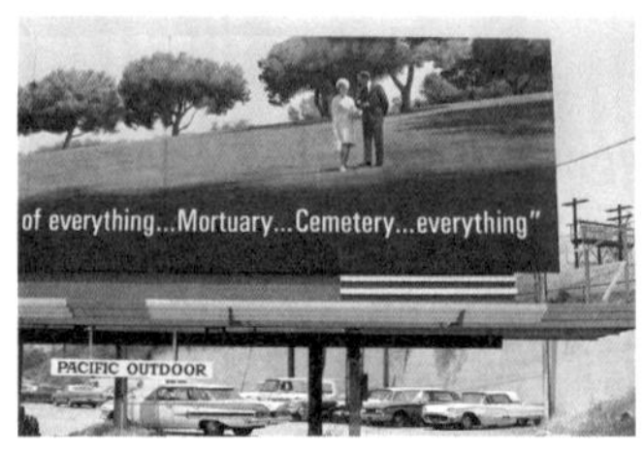
of everything...Mortuary...Cemetery...everything"
PACIFIC OUTDOOR

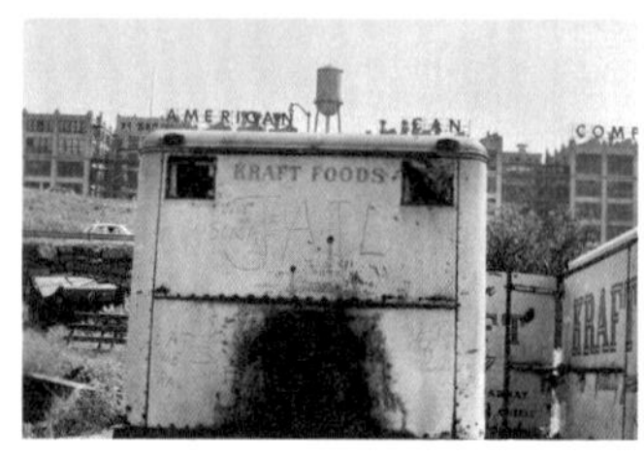
KRAFT FOODS

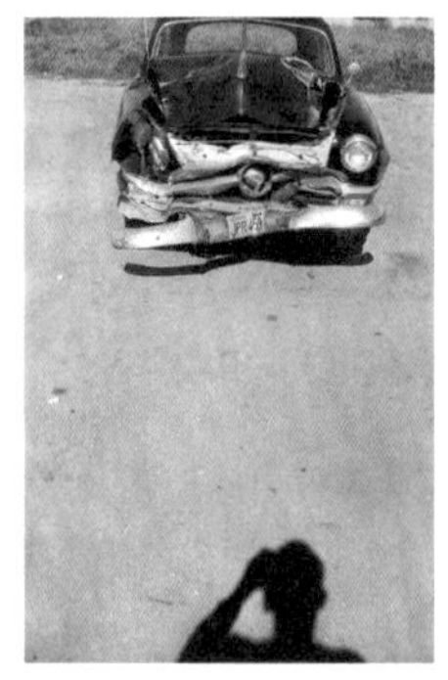

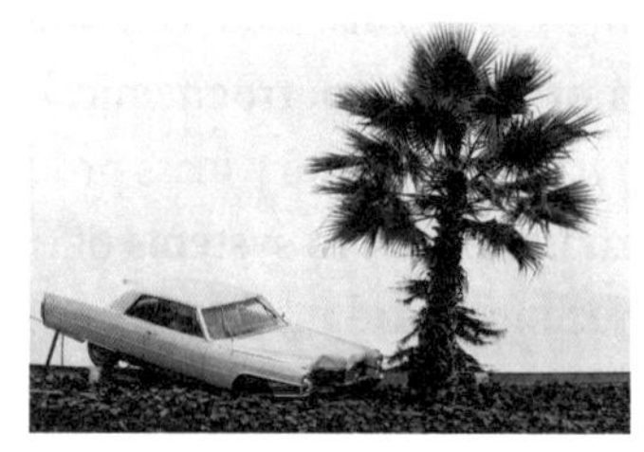

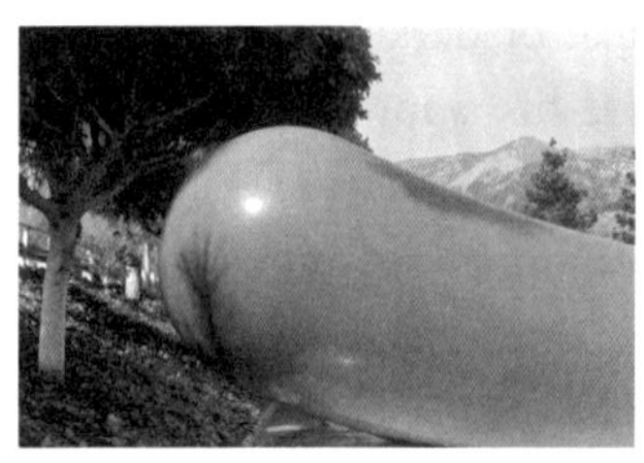
PACIFIC OUTDOOR

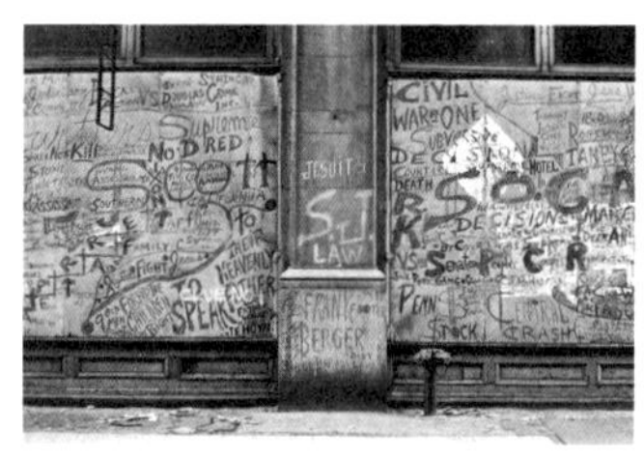

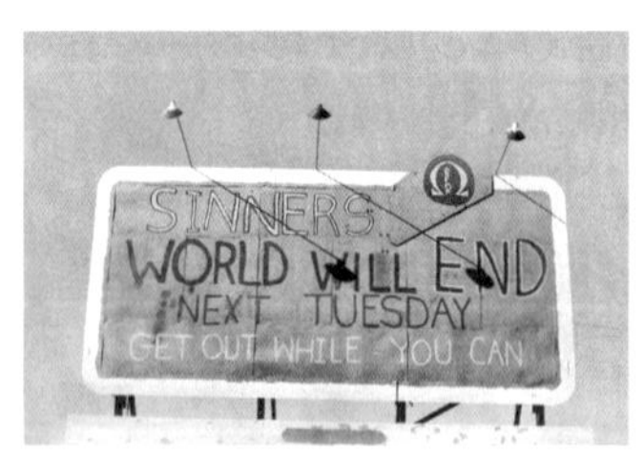
SINNERS
WORLD WILL END
NEXT TUESDAY
GET OUT WHILE YOU CAN

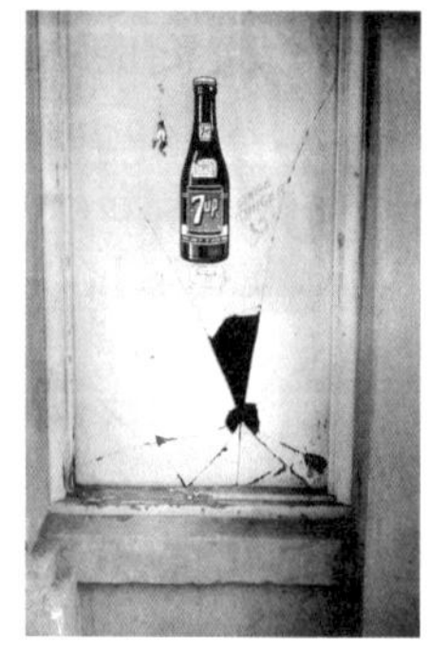
7up

PAT O'NEILL

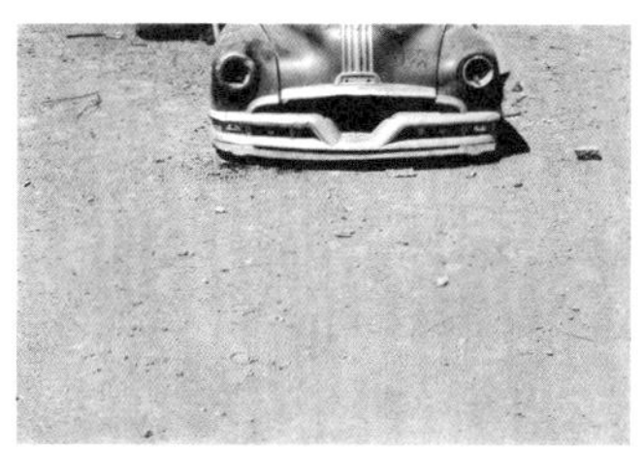
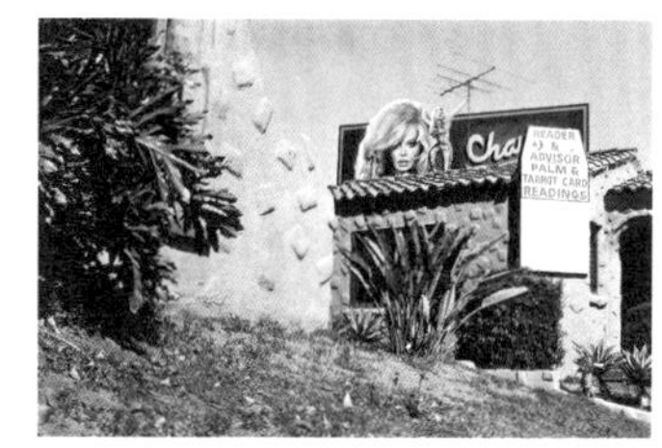
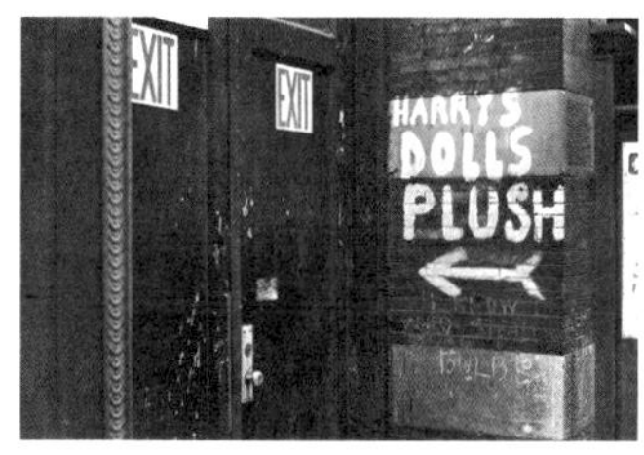

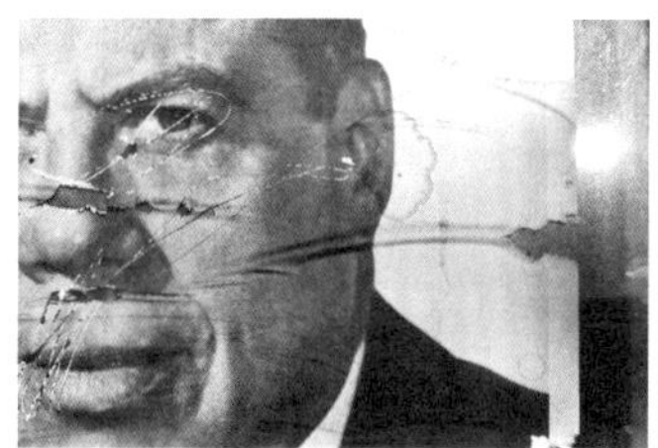
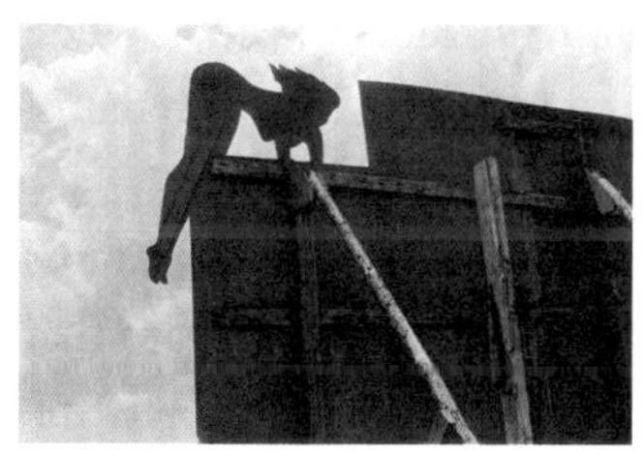
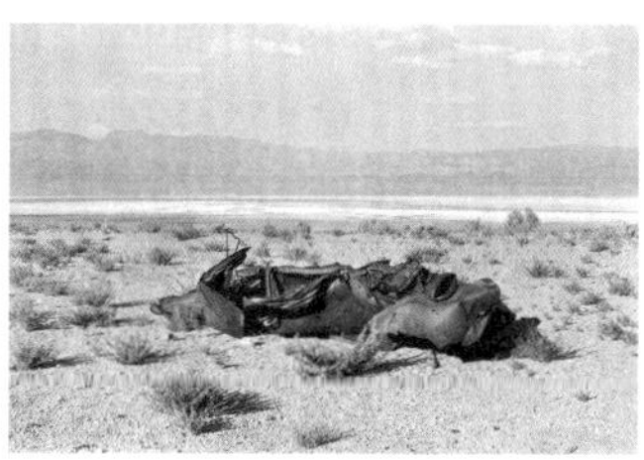
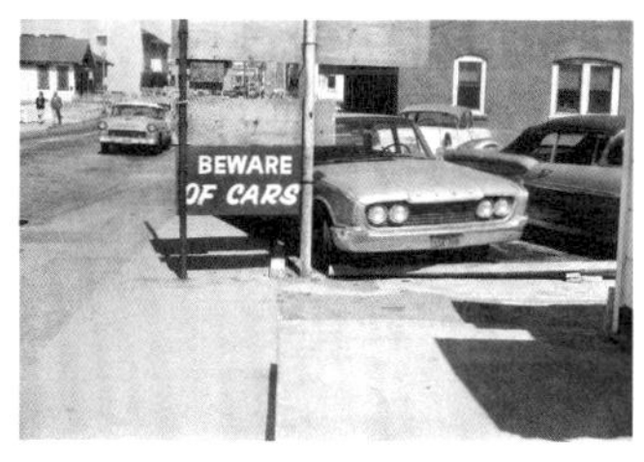

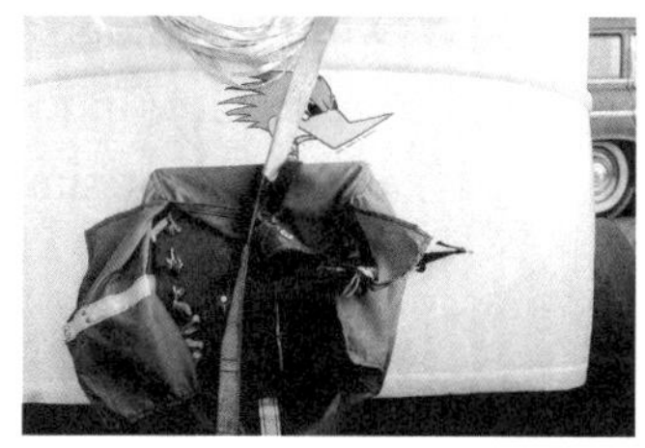

Selections from Pat O'Neill, *Cars and Other Problems*, ca. 1960s

leaning against a cylindrical yellow form, with a puddle-like red shape spread at its base. The composition is boldly absurd and slightly subversive—the pickle's comically oversize, phallic appearance and the dripping red "spill" suggest a playful eroticism. At the core of the work is its sense of balance; the forms hold each other up, emphasizing the work's movement and narrative.

Before too long, recognizable subject matter began to recede in the artist's sculptural production. O'Neill's signature "sweeps" are sculptural forms created with industrial techniques often used in boat making. The works appear to emerge and disappear back into the floor, rising and falling with smooth curved lines. Like *Safer Than Springtime*, *British Columbia Sweep* (1968) contains variable elements that fit together in different ways. Other works, like *Virian Red* (1969), consist of only one sweeping form. The process of painting and adding color, O'Neill has said, is when the works reveal themselves to him, changing from flat industrial forms to dimensional, mysterious objects.

Despite the aesthetic divergences between his films and sculptures, it is at the level of material substrate that O'Neill's practice reveals its greatest continuity. His sustained engagement with plastic—both literally, in terms of petrochemical compounds, and conceptually, in terms of mutability and transformation—offers a lens through which to understand his work as a unified exploration of modernity's industrial base. From this perspective, O'Neill emerges not simply as a technician or formal innovator

192

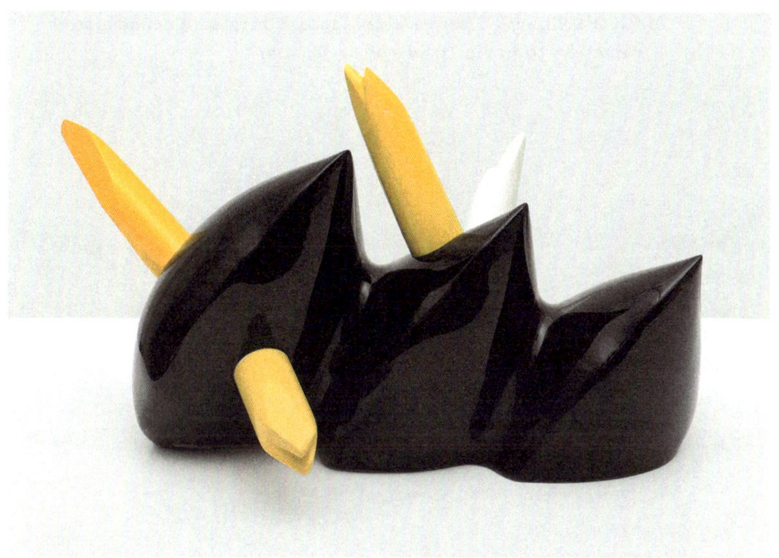

Pat O'Neill, *L'il Neverbetter*, 1969. Polyester laminate, wood, lacquer. 18 ½ × 32 × 24 in. (47 × 81.3 × 61 cm)

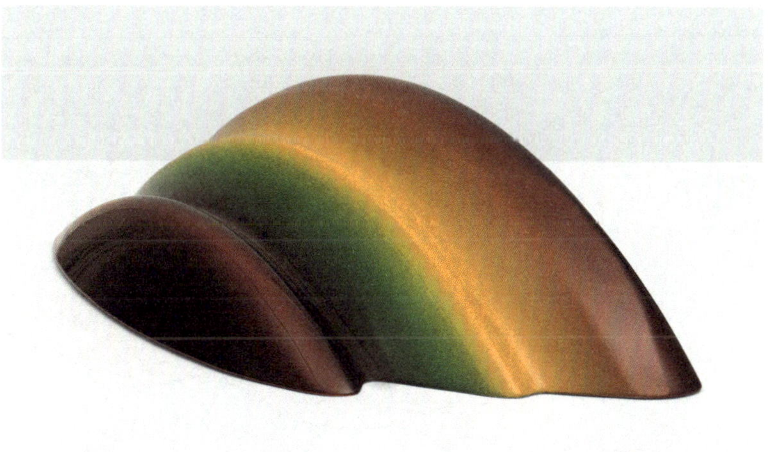

Pat O'Neill, *Large Sweep (1012 Pico Series)*, 1968. Fiberglass, wood, lacquer. 40 × 72 × 19 in. (101.6 × 182.9 × 48.3 cm)

Pat O'Neill, *Safer Than Springtime*, 1964. Fiberglass, aluminum, steel, paint. 48 × 39 × 30 in. (121.9 × 99.1 × 76.2 cm)

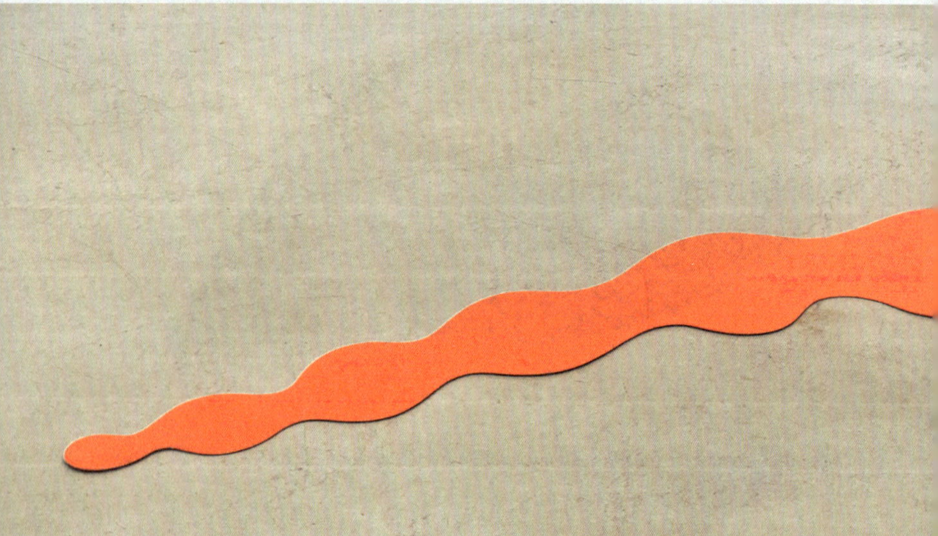

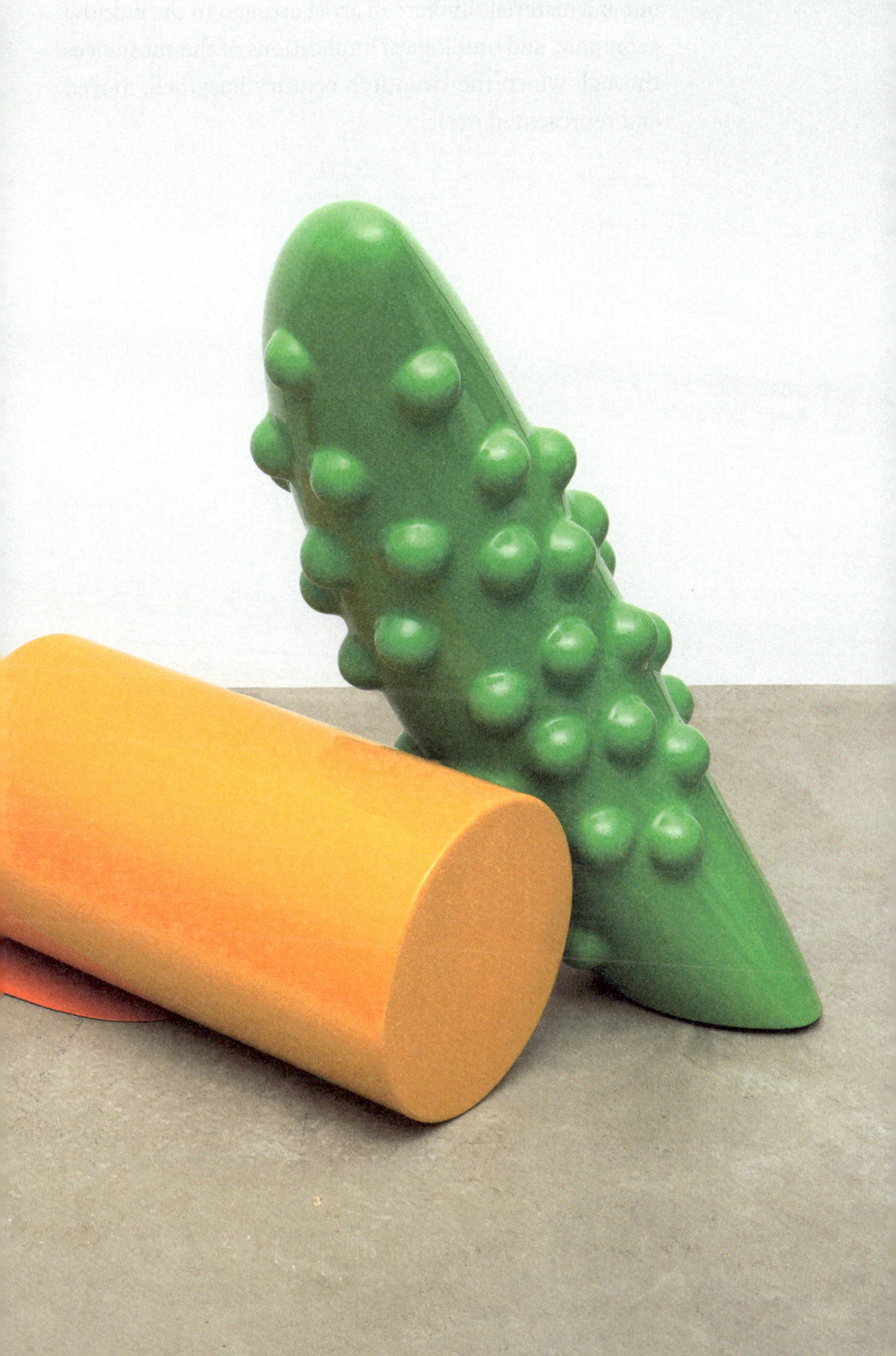

but as a material thinker: an artist attuned to the cultural, economic, and ontological implications of the substances through which the twentieth century imagined, moved, and represented itself.

Will Rawls

in conversation with Taylor Renee Aldridge

Constructing Your Liberation(s):
Freedom Pathways Through Choreography

Will Rawls is a Los Angeles–based choreographer from
Massachusetts. Rawls has long been interested in language
and various modes of coherence and meaning making. In
using dance, language is situated to the body as an ever-
changing regime of representation. When bodily movement is carried out on a stage or in a black-box theater with
an audience—spaces designed to encourage perception—
desires for coherence and legibility are heighted. And yet,
Rawls aims to subvert and untangle common signifiers,
correctness, and legibility through dance while calling attention to the limitations of vocabulary-based dance forms.

In December 2024, Rawls and I met to talk about his
time in Los Angeles, his recent works *[siccer]* and *Parable
of Guest*, and the economies of dance.

TAYLOR RENEE ALDRIDGE   I'm curious about your view of
the contours of the city of L.A. and how that informs
your practice, which is particularly interested in different
language forms through the body. What does the city of

197

L.A. offer you? How does its built environment impact your practice?

WILL RAWLS L.A. has rhythms, I think, that create a particular kind of holding pattern. There's a rhythm of people constantly coming together slowly through traffic and across time to then dissipate again or evaporate. When I think of L.A., I think about it in terms of slowness and acceleration symbolized by a car and the various shifts of gear. But I am also thinking about L.A. in terms of condensation; plants take whatever water that is possible out of the air. I found myself struggling against the fact that it's not easy to establish a sense of containment in L.A. New York is a city where you're pressed into spaces constantly with other people, and you have to negotiate so many different social typologies and agendas as you walk through a subway station. L.A. is more a city of solitude, isolation, but also, paradoxically, a kind of evaporation or spatial extension of self. Here, I can continue dwelling on notions of undoing, which are key to my choreography, as is running interference into regimes of representation that surround the Black performing body, and the dancing body writ large.

T.A. In 2024, you were commissioned by the Whitney Museum to choreograph a dance in honor of their exhibition *Edges of Ailey*. We have this history of Alvin Ailey as a highly politicized figure in modern dance, a generous resource and world maker for a lot of Black dance discourse throughout postwar America. All of that is really present

198

for me as I think about your work as providing new forms
of communication for us to engage with.

W.R.	In being invited to contribute to the Alvin Ailey leg-
acy, I first wanted to run away. [*laughs*] I studied at the
Ailey school for a summer. I love the dancers. I would not
have pursued dance if there wasn't an Alvin Ailey company.
But since being in the school in 1996, I have diverted my
focus to other forms of dance making and different kinds
of choreographic questions.

What I experienced while building my commission,
Parable of the Guest, for the *Edges of Ailey* exhibition is a deep
conundrum in the commitment, legacy, and inheritance of
expressive gesture, and the way in which Black people and
Black bodies historically both generate and are conscripted
into regimes of expressivity, both for and against their
well-being. I wanted to go there and make a dance that is
beautiful and symbolic and communicates through symbolic and expressive gesture—movement that is framed and
sculpted and formalized to be read as symbolic in ways that
differ from other dance material that I make.

T.A.	I saw your piece *[siccer]* at the Museum of Contempo-
rary Art Chicago in 2023, and you and I engaged in a public
conversation during its run in the city. I love it so much. It
makes so much sense in relationship to Ulysses Dove, this
figure who is a beneficiary of Ailey's work and generosity
but who transgresses these notions of refinement and re-
spectable representations that Ailey sought to render of

199

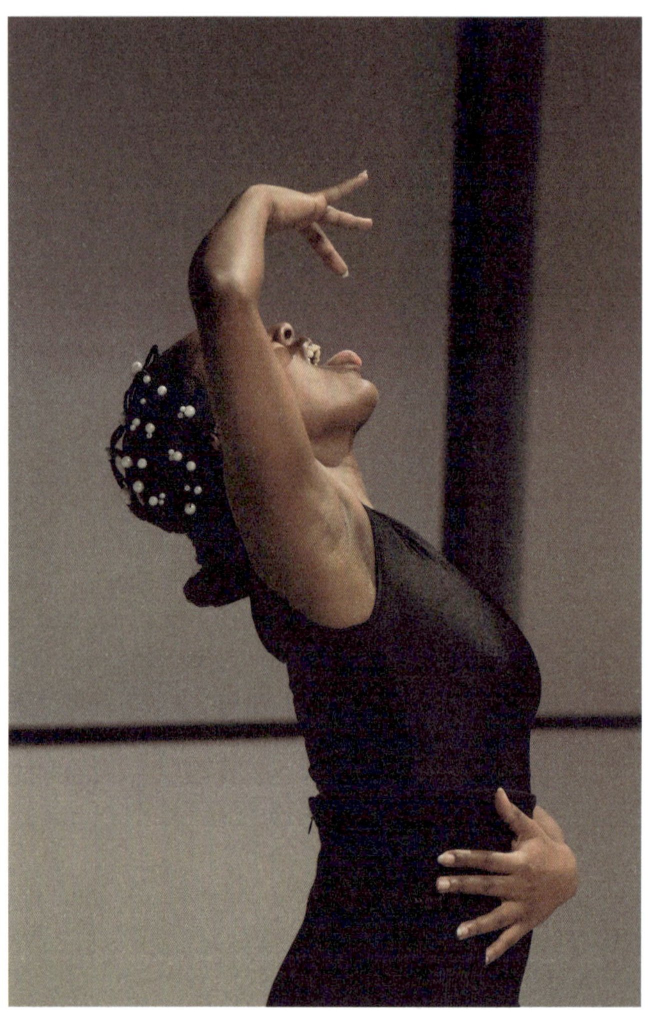

Will Rawls, *Parable of the Guest*, 2024. Performance

200

and for Black culture. One of the things I really appreciate about *[siccer]* is this constant blurring of form and language. There are moments of illegibility and legibility in terms of Black vernacular signifiers, vocality, polyrhythms, all these things that are very recognizable through various senses, via an intersubjective space. Caretaking, too.

w.r.   In *Parable of the Guest*, caretaking is happening as well, although in the final form of the piece, which is virtuosic dance, the care for and the agency of the dancer are thrown into question and oftentimes subjugated to the physical demands of presentational performance. A dance is, among many things, a staging of power dynamics—the power dynamic of how the choreographer's vision traffics through the dancer's body.

The dance field is primarily directed by men and primarily populated and danced by women, and this intensive gender economy structures all virtuosity in dance. In making *Parable*, I was really aware of honoring the legacy of Ulysses Dove while working with two Black women dancers and thinking deeply about the ways in which I was asking them to perform movement—and telling these dancers how to move. But in some ways, quite simply, this is the job of the choreographer. So, there was this homage to a more classic form of dance making, as well as an attempt to thematically center sisterhood and its complexities in a way that tries to push through and maybe beyond how certain relationships among women were expressed in Ailey's work and Dove's work. The piece ends with an

201

interview with a former Ailey dancer, Nasha Thomas, who worked very closely with Dove during his guest choreographer gigs with the Ailey Company. From Nasha, we get a history lesson from a Black woman about her experience working with Ulysses, and she exposes some of the dread and bodily harms that are embedded in a gender economy that is unfortunately customary in concert dance.

It's also sometimes just scary to make a beautiful dance. I think a lot of Black performers have digested the pressures according to which Black virtuosity was constructed across the twentieth century. There are new approaches to form emerging now that break these rules and embrace alternate strategies that subvert or expand what is identifiable as beautiful, as African American performance. Black queer aesthetics in particular have facilitated a transition from certain classic, defining African American tropes into a rich malleability of subject, material, and underexposed aspects of Black embodiment today. Even though *[siccer]* and *Parable* look really different, they're both asking questions around the power of the choreographer over the dancer, and the malleability, or transformation, that is possible for the dancer in a moment of public consumption, like performance.

And so *[siccer]*, as you say, is me trying to stage that power dynamic through staging a film shoot as a device that enacts the heightened apparatus of photographic capture built into stop-motion animation, then twisting it to put real people in that situation. There's a head-on presentation of that power dynamic and the eye of

202

the director and my eye collapsing together and, over the course of the piece, working to challenge those givens, undo those dynamics, explore different layers of agency in this situation. This is evident through whispered side discussions among the performers that happen onstage, in plain sight, while other dialogue or material is being performed in a more, let's say, explicitly frontal way for the audience. The great and devastating thing about a performance is that it doesn't always get read by audiences in its preferred way. It might feel like they hate it (even when they love it). And you have to live that while the performance is unfolding. How might a choreographer attend to or address that dread in and through the performance itself?

T.A.   This practice of reimagining improvisation through common sense lends itself to a kind of emergent strategy building onstage, in ways that enable the performers to reach whatever desires that you're wanting to achieve as choreographer and director without it being prescriptive and authoritative.

W.R.   One of the most exciting things to experience as a choreographer with a performer is the moment when they start *wanting* to perform the material. That there's a moment when the performer's voluntary will to enter into the material and take hold of it, and interpret it with their full being, is what allows the piece to move forward. Ulysses Dove spoke about this. So, when you're in a cast and you see

203

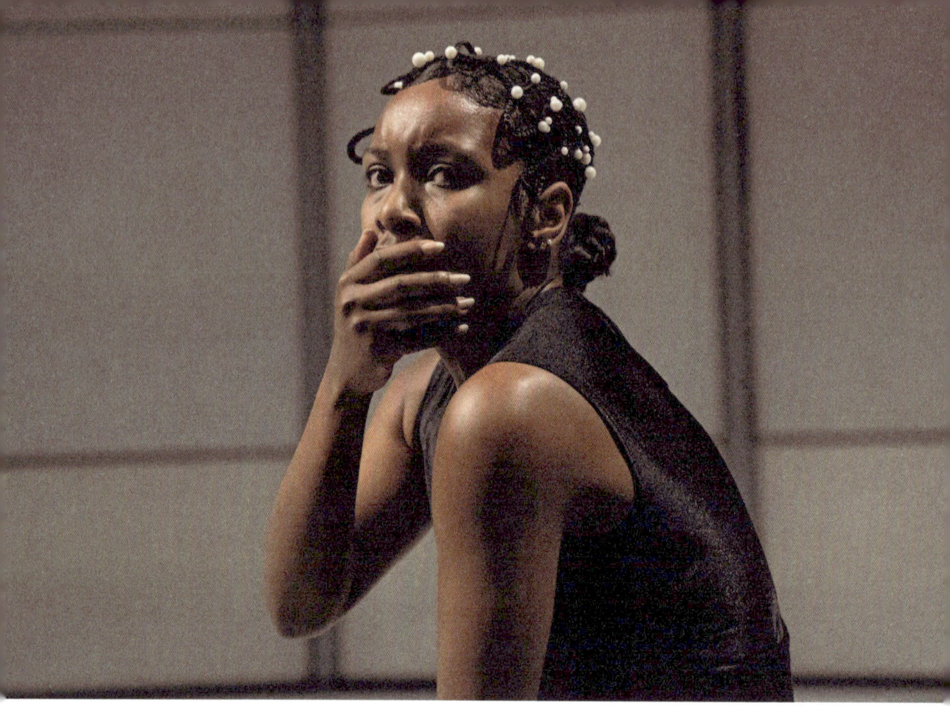

Will Rawls, *Parable of the Guest*, 2024. Performance

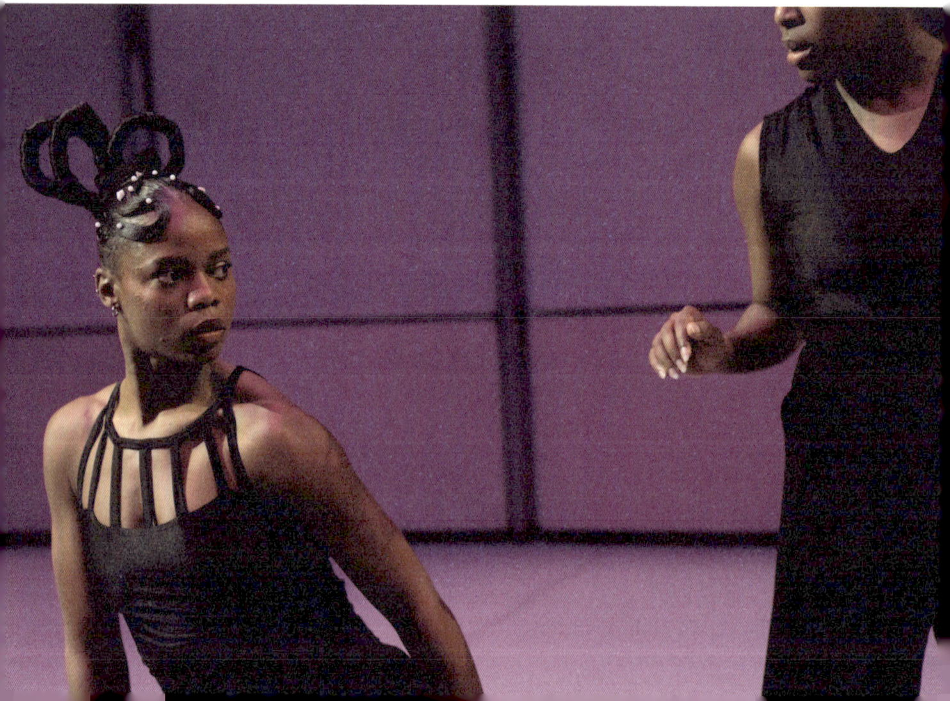

other dancers doing this, you're like, I'm not that performer, but I see how this performer has understood the situation and is able to produce responses to it that throw the situation into relief as a constructed predicament. Then I as a performer can find *my* ways of doing that, but it will be different. Those emergent strategies happen in rehearsal, and they are challenging to script into the performance but can become a kind of common sense that develops through fucking around in the studio. Once we decide what the material of the show is, then it's about how the performers maintain that emergent, strategic consciousness within the performance situation. How do they take things to the next level. And this happens with improvised or set material, with greater and lesser margins of choice for the performer. Working on *[siccer]*, we talked a lot about the term *[sic]* as an anti-Black framing of language, e.g., *[sic]* as used to point out improper Black speech that appears in a standard English text. If we think of the stage as a standard text, and the performer as nonstandard speech, how might the performers then *[sic]* the performance themselves, i.e., call out its frame? This is perhaps what it means to be *[siccer]*.

T.A.   Yes, the device of *[sic]* in written language as marking the indecipherable becomes not only a prompt for calling out the myopic understandings of certain kinds of illegibility through language but also critiques correctness as something that is Western, anti-Black, and oppressive. *[Sic]* becomes a verb in the piece, calling out the farces and limitations within colonial language schemata.

205

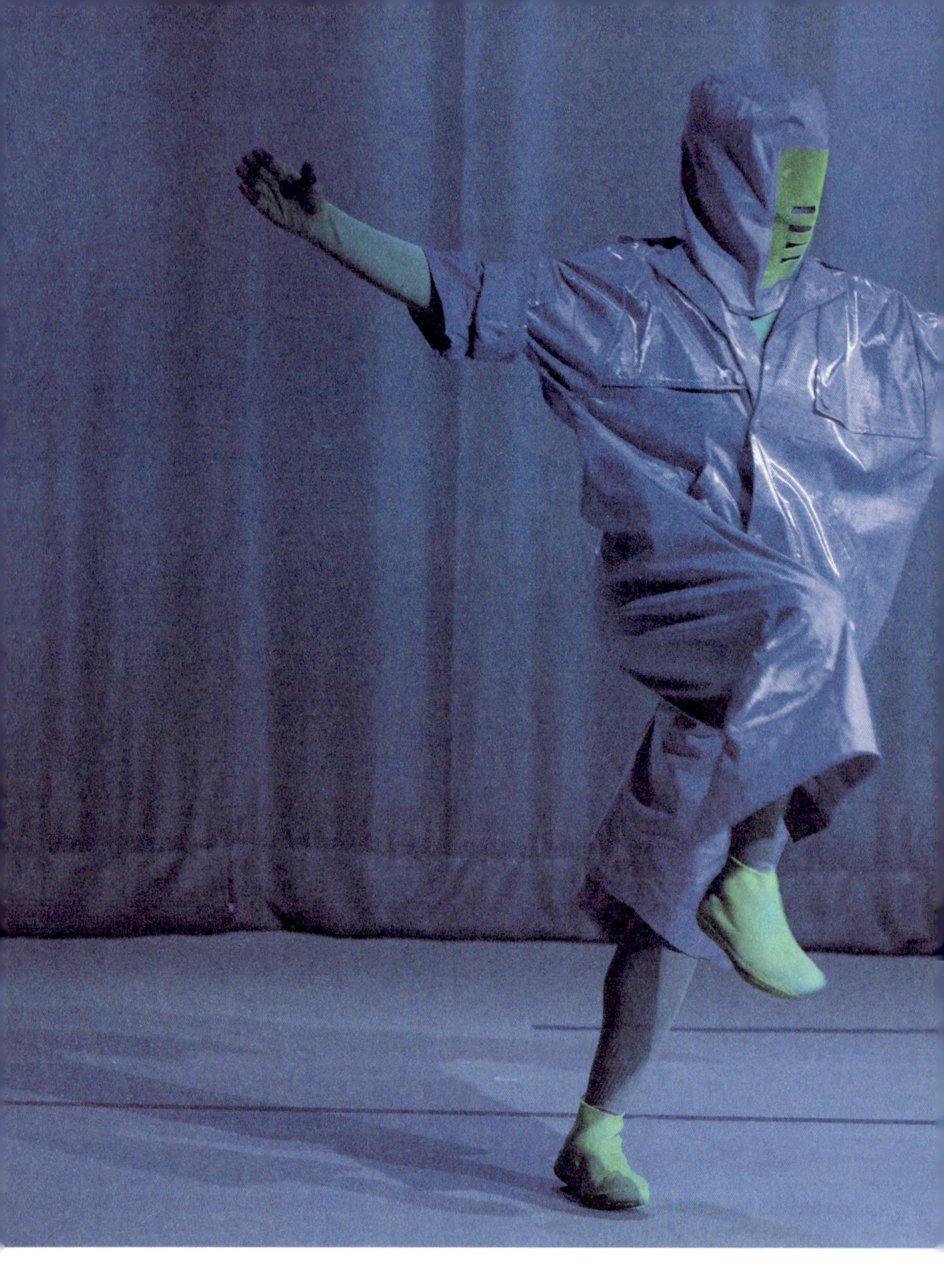

206

WILL RAWLS

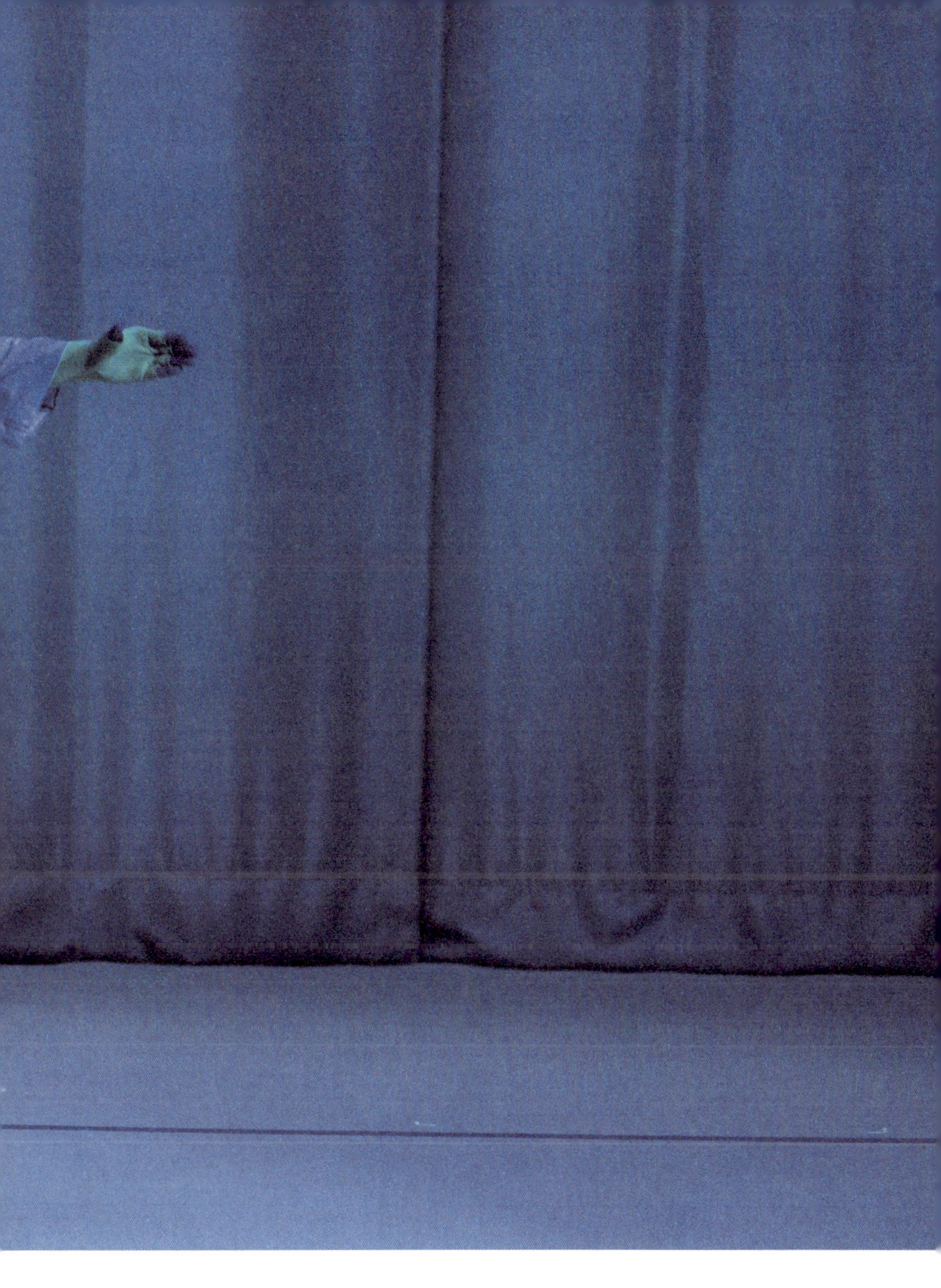

Will Rawls, *[siccer]*, 2023. Performance and installation diptych

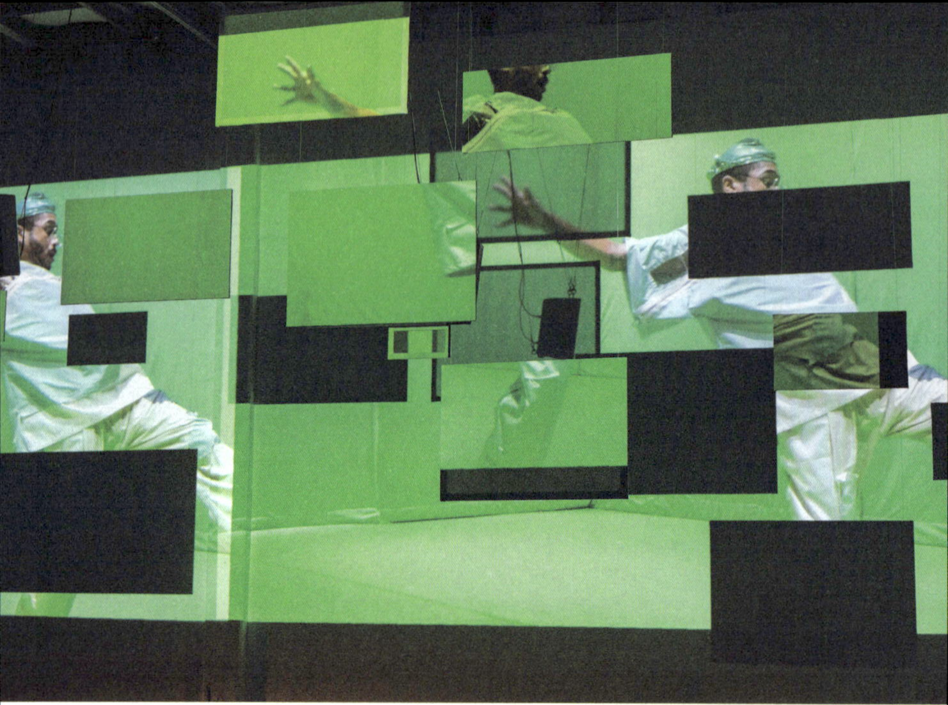

Top: Installation view, Will Rawls, *[siccer]*, Portland Institute for Contemporary Art, Oregon, September 23–November 5, 2023. Bottom: Installation view, Will Rawls, *[siccer]*, Institute of Contemporary Art, Los Angeles, April 5–August 31, 2025

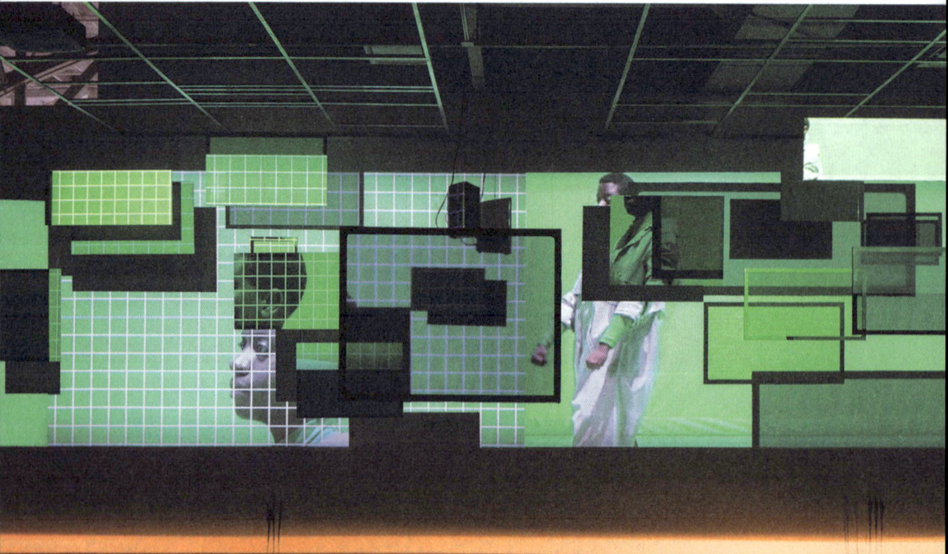

W.R.   I will say, too, that among the performers, "siccing" each other is about ribbing, joking and capping on each other—not to call each other out or reimpose proper linguistic rules, but to actually *call in* the play and mess that is foundational to the intimacy that makes performance electric. There's nothing more exciting to me than seeing performers who are comfortable making fun of each other onstage. So often, due to so many histories of degradation, the desire to exalt Black performers onstage is a potent reparation. We can witness and enjoy exaltation, but most performances are not interesting without some form of antagonism and friction. So, that is what I look for—ways to present the predicaments of Black being, through a certain distortion that suspends the binary of exaltation and misery. And hopefully it's playful, too.

T.A.   I wonder if you can talk about the invisibilized labors that go into performance work and particularly *[siccer]*. Why these collaborators? How do these things get developed through relationship? How do you make it work with all these schedules, with all these practices spread across different parts of the world? So much of performance is contingent on you all being together. How do you make that happen?

W.R.   I guess one could say that I'm a postclassical or *postmodern* dance maker, in that, for me, you can make an excellent performance with anybody as long as the choreography is sensitive enough to hold that body to deliver

209

something powerful. Anyone can *do*. Anyone. The performers in *[siccer]* are people that I admire as people, and I want to collaborate with, channel, and also capitulate to their ways of being inside a world that I'm trying to create.

The performers in *[siccer]*, Jeremy Toussaint-Baptiste and Holland Andrews, have approaches to sound that are so different, but they both question the limits of how spirit, self, form, mythology, and emotion can exist inside music. Really, I attribute that to Holland's practice. Jeremy is thinking about the concrete sculptural performativity of sound: How does sound do something consequential, and how is there a way to point to a particularly Black aesthetic in sound, especially at the minimal sculptural level that can produce an impact? The fantastic dancer jess pretty is also a fantastic comedian and thinker, and down for whatever risk. Same with keyon gaskin, same with Katrina Reed—performers with broad and profound experience in a variety of contemporary work. These are people who are hyper-professional, have performed in multiple situations, and are the kind of quintessential contemporary twenty-first-century dancer. In a complex way, they're sort of like the neoliberal subject in their ability to do any kind of work at any time. But they're also extremely critical and clear about their commitments to choosing projects that feel aligned with their own politics around being Black people in the world.

T.A.   You're a professor of choreography at UCLA, a person who has the opportunity to engage with young folks,

210

Gen Z in particular. I'm really curious how that sort of cross-cultural exchange in an educational space might have been informing your practice over the past couple of years. Young folks, we learn from them too. And I've watched you become a refuge for many students on campus who want to protest and evolve through forms of resistance while also desiring safety from state harms that are becoming more and more ubiquitous. How do you navigate those dynamics in addition to your practice?

W.R.   I don't claim to understand Gen Z. But like all dancers, they are facing intense precarity as well as intense consolidations of aesthetics through social media. I can identify with the world being precarious. For many years, my income changed all the time. I've been evicted. I've had to sell half my belongings to make it to the next apartment. I cashed checks through friends. Significant precarity for years and years on end. Over time, I decided that my art should reflect my life; therefore, inconsistency and change-ability became foundational to my practice, to my forms, to my choices of media. I became interested in questions of how reliable structures force a consistency into an artist's practice that isn't necessarily reflective of their life but more reflective of the artworld's needs. I bring that question into the classroom and throw multiple approaches to working with objects, language, movement, image with these young makers so that they can also spend time being inconsistent and experimental before they cohere. There are some students who cohere a style and it's great. I'm not against that,

211

but it just couldn't be true for me based on what I lived as a young performer. I want to play and play and play and push and break and break until I am convinced that I've found the form that expresses my feeling or idea.

T.A.   In that, the work that you're doing edges toward making some sort of freedom within these traditional structures of movement, performance, and dance.

W.R.   You have to construct your liberation. And liberation is temporary and must be remade again and again. Which is kind of a beautiful conundrum of performance and the reason time matters so much. Questions of liberation exist both inside and outside performance. The way you structure and commit to time as a medium that holds you and your audience can produce resistance or breakthroughs in various situations. Liberation is temporary, but choreography is forever. And you can quote me on that.

Brian Rochefort

by Annika Bohanec

Earthbound and Otherworldly

What began as a childhood obsession with gathering natural artifacts has evolved into a lifetime of exploration and experimentation for Los Angeles–based artist Brian Rochefort. Drawing from his travels and childhood memories of collecting beehives, bird nests, and robin's eggs, Rochefort's ceramic vessels emerge as abstract, sculptural portraits of the world around him, capturing both its beauty and fragility. Through layers of carefully selected glazes and pigments, his work offers a personal evocation of nature, rich with texture and color.

Rochefort's passion for ceramics began at a young age. "I've enjoyed clay since I was a freshman in high school," he notes. "It has the perfect balance between control and surrender, which I practice in the studio. The transformative quality of clay and glaze initially drew me to this notoriously complex material, one that is still relatively unexplored." The artist attended the Rhode Island School of Design, where he honed both his technical skills and conceptual approach. "I would go places, absorb my surroundings, and then come to my studio and make abstract representations

213

of these memories and feelings," he shares. "It was all about turning what I experienced into something new."

After graduating, Rochefort embarked on a two-year residency in Helena, Montana, before relocating to Los Angeles, where he has spent the last fifteen years further developing his practice. For the artist, his interpretation of the vessel and how he activates the surface is key. Working with multiple glazes, each piece undergoes several firings—typically four or more—to build cumulative layers that react dynamically in the kiln. His aesthetic draws heavily from abstract expressionism, nonrepresentational painting, and sculpture, pushing the boundaries of material and expression.

Rochefort's sculptures serve as responses to the places he has visited, and his studio, a space where he re-creates the atmosphere of those locations. Color, texture, and form all reference the natural world. The interiors of his works often possess a glossy, molten quality—mimicking lava or tropical waters—while the exteriors are more tactile, evoking the rough texture of tree bark or weathered landscapes. "I rely on heat and layering to arrive at the final piece," he says, "which can be flawed by too much or too little saturation." By using different slips, clays, and sands, he creates forms that look like they came from outer space, a tropical rainforest, or even the bottom of the ocean.

Each piece bursts with myriad colors—vibrant blues, mossy greens, bubblegum pinks—layered in shifting fields or winding like tributaries across volcanic stone. From cratered bowls to towering vessels, the works carry a quiet

214

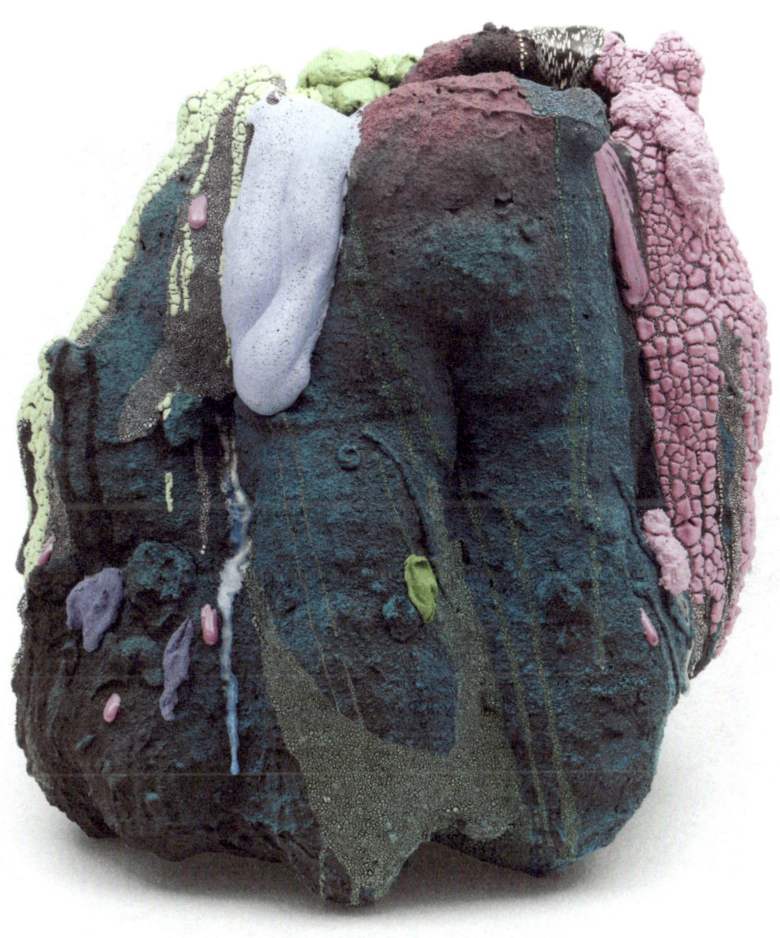

Brian Rochefort, *Lichen Code*, 2025. Ceramic, glaze, glass fragments.
22 × 22 × 22 in. (55.9 × 55.9 × 55.9 cm)

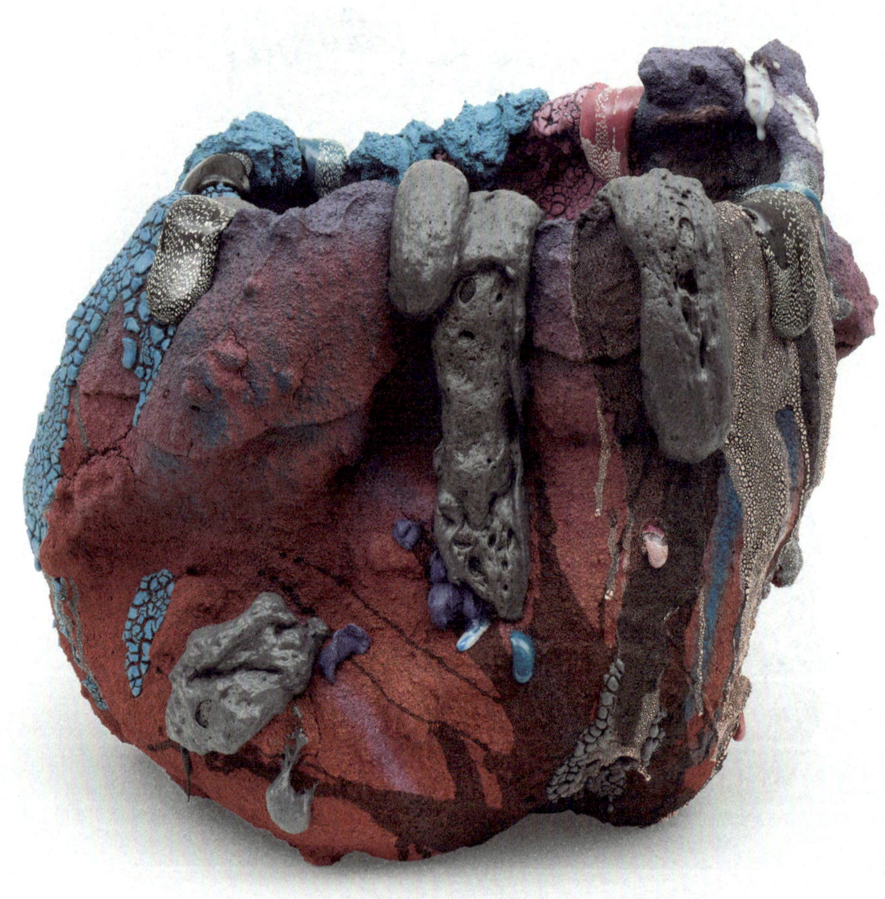

Brian Rochefort, *Scald Rain*, 2025. Ceramic, glaze, glass fragments. 22 × 20 × 19 in. (55.9 × 50.8 × 48.3 cm)

elegance. Their tactile surfaces evoke charred earth and obsidian, while a subtle iridescence suggests breath beneath the glaze. Titled after memories from the artist's travels—animals, flora, specific landscapes—they offer glimpses into abstracted impressions of place and experience.

"I want some kind of chaotic feeling in my artwork, erratic glazing and broken appearance, yet refined, layered, and beautiful," he explains. This tension between beauty and risk permeates his sculptures, which capture an energy mirroring the unpredictable forces of nature. His works appear as though they could either emerge from or collapse into the earth itself, teetering between becoming and falling apart. The surfaces often show marks of brokenness—cracks and fissures—suggesting fragility beneath their glossy exteriors. Though unbroken on the inside, the exteriors capture a rawness, reflecting the world around us: beautiful yet fragile and constantly on the edge of something else.

Rather than focusing on literal representation, Rochefort seeks to translate the essence, memory, and energy of nature into abstract forms. His work captures a visceral response rather than a conventional interpretation. For him, transforming an experience into an abstraction is what allows for personal and emotional connection, without the constraints of traditional imagery. This tension between the fragile, the beautiful, and the catastrophic imbues his work with a mesmerizing quality. Grounded in memory and capturing the world, Rochefort's work invites us to consider the delicate balance between creation and destruction.

217

Amanda Ross-Ho
by Chinaka Hodge

On Devotions and Archive

I meet Amanda Ross-Ho on a particularly chilly Los Angeles morning, one that made us both shiver in its wind. We chat over tea in her Lincoln Heights studio; traffic was light from Leimert Park, streets deserted this time of year. Still, I'm mindful of my "hard out" after we talk. I'll rush from here to make a cake for my kid's school's holiday party. Amanda has our interview and studio visit, then it's on to finish inputting grades for her university students before she's finally done for the year. It's 2024. We both admit we're bracing for whatever foolishness comes late January.

Amanda's nails are clean, short. The mug she hands me feels sturdy, the water not overly hot. I ask where she's from originally. *Chicago.* I ask how long ago she left and she has to stop to figure out the number of years. I ask if L.A. is home now. *Yes.* Then she qualifies that with *in many ways.* Her partner is here. Her students are here. I ask what questions she is sick of answering about her art; she says scale. I don't have a single question prepared about scale. Didn't even think to include it. Everything I'd seen on my phone in prep for this meeting looked the same size.

My prepared questions are about legacy, mostly. About whose work she inherits. I have questions about for whom Amanda makes, and why. Who are her people? Whose histories does she inherit? What does she hope to leave behind?

More specifically, I ask Amanda about a piece of hers: an image of her father, commercial photographer and studio artist Ruyell Ho. When I saw it, something made me pause. A sadness in it, a freedom, maybe. She tells me about that image, how the original film was over the years carefully saved and revived, a blue stain patinaed over her dad's straight-ahead expression. It is clear that in both language and approach, Amanda intends to honor her father. I ask Amanda about her mother, her mother's presence in her work. She is vulnerable and honest in her response, detailing family nuance gently and truthfully. She is courageous and nonhyperbolic, which makes me think I can trust her art.

I mean to be focused, but I'm neuro-atypical and I tend to self-soothe by looking around the room. A light fidget. A sip of tea. A shift in my chair. A reminder to myself to make eye contact. We haven't walked into the chest of her studio yet, haven't begun the tour per se. But from this anteroom, from this metal work table slash lunch stand where we sit, I can see prints and works hanging above and around me. In my periphery, I see a wooden table covered in objects, meticulously arranged into a neat chaos of display. It's familiar and clinical at once.

220

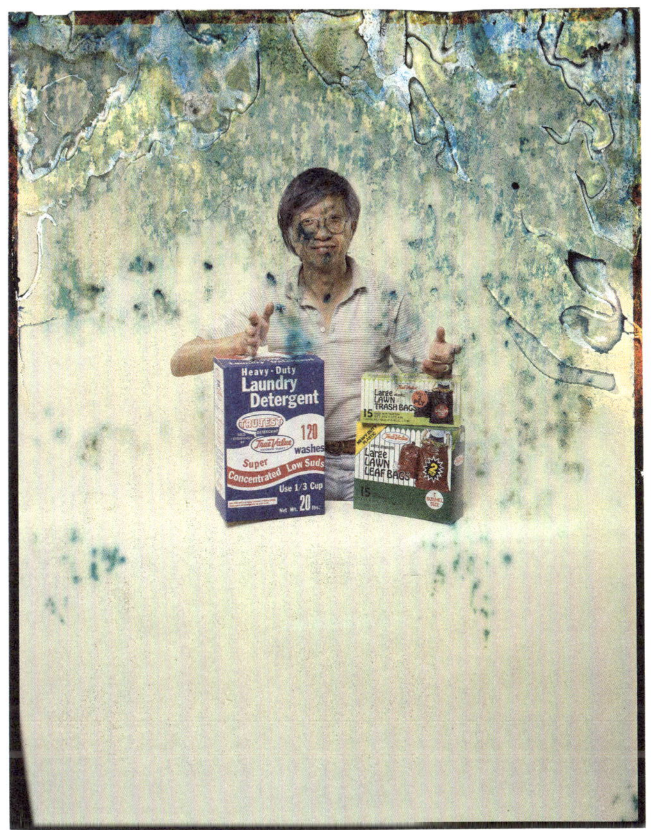

Amanda Ross-Ho, *Untitled Waste Image (HEAVY DUTY)*, 2024.
Duratex transparency print in custom lightbox. 73 × 59 ¾ × 3 in.
(185.4 × 151.8 × 7.6 cm)

221

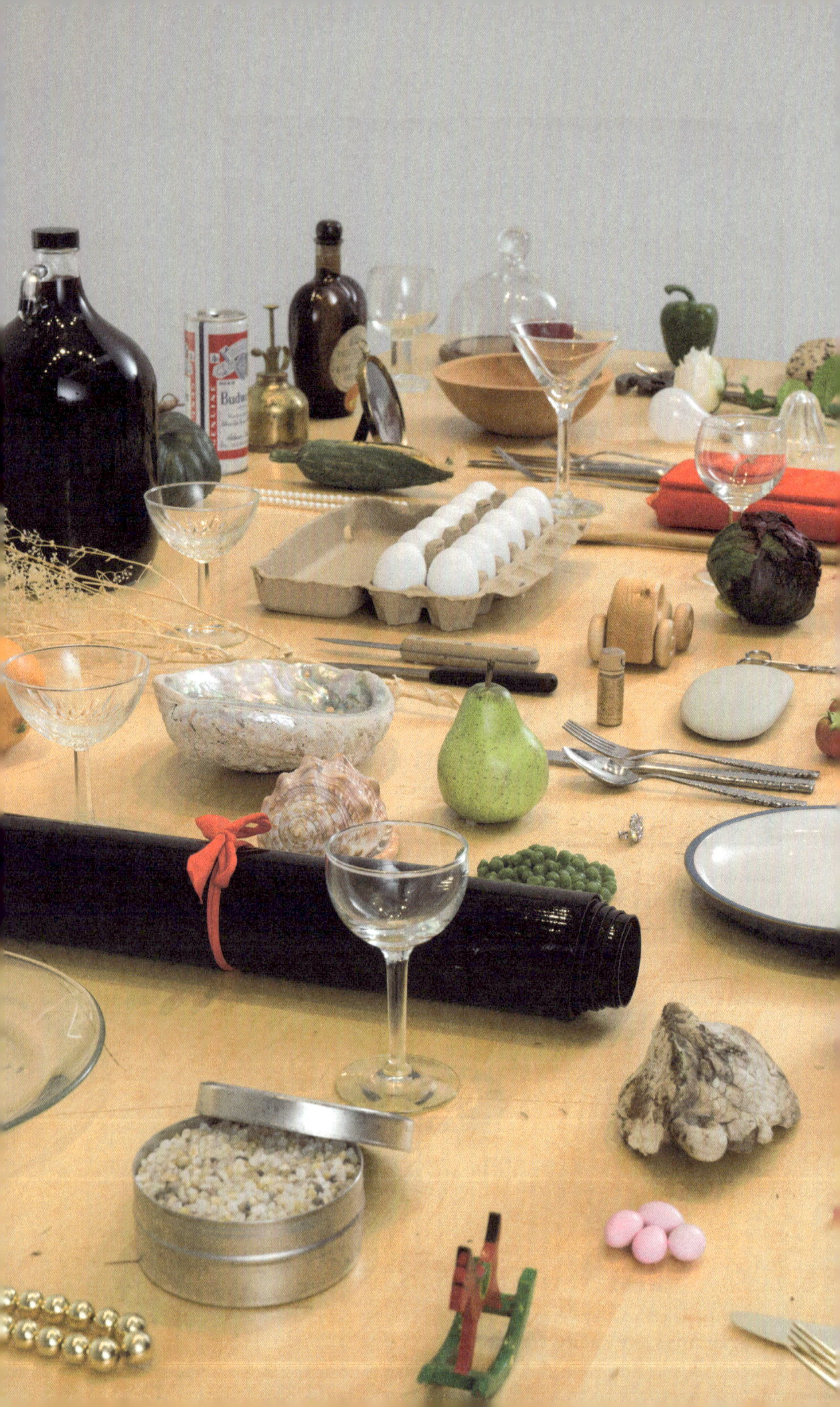

I can't pay attention to Amanda's answer to my question *and* detail each of these objects on the table like my mind is begging me to do, but I find myself trying to figure out what these things—what my grandmother might have lovingly called bric-a-brac—have in common. I can't even quite make out what that assortment is? Vials. Binoculars. Pill jars, glass, and plastics from the 1960s and 1970s. Something about the table makes me feel very much at home.

Maybe it's because the women in my family hold onto things, make plans to make use of them later. I'm one of those women, I know, who finds herself obsessed with tinted glass jars you just can't find anymore, muffin tins, heart-shaped ceramic pinch pots, smoking pipes. I spend my spare time online trying to find the exact ceramic Bundt dish my Aunt Hazel used to make her pound cakes, in case the two I have ever break or come to some disaster. I wonder how long it took Amanda to find a table full of this generation of delights—an entire four feet of things crafted decades ago, all in pristine, photographable condition.

When I turn my full attention back to our tea, Amanda is telling me everything she makes is either *archival, devotional, or both*. I understand the *archival* part

Left: Amanda Ross-Ho, *Untitled Prop Archive (THE PORTFOLIO)*, 2024 (detail). Reproduction Magnolia Street Kitchen Table (154.84%) (Combination core plywood, ash end-grain veneer with fleece backer, plank matched plain-sliced maple veneer, steel surface mount corner brackets, oil and hard wax finish), preowned, modified, and prop objects sourced from an online marketplace. 56 × 96 × 46 ½ in. (142.2 × 243.8 × 118.1 cm). Installation view, *Scratching at the Moon*, Institute of Contemporary Art, Los Angeles, February 10–July 28, 2024

223

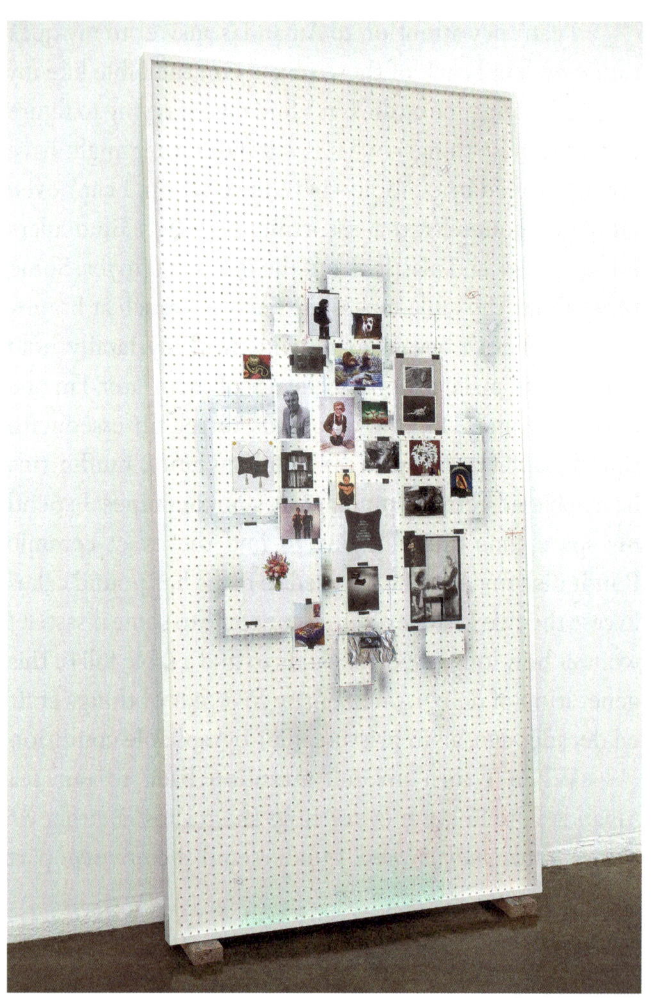

Amanda Ross-Ho, *Local Search and Seizure*, 2008. Hand-drilled sheetrock, inkjet prints, laser prints, acrylic, graphite, colored pencil, pushpins, linen tape, reproductions of original photographs and artworks by Peter Dean Rossi, Ruyell Ho, Laurel M. Ross, Pei-Lee Ho. 96 × 48 × 12 in. (243.8 × 121.9 × 30.5 cm)

224

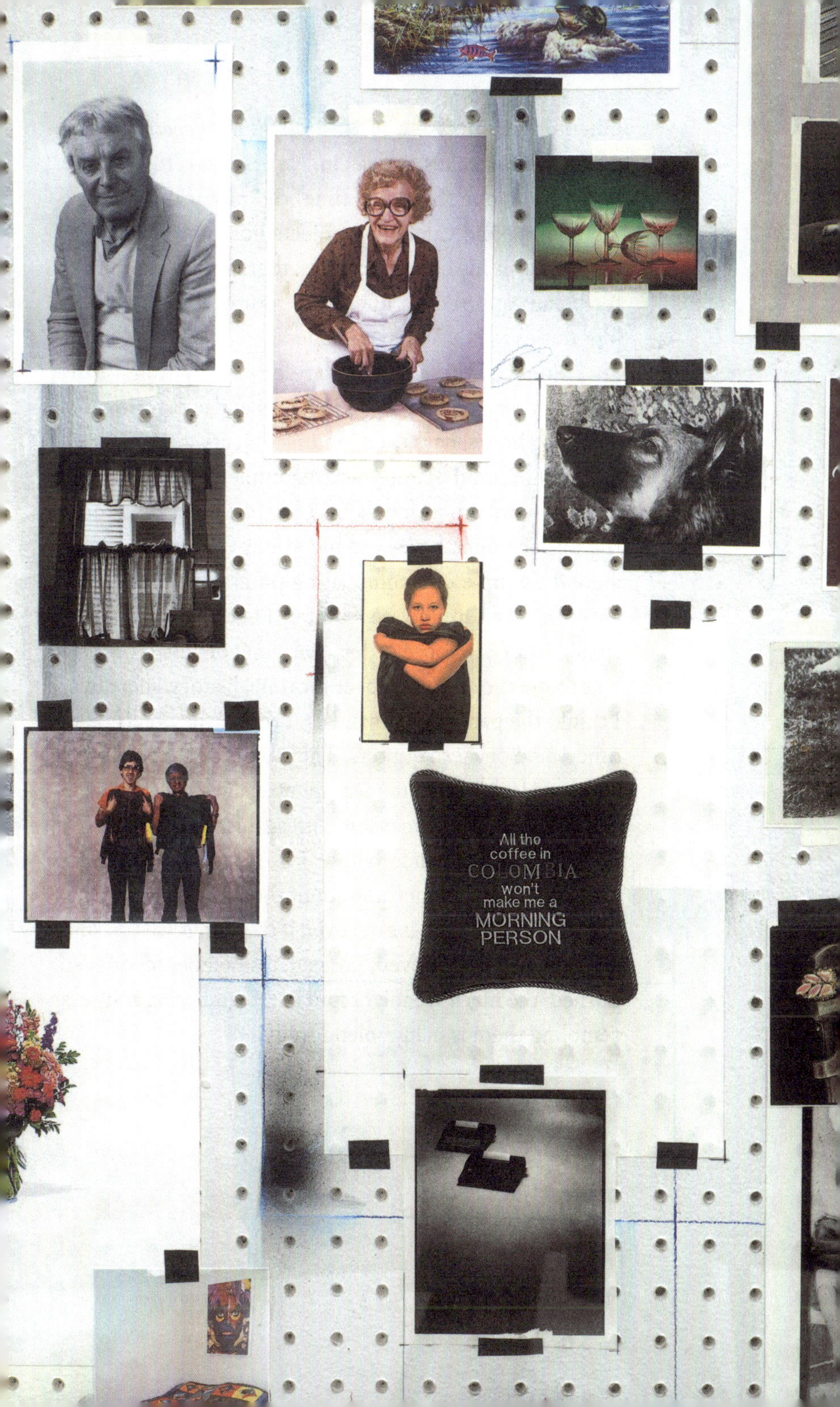

All the
coffee in
COLOMBIA
won't
make me a
MORNING
PERSON

inherently, completely. Intrinsically. That *devotional* part, though. That makes me lean in. I ask Amanda to say more. She talks about the sheer time, the physical acts of re-membering and cataloging objects like those her father employed in his commercial photography, that often, af-ter being captured on film, were returned to their hum-bler duties as household ephemera.

Some of these things were broken by time or dis-placed by the same. So sometimes, Amanda's devotion is in spending hours, days even, finding objects she knew well in her childhood—lamps, writing implements, glass vials, brushes—and procuring them. The table in the next room, the one she must have seen me eyeing our whole talk, is a good example of a culminating point of that devotion. Up close, I can appreciate it better. There are hundreds of small objects, in loose order, every one of which now sig-nals to me the artist's respect for time, history, specificity. I think: the patience of mandala. I think: the precision of American Southern quilters. The table is sized to make its audience feel smaller, to measure up against us how Aman-da's childhood table measured up against her.

I visited Amanda before Los Angeles was forever changed by fire. Something about the work is comforting to me. Something in it says, even if the things we treasure are drowned or removed, ravaged, dismembered, or even burned, the merit we might find in remembering and reas-sembling them is many splendored.

226

Gabriela Ruiz

in conversation with Kate Durbin

Dream Houses

Gabriela Ruiz's vibrant, trippy artworks span mediums from painting to performance to video installation to sculpture. Using readily accessible materials, Ruiz's foam and brightly colored glossy paint transform thrift-store chairs and dressers that she places inside altered gallery spaces. For her first solo show, *Haus* (2017), at Little Tokyo Art Complex in Los Angeles, the gallery's rooms became monochromatic, primary-colored dream environments that, at equal turns, resembled the rooms of a house, a fashion-shoot backdrop, and a mise-en-scène for her performance art.

Growing up in the San Fernando Valley as part of a large family, from a young age the self-taught artist escaped the busyness of her environment by finding inspiration in the colorful houses of Mexico, the splashes of neon in *Ren and Stimpy* cartoons, and the decadent music-video sets of 1990s MTV. She also cultivated her singular personal style, which she developed further when she began performing at Mustache Mondays, a staple of L.A.'s queer nightlife scene from around 2007 to 2018, and her fashion is central to her performance work in galleries and museums now.

I spoke with Ruiz on Zoom in late December 2024, right after she moved into her very first apartment by herself. Although she had just arrived, she had already decorated with colorful chairs and brightly painted cabinets.

KATE DURBIN   You have such a joyful use of color in your practice. You've said elsewhere that that fascination goes back to your childhood.

GABRIELA RUIZ   Growing up as the second youngest in my family, I often had to find ways to entertain myself. My parents were usually at work, so my siblings cared for me and my younger sister. Television became my escape. Cartoons and music videos were where I learned so much. I spent a lot of time watching and examining the sets, the garments, and the props. The 1990s especially felt like an exciting time of experimentation.

Another big influence was visiting family in Mexico. I was always struck by how color was a natural part of everyday life, from the food and decorations to the way people dressed. It felt so alive and intentional. Even though I had a hard time expressing myself verbally, I found other ways to communicate, like through what I wore. Over time, color became deeply personal to me. I went through phases of being obsessed with different colors—everything I owned or surrounded myself with had to be that specific color at the time.

228

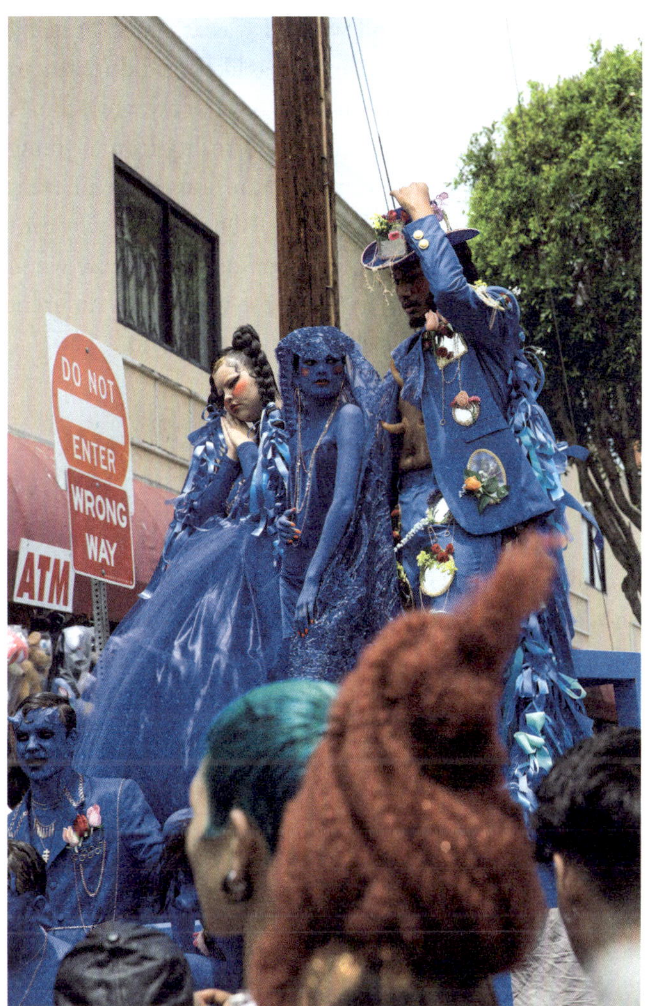

Gabriela Ruiz, *de la Calle*, 2018. Performance. Part of *de la Calle*, curated by rafa esparza at Santee Alley, Institute of Contemporary Art, Los Angeles, June 22, 2018

229

There was a period where I was ashamed of being who I was, because at the time it was like you didn't want to be associated with who you were. A lot of my work comes from looking for ways to cope with reality from a young age. I would see how in Mexico all the houses are different colors and I was obsessed. I'm like, "Oh my God, why can't it be like that?" I remember dreaming about how when I was older every room in my house would be a different color. It felt like I was building my little world.

K.D.   How do you build your own worlds in your work now?

G.R.   One way is in how I make little homes and spaces for my works. If I'm going to show a painting, I want to show it on a beautiful red wall or purple wall, because I want to create a home for it. It doesn't matter if it's just a small painting. Making my objects, I want them to feel like they're in this safe space; they're in their own little world, and I love that.

K.D.   Even the work that is a home itself needs a home. I think that's beautiful. Especially when rent is getting worse and worse. Homes are becoming more and more inaccessible, especially in L.A. So I love your idea of the space of a home being this place of safety in the world and also a place to reclaim color.

230

G.R.   It's interesting that you talk about high rent, because
I'm thirty-three years old and I just moved to my first place
all by myself.

K.D.   Congratulations!

G.R.   Yeah. It's a little dirty, but at least I get to have my little chairs.

K.D.   Oh, your colorful dining room chairs are cool. They
almost seem like they could be for one of your installations, since your work often features brightly colored furniture, like the canary yellow, insulation-foam-covered
chairs in your piece *Reflexion* (2018), or the red ones in
your show *Haus*.
     Speaking of transforming everyday objects into art,
your fashion is a huge part of your performance work as
well as your daily life. Your style is next-level.

G.R.   Thank you! Fashion for me has been a shield, a sort of
defense mechanism. Growing up being the biggest person,
you're immediately shut down—"You're not as pretty as
other girls." I started to be really conscious of what I wore.
Fashion gave me this way to not get bullied and to be witty.
I stopped getting picked on.
     This country has a way of making you feel like be-
ing different is a problem, like standing out is something
you should avoid. For a while, I tried to blend in, to tone

231

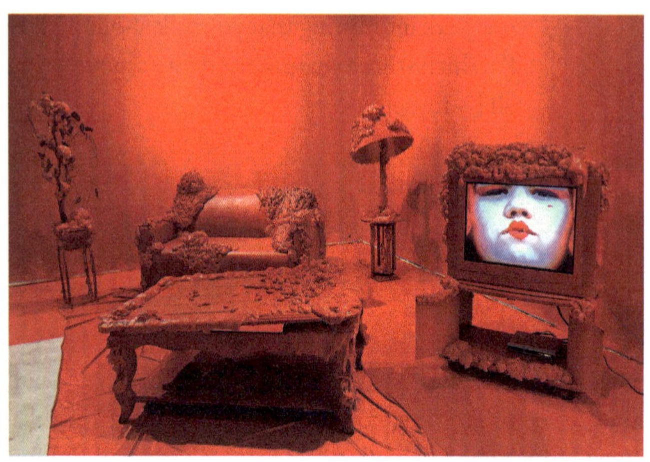

Installation view, Gabriela Ruiz, *Haus*, Little Tokyo Complex, Los Angeles, July 13–15, 2017

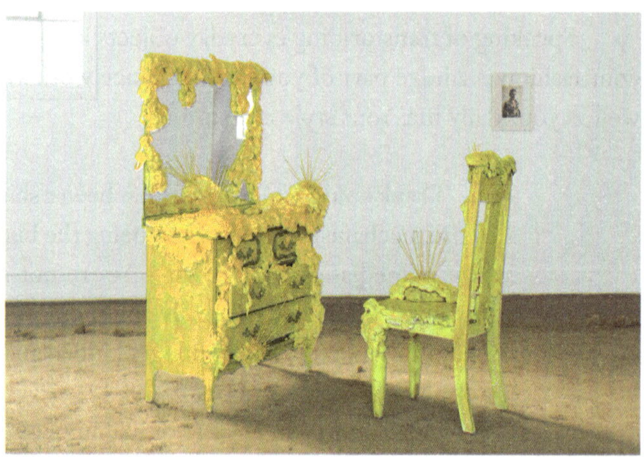

Gabriela Ruiz, *Reflexion*, 2018. Insulating foam and spray paint on furniture. Dimensions variable. Installation view, *Pasado mañana*, Commonwealth and Council, Los Angeles, January 20–March 3, 2018

232

myself down, just to feel like I belonged. But over time, I realized how important it was to hold onto who I am. I'm glad I didn't give in to that pressure to assimilate in order to make others comfortable.

K.D.   This is an impossible question to answer, but do you think you would have developed this highly unique style otherwise?

G.R.   I think about this all the time! I'm kind of grateful for all the trauma I've experienced. Sometimes you have to be a little seasoned, you know, to creatively deal with life. I feel like the more restraints you have, the more you can develop as an artist. I was really pushing the boundaries. A lot of the girls back then, they were wearing their American Apparel stuff and so they would only wear leggings and a shirt, right? When I did it, all hell broke loose. They're like, "Oh my God, why aren't you wearing pants—your legs are showing!" I was like, "This girl is doing the same thing, and it's just because she was thinner it didn't look like that on her!"

I made it a goal every day in tenth grade: I would wake up and just create an outfit that morning. I would go nuts and stick things on shirts. On special occasions I would use Easter eggs, or Christmas stuff, or Halloween stuff.

K.D.   You've mentioned elsewhere that the funhouses and carnivals that came through the San Fernando Valley where you grew up are an influence. I can really see that

233

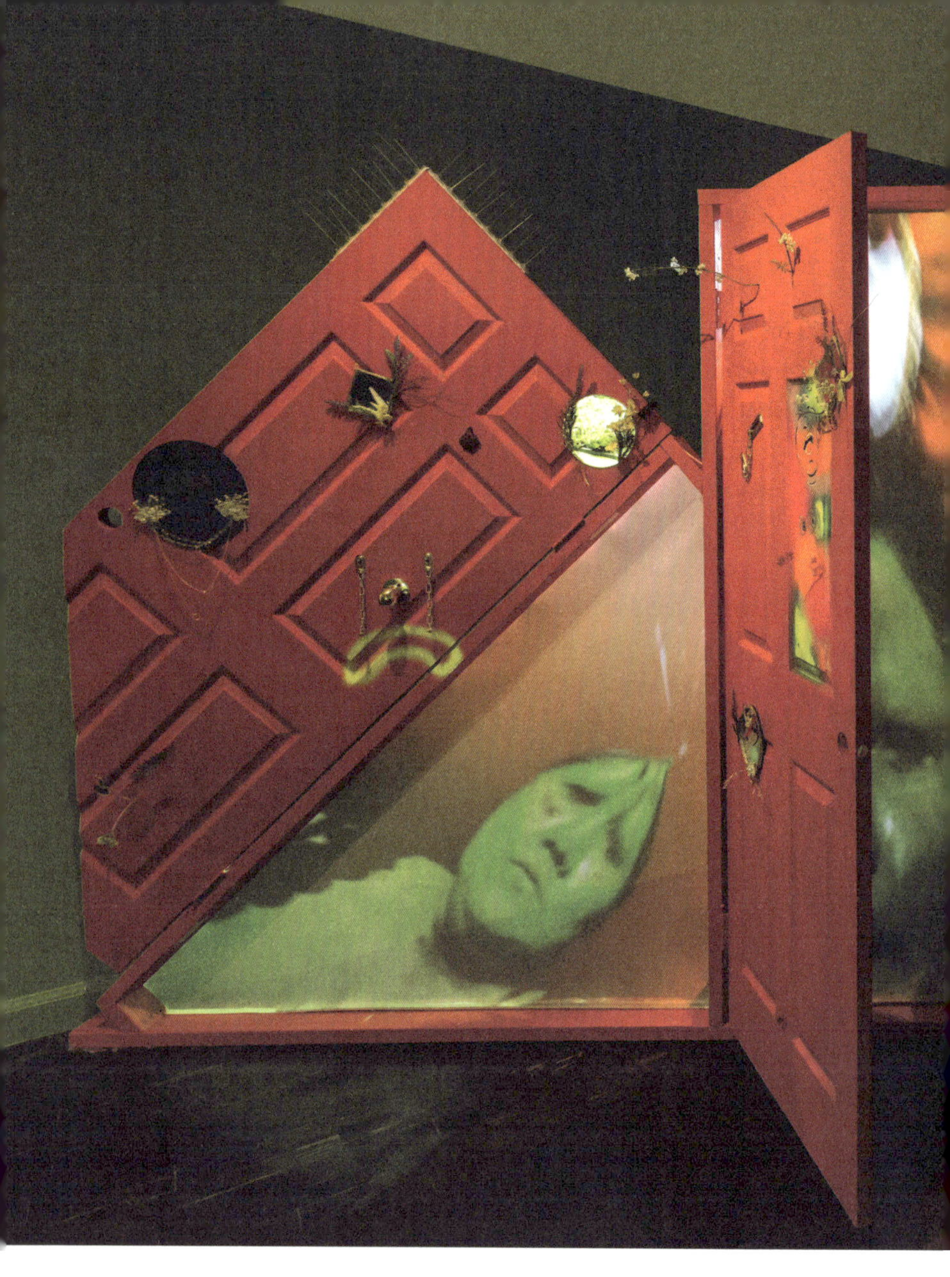

234

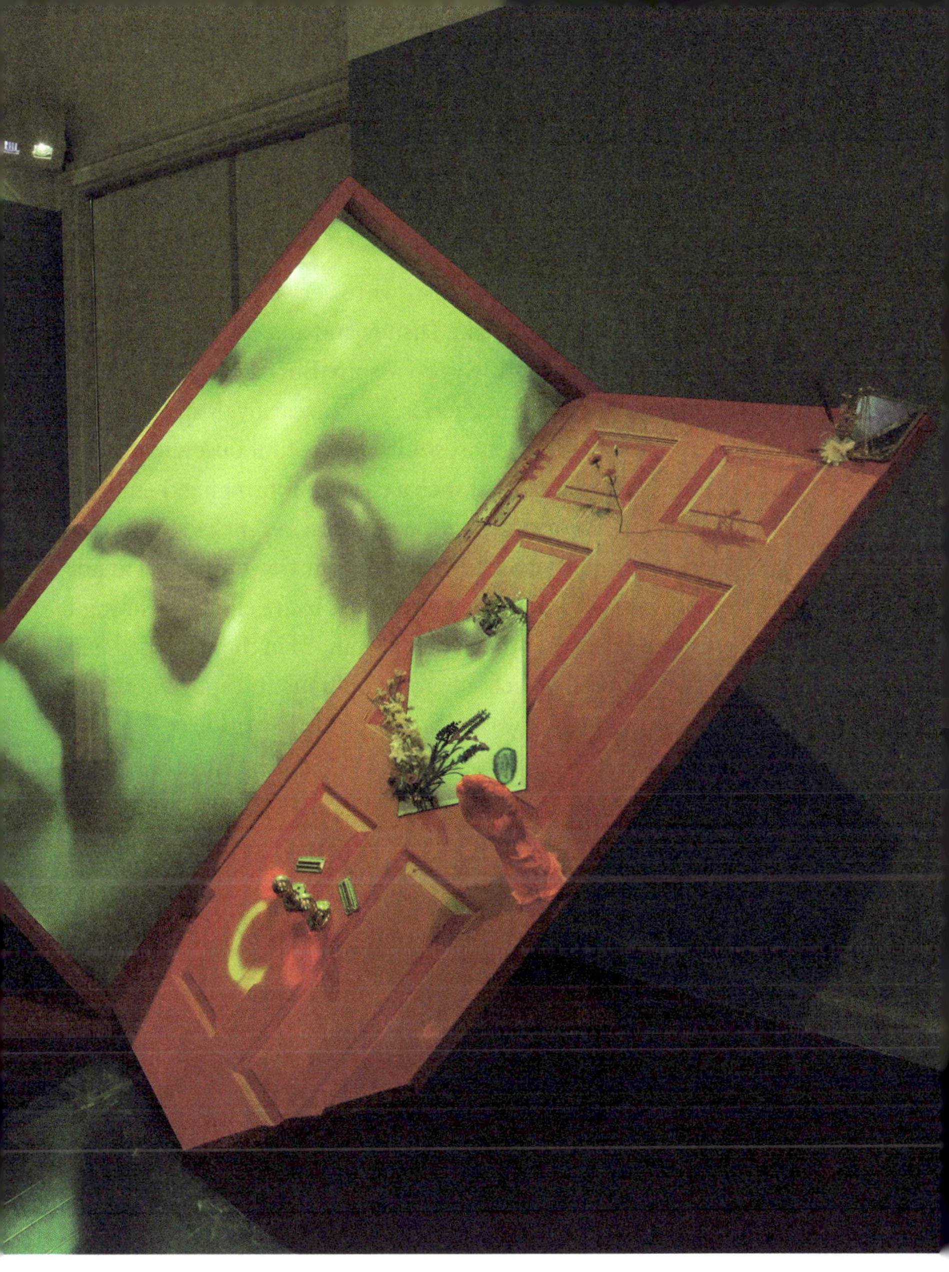

Gabriela Ruiz, *Full of Tears*, 2019. Wooden doors, mirrors, doorknob, chain links, plaster cloth, artificial flowers, acrylic, temporary tattoos, door locks, mesh fabric, and bird spikes on wood frame. 98 × 192 × 43 in. (248.9 × 487.7 × 109.2 cm). Installation view, *Gabriela Ruiz: Full of Tears*, Vincent Price Art Museum, East Los Angeles College, Monterey Park, CA, September 21, 2019–February 15, 2020

with the piece you made for the Palm Springs Art Museum, *Stream* (2022), which features an immersive mirror maze, sound installation, and video works.

G.R.   Here in Los Angeles we're very close to all of these amusement parks, like Disneyland and Six Flags, and we would go frequently growing up. But my favorite things were in the neighborhoods, pop-up carnivals and circuses. I remember being obsessed with the funhouse specifically. I think because I had such a chaotic upbringing, I enjoyed this intense environment where you get sucked into a mirror maze and you have to figure your way out. "Oh, I'm not on Van Nuys Boulevard anymore." You're climbing through these things and then you see yourself in these warped mirrors. It was a place where I could just escape, where my brain thought I was in this other little world.

Alake Shilling

in conversation with Ali Liebegott

Ladybugs Are Underrepresented in Art

As soon as I entered Alake Shilling's jam-packed studio—the living room of her mother's Los Angeles home—I was transfixed by both the artist and her work. We drank coffee and talked for two hours. Shilling was raised by her mother. As a teenager, she fell in love with fashion as a way to express herself without having to speak. She dropped out of college after a year, unable to deal with the culture shock of being around wealthy peers. Instead, she learned an immeasurable amount as an intern at the Los Angeles gallery and community space 356 Mission, which closed in 2018. Shilling's brightly colored paintings and sculptures often feature fantastical creatures like snails, mushrooms, and psychedelic train-conductor bears, all with cartoon-style features. Despite their childlike whimsy, all these characters seem to hold a deeper knowing in their giant eyes.

When we met, on the floor of Shilling's studio lay an unfinished diptych of paint, glitter, rocks, and sand picturing a dinosaur whose spots were ladybugs. I asked her about an unpainted gray rock in the dino's mouth, and she said cheerfully, "Oh, that's going to be a ladybug! This is

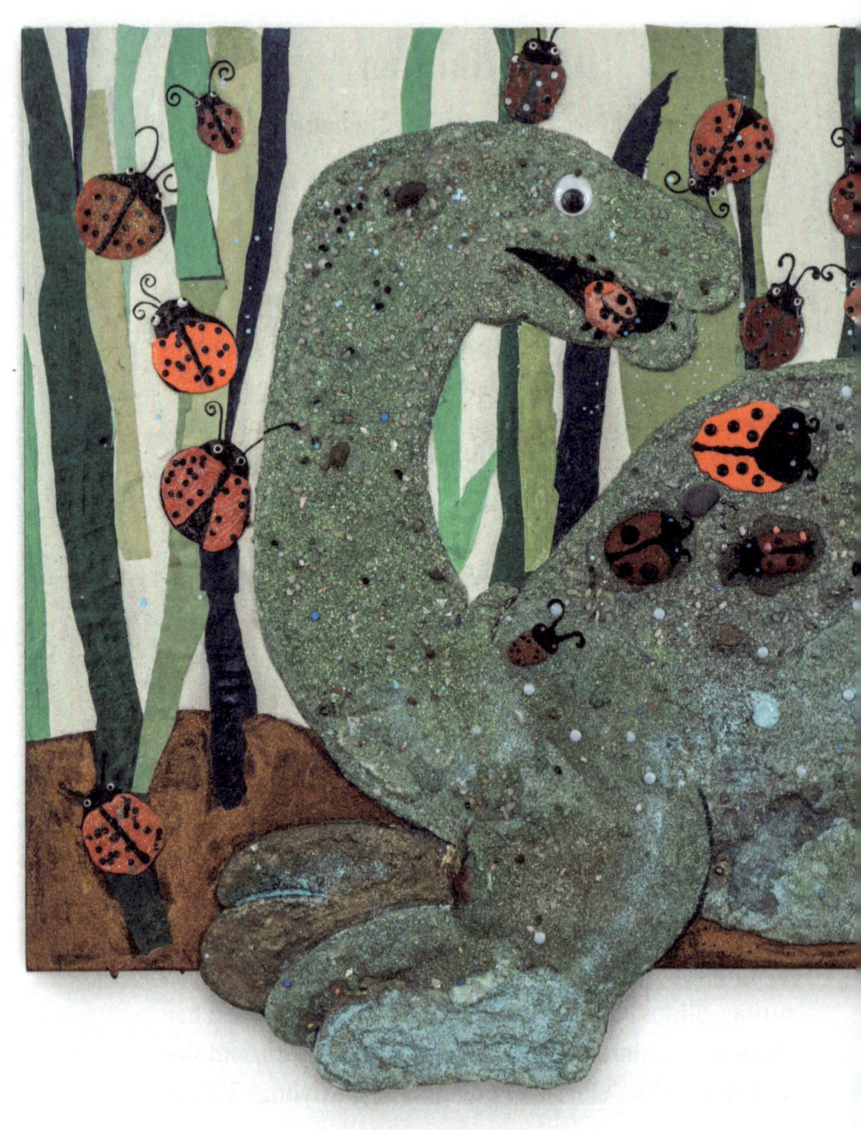

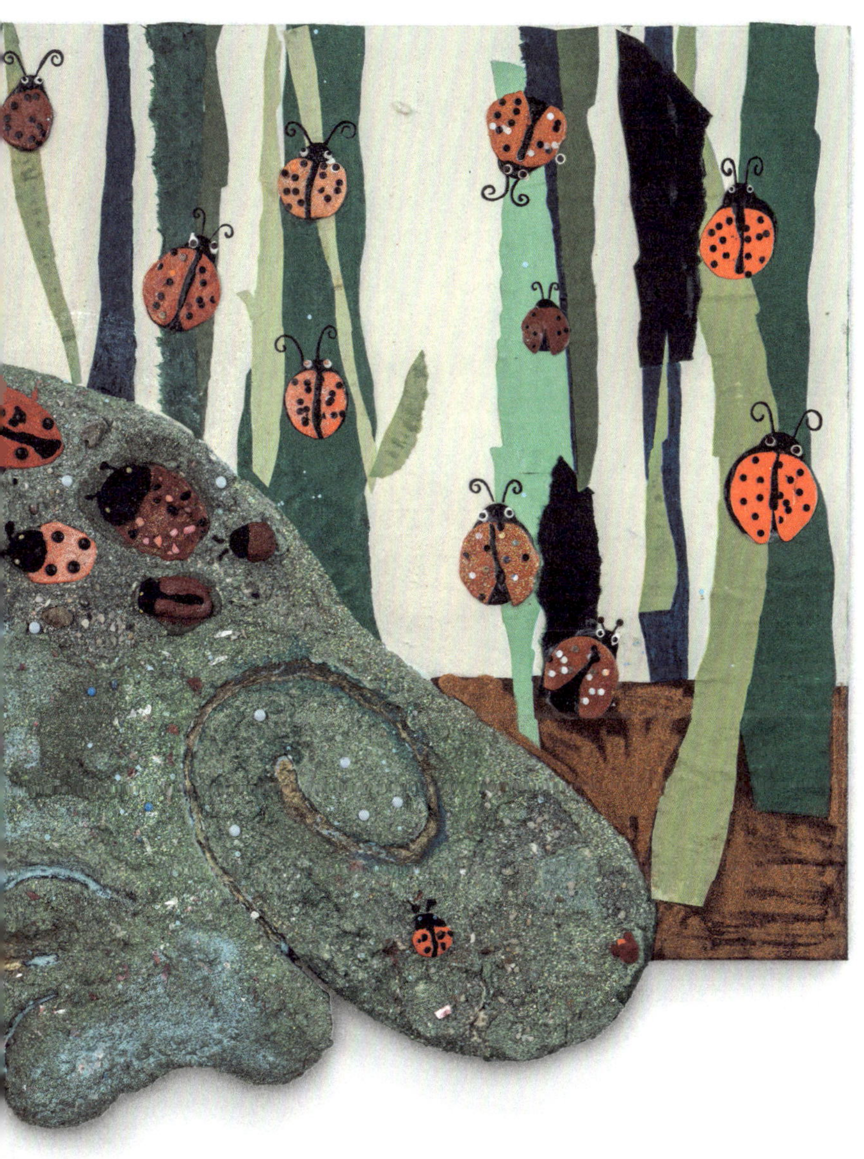

Alake Shilling, *Dino's Fine Feast*, 2025. Sand, glitter, tile, beads, construction paper, air-dry clay, ink, googly eye, cardboard rocks, pebbles, flashe, Swarovski crystal, and acrylic on canvas. 40 × 60 in. (101.6 × 152.4 cm)

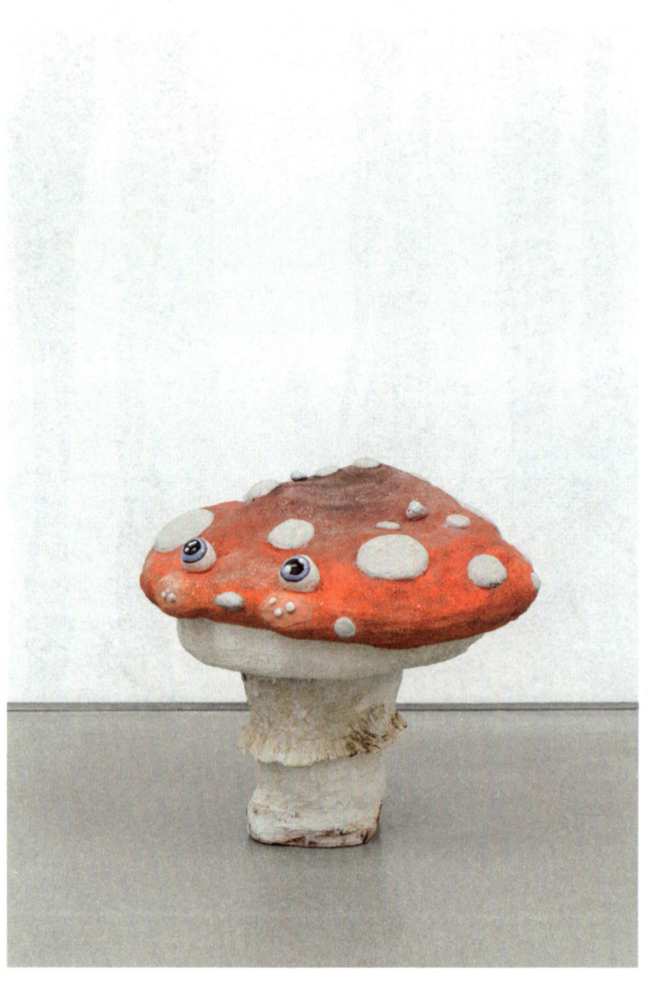

Alake Shilling, *I'm Just a Fun Guy*, 2023. Glazed fired clay.
20 ½ × 19 × 17 ½ in. (52 × 48.3 × 44.5 cm)

240

called *Dino's Big Feast*!" The tragedy quickly came into focus; the sweet-faced dinosaur was about to swallow the insect in its mouth, then devour the rest of the "spots" on its back. Just like that, Shilling captured the heartbreaking duality of life: Dino's feast is a ladybug massacre.

ALI LIEBEGOTT   What kind of art do you make?

> ALAKE SHILLING   My work is playful, with a nostalgic approach to visual storytelling. I paint fantastical worlds populated by vibrant, cartoonlike characters.

A.L.   Who is someone that inspires you by how they live?

> A.S.   I'm a huge fan of Miuccia Prada. She had a crazy fast slide installed in her office. She uses it as an exit after her workday. It shoots down three stories! I think she's mastered a lifestyle of whimsy. I can only dream of such a life.

A.L.   Dream fashion designer to work for?

> A.S.   I have a long list, but I'll narrow it down to Rei Kawakubo.

A.L.   What can you express in sculpture that you can't express in painting?

> A.S.   Sculpting, especially ceramics, is magical because you can cook your art and transform it into something

amazing, and it's out of your control to a certain degree (no pun intended). I like the idea of hand-building my own 3D world that you can actually walk through and touch and experience. While painting is also transportive, I like the idea of really taking someone there and immersing them in my imagination.

A.L.   What is your class background? How would you say it affected your journey in becoming an artist?

A.S.   I suppose lower middle class? Just barely squeaking into the middle-class category. I think taking art seriously can feel like a gamble. Financial stress makes it hard to figure out how to move forward, and makes me question if it's something I can sustain.

A.L.   Describe an artistic breakthrough.

A.S.   I was in the studio working on my first assignment in freshman year of college. It was a Friday or Saturday night, so the studio was empty and quiet. I ended up painting a frog in a Dr. Seuss–inspired landscape, and a light switched on. It was that simple. I found my style that night. It was a moment I had been waiting for since I was a child looking at cartoons. I'd ask myself, "When will I have my moment when it all makes sense?" I loved art, but I didn't have a cohesive language or world that I was excited to build upon.

A.L.   Tell me anything you want about your color palette.

242

A.S.   It always comes out the same, even when I make an effort to use different colors. It's frustrating.

A.L.   Who are you rooting for to make it in the art world who hasn't gotten their due?

A.S.   I need to think about this one.

A.L.   Do you ever destroy your own work?

A.S.   No. I tried destroying one or two paintings, but it didn't feel right or necessary. I used to throw stuff in the trash, but when I did people took it out, so I stopped doing that as well.

I feel the work has a spirit and a soul. It's almost like a living thing. I have conversations with my work and the characters in it. I usually leave things to sit, and the work somehow develops into something interesting or finds a home somewhere.

A.L.   What are you proud of?

A.S.   I had a dream of being an artist when I was a young bean sprout. I had no idea if it would be possible. When I went to college, I knew very little about the art world and the steps it would take to become a fine artist. I found the art world confusing, and the advice I was given pretty vague. I'm proud of what I've learned and what I've accomplished.

243

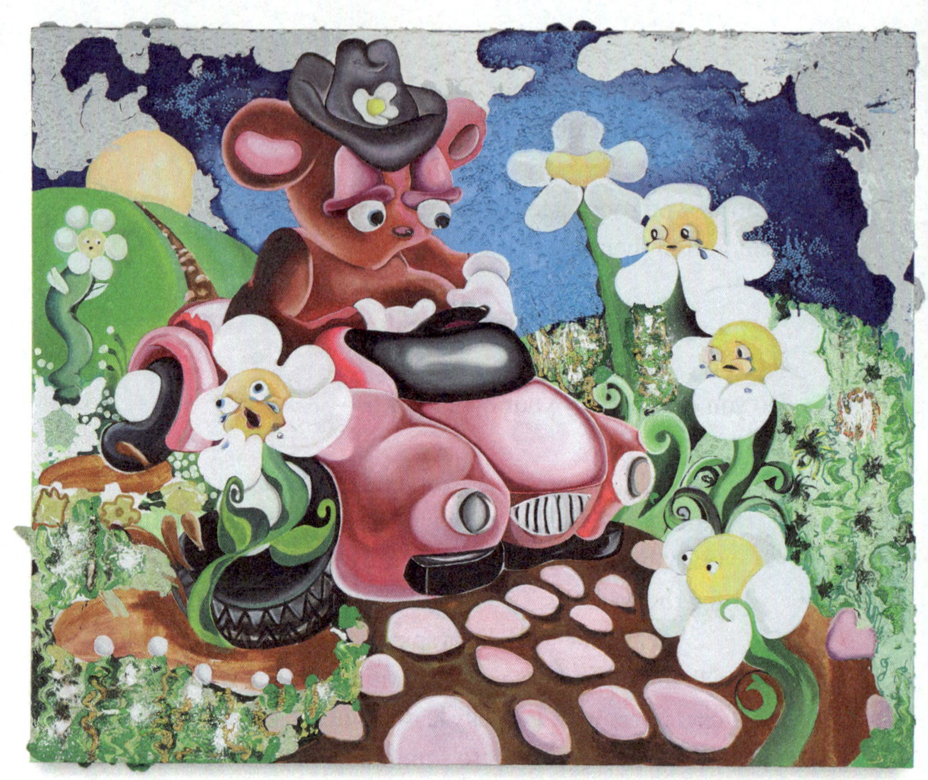

Alake Shilling, *Buggy Bear Is Out of Control on the Long and Winding Road*, 2019. Oil, Flashe, acrylic, Styrofoam, glitter. 50 × 60 in. (127 × 152.4 cm)

244

A.L.   What makes you anxious about being an artist?

A.S.   Sales, the art-historical canon, the business of being an artist.

A.L.   What do you hope your art will do in the world?

A.S.   I hope it inspires people to be artists as well and become fascinated with fine art, to use their imagination. There's no better feeling than seeing art that makes me want to drop everything and make something. It's so rare when it happens, but I'd like to make work that does that for others.

A.L.   What do you consider a "successful" painting?

A.S.   I suppose I judge this two ways. One is when a painting is totally finished, and there's nothing I would change or add to it. I could probably paint one painting for years if I didn't have deadlines. The second is painting that is popular. The point of making the work is to have a special connection with different people, so if that happens, it's successful! I've had some really bad technical failures in some of my work, but these pieces are some of the most popular works I've made. I find that very interesting and funny.

245

Nicole-Antonia Spagnola

in conversation with Summer Kim Lee

Using Irma's Green Stockings

Nicole-Antonia Spagnola's work is often shaped by what she is consuming. Obsessions take hold, and she works through them by giving them form. When she and I first met, she told me that lately she had become fixated on the work of filmmaker Billy Wilder. She was in the process of watching and rewatching his oeuvre. Most recently, Spagnola had been thinking about Wilder's 1960 film *The Apartment*, starring Jack Lemmon as C. C. Baxter, a New York insurance company employee who lets his managers borrow his apartment for their extramarital affairs, and Shirley MacLaine as Fran Kubelik, an elevator operator in the company's building who unknowingly has been to Baxter's apartment as the lover of his married manager, Jeff Sheldrake, played by Fred MacMurray. I had seen *The Apartment* before, but since it had been on Spagnola's mind, I watched the film again to follow her obsessions and see what form they would take for me, too.

SUMMER KIM LEE   I'm so glad you gave me a reason to watch *The Apartment* again. What initially drew you to the film?

247

 It was actually work. I had to teach the film last fall. You know when something is duh-good? Like, the image precedes itself so heavily you almost can't see its parts? I find Wilder's hits to be like this, anointed a "good movie" to the degree that it's a distraction. Watching it with a bunch of eighteen/nineteen-year-olds opened up random parts. They didn't want to talk about the implied sex or suicide attempt, so we awkwardly circled back to the significance of the key over and over again. Then I decided to try to watch all of his films. I watched his 1963 film *Irma La Douce* immediately after. Again, commerce and sex in an apartment with Jack Lemmon and Shirley MacLaine, recast as a Parisian policeman and a prostitute who've fallen in love. What did you think of *The Apartment* the second time around?

s.l.   I loved it all over again. What stuck out to me this time was the song "Jealous Lover," composed by Charles William. We first hear it played by a pianist in a Chinese restaurant, where Fran meets Jeff in secret, and then we hear it again on a record that Fran plays in the apartment after Jeff has left her there alone.

Obsession can reproduce or preserve its object, but it can also wear it down, like playing a song on loop or watching a film over and over again. Is it a way of taking the "duh-good" and breaking it down so that you can see and appreciate all of its parts? What damage or destruction do we do to our objects of obsession by consuming them so many times? Is it akin to being a jealous lover?

248

N.S.   I guess you wouldn't have discernment without repetition, but then taking it too far throws the whole thing into question. I have a bad habit of eating the same thing until I can't taste it anymore. I do this annoying thing where I ask others to taste my food because I've eaten it so many times I can't tell if it's gone off. But I don't think about it as breaking down. Looping displaces the origin, and without a beginning you can't assess damage. The second time "Jealous Lover" plays, it generates something different but not less? Wilder's films almost always start amid the action. He says, "I don't like to get too much into backstory. I believe only what you need should be forced out." The plot of *Irma La Douce* feels like this, some slapstick propulsion toward fidelity when all the odds are stacked against it.

S.L.   I like how you're seeing the relationship between Wilder's resistance to backstory and the propulsion of his repetitive slapstick. It reminds me of the scenes interspersed with the opening credits of *Irma La Douce*. Over and over, we see MacLaine as Irma with different johns, and each time she gives them a different sob story, because she knows these men are expecting one. She tells one man that she used to be a concert pianist before she broke her fingers, she tells another that she grew up in an orphanage that was destroyed on D-Day, and so on.

N.S.   "Why does a girl like me have to do this for a living? Well…"

249

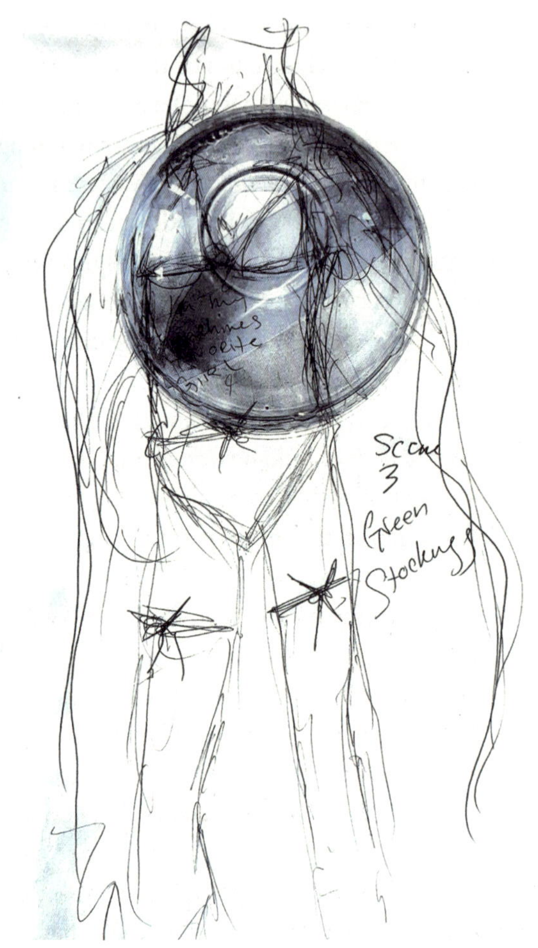

Nicole-Antonia Spagnola, *Study 2*, 2025. Pen on paper. 11 × 8 ½ in.
(27.9 × 21.6 cm)

250

s.l.   Yes! In the film, there's a running gag that involves the local tavern's proprietor, known as Moustache. It's rumored that he's a Romanian chicken thief, but then he mentions that he once was a professor at the Sorbonne, and he turns out to also be a (not very good) lawyer. Every time he shares a bit about his past, he stops himself and says, "But that's another story." The film ends with Moustache looking directly to the camera and delivering that line. I feel like that's Wilder talking, and that's what you're saying, too. There will always be another story. To not give a backstory does not mean things will break down. Like you said: It generates something different but not less, not a lack of taste from eating something so many times, just another taste to work with.

n.s.   And here the proliferation of work and sex makes new life. Lemmon as Nestor, the policeman/packer/pimp, becomes Mr. X, the john/English lord who pays Irma enough so that she doesn't have to see other clients. In the end, both Nestor and Mr. X appear in the same place as Irma has their (who's *their*?) baby. Prompting Moustache's final "But that's another story."

s.l.   Instead of a backstory there's just another character with another story. Everyone is working overtime. When watching *The Apartment* and *Irma La Douce* together, I realized they're all about work. Lemmon in particular is always doing too much. In *The Apartment*, he's struggling to run his side hustle of managing his own managers' extramarital affairs, and in *Irma La Douce*, he's a policeman, then he pretends to be Mr. X, and he must also work long nights at the food market to pay back Moustache, who's lending him the money he's been giving to Irma while posing as the Englishman. Lemmon's characters are stretched thin because they struggle with the ways that sex and work are inseparable from each other. Meanwhile, Mac-Laine's characters, who are working women, know better and wait for Lemmon to catch up, to get wise. Wilder knows what she knows, which is why he is able to comedically capture the contradictory, collapsed boundaries between work and play, between commerce and sex, as you put it.

This must be why your students fixated on the key to Baxter's apartment but didn't want to talk about what went on *inside* that apartment. They hadn't found a way to enter the apartment, to cross that boundary or threshold, or unconsciously they did not want to, not yet. I wonder which way in they were looking for.

> N.S.   Maybe because these boundaries are so far gone, there's some desire to reproduce them. For roles to be clearcut. And this is projected upon the narrative. I think there's a real difficulty in trusting that what's given is enough; it's easy to get stuck on the key, looking for a right way in. And I don't really care about that. I'm more into Irma's green stockings; they're versatile...useful in Nestor's jailbreak.

252

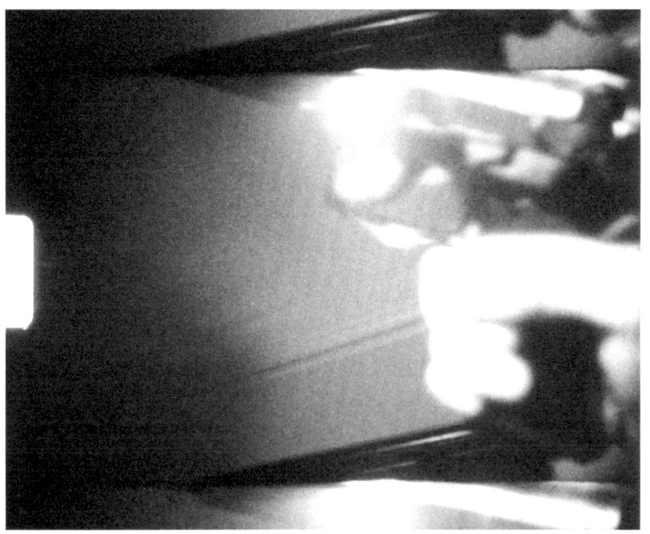

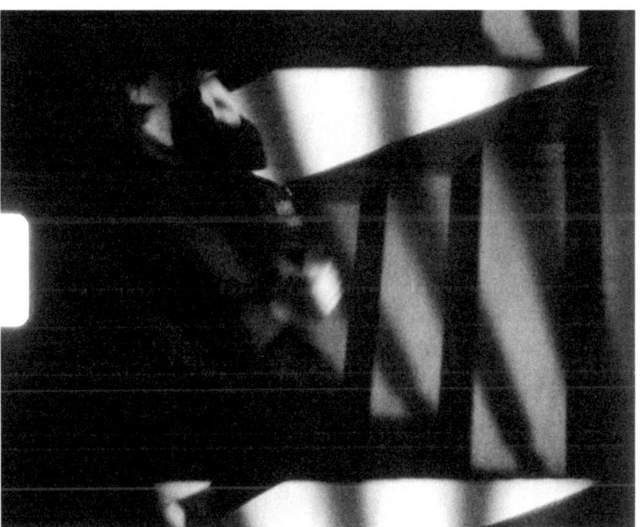

Outtake stills from Nicole-Antonia Spagnola's 16mm silent film *1-2-3: Apartment Gallery*, 2025

253

s.l.   Are these objects, the key and the stockings, useful
to you in the work you're making for Made in L.A.? What's
your way in, or your way out?

    n.s.   Not sure, I haven't made anything yet :)

Mike Stoltz

in conversation with Esti Giordani

Time Machines

I met with Mike Stoltz over video just days before the Los Angeles wildfires would take hold of the area. The winds hadn't quite picked up, but we were both consumed with anxiety. The last song he had listened to was "Another Flaming Tune" by Flaming Tunes—on vinyl. You could call him an analog guy.

An L.A.-based moving-image artist, Stoltz grew up outside Orlando, Florida, near an Air Force base and NASA's Kennedy Space Center. He describes his hometown as a "cultural vacuum" that had a type of "*Leave It to Beaver* overlay over real life." For the bored kids living in the shadow of Disney World, however, subculture was exploding, particularly in music. Emerging from somewhere between massive retirement communities and the local Elks Clubs, Florida's 1990s DIY punk scene became an avenue for Stoltz and his peers to experiment with music and art, like making zines—"seeing what we could do with scissors and a Xerox machine," as he puts it—and his eventual discovery of experimental film. In retrospect, the scene was an outlet Stoltz didn't know he needed.

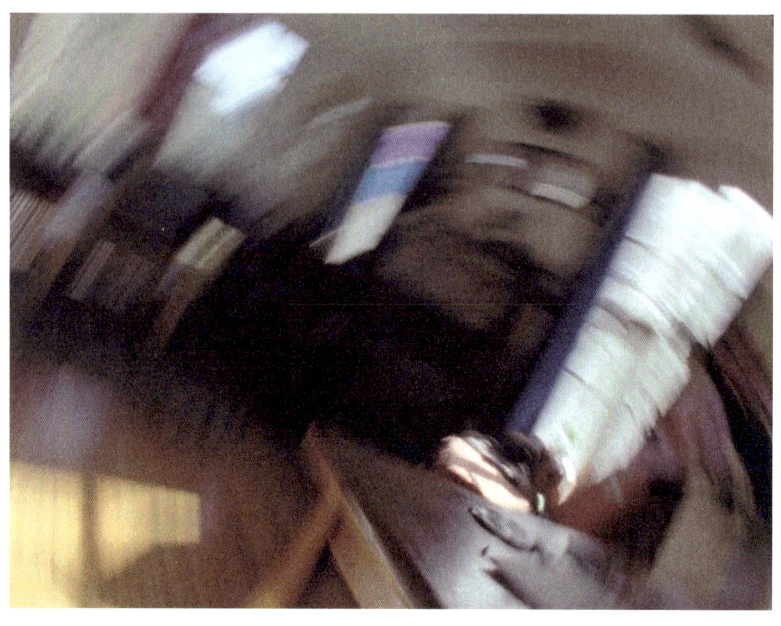

Stills from Mike Stoltz's 16mm film with optical soundtrack, *Holographic Will*, 2023

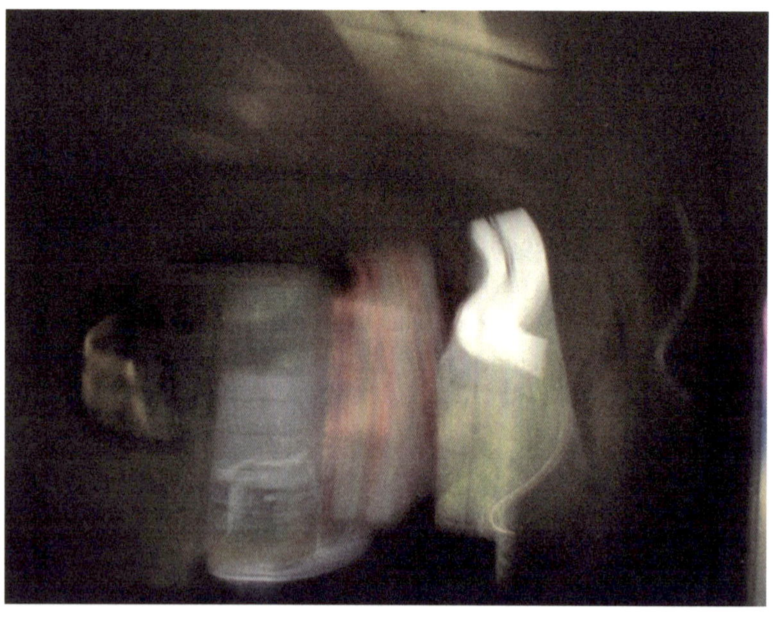

Informed by MTV, zine culture, mail-order records, and the advent of the internet, the future was not only uncertain, but there was an understanding that it would be unrecognizable. Even today, Stoltz's films capture this energy. His work moves across time, moment to moment—sometimes in minutes, sometimes over decades, folding time on top of itself—in what he describes as time travel. The images are driven not by linear narrative but rather by sensation and intuition. Collapsing layers of time and place, the artist distorts reality from the moment the camera captures an image to the final splice of the edit.

Stoltz's films are immersive—chance encounters; visceral, pulsing, sometimes frenetic movements flashing in and out of frames. Yet, in other instances, his work is languid—unhurried and open-ended. His films are deeply personal without oversaturating the viewer with autobiography. In *Holographic Will* (16mm, 2023), Stoltz, a longtime renter, captures what he calls the "domestic swirl" surrounding the sale of the building in which he lived. The ultimate question? "How much longer can we afford to stay?" Process driven, Stoltz meticulously shot the film frame by frame, adjusting the camera between every image. He describes the piece's interplay of sound and sight: "Single frames move forward in time, creating afterimage combinations without superimpositions. A phased drum machine soundtrack emphasizes the percussive quality of the image."

Stoltz's more abstract works are playful, rigorous, and formal, yet also intoxicating, even enchanting. *Tomorrow: it's not too late to join* (2021) is a "cameraless video

257

that uses shaders, digital oscillators, and feedback to push out against the edges of the screen." Rich blues, deep reds, and thermal glowing greens and yellows pulse alongside bouncing, glitchy lines. Though the images are carefully composed, they feel erratic and spontaneous. The sound is multifaceted: Piercing feedback loops are met with cinematic, almost Hitchcockian scores that eventually resolve into the divine harmonies of a synth.

Working with celluloid and other analog formats, Stoltz creates sensory, somatic, experiential films. The work's material and formal constraints set parameters while leaving room for discovery. A meticulous craftsman, the artist brings a distinct and laborious physicality to his practice. He edits his work by hand—a meditative yet intensely demanding process. "There's no Command-Z when you're using a tape splicer and a blade," he quips; mistakes are part of the stitching. "That kind of logic and that kind of rhythm is how I think about editing the moving image."

Preferring a black box to a white cube, Stoltz believes in the collective experience of the cinema, where an audience can "feel each cut" and be physically engaged. Similar to a punk show, he says, "There's this bodily experience…an understanding that it is going to affect the nervous system." It's what he describes as a contract with the audience, the contract of cinema.

When I spoke to Stoltz, he was working on a project exploring Los Angeles through an archive of slides from the 1970s documenting the locations of movie posters put up by the Fox Theater in Venice. An art-house cinema at

258

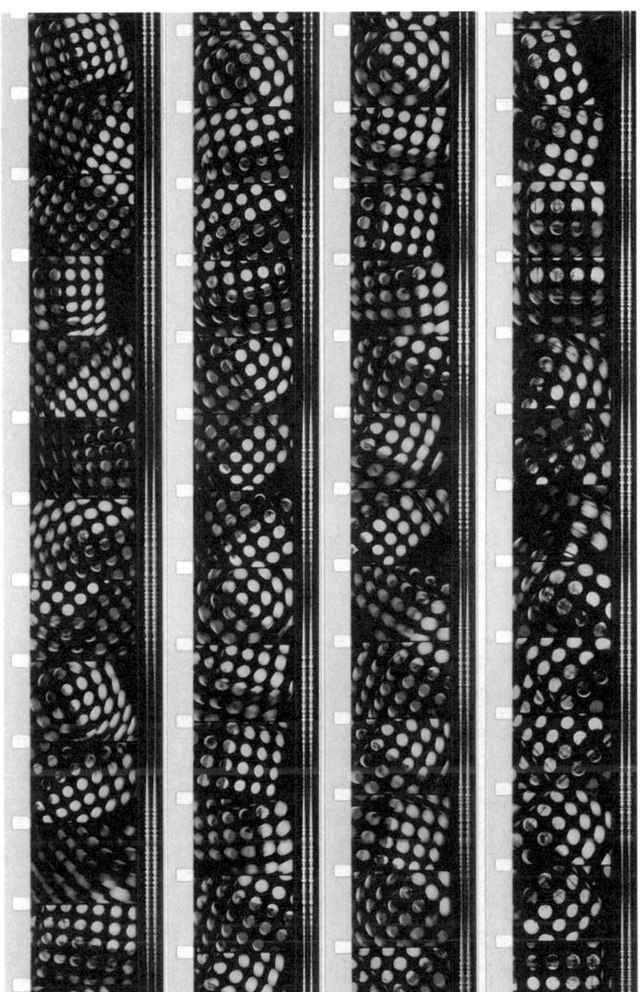

Still from Mike Stoltz's 16mm film with optical soundtrack, *With Pluses and Minuses*, 2013

259

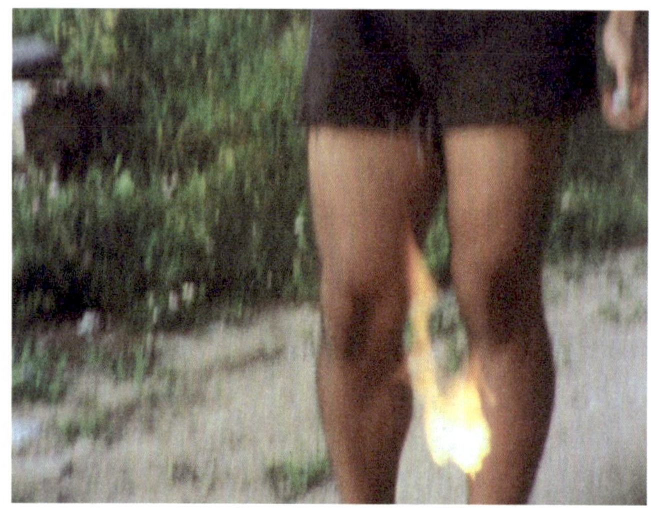

Still from Mike Stoltz and Alee Peoples's 16mm film with optical soundtrack, *Spotlight on a Brick Wall*, 2016

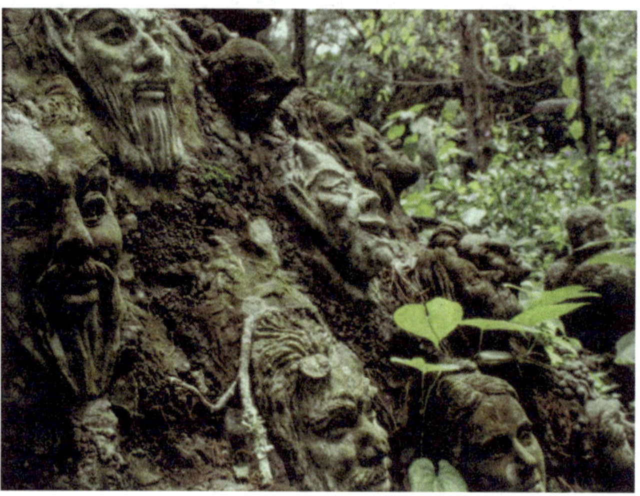

Still from Mike Stoltz's 16mm film with optical soundtrack, *Half Human, Half Vapor*, 2015

the time, the Fox had an employee wheat-paste posters of Emile de Antonio's polarizing 1976 documentary *Underground*, about the militant SDS offshoot the Weathermen, throughout the city. The slides, often shot from the dashboard of a car or the hip, capture street life alongside the posters, the pedestrians and traffic of a bygone era. Using a blend of this archive and his own contemporary footage, Stoltz's approach is thorough and iterative. Over the months we were in touch, the project was in a steady state of motion, its identity evolving as he immersed himself deeper into the material. New mysteries unfolded alongside the hidden histories of the city. In its final form, the work will offer multiple points of entry, inviting viewers to discover the space between what is visible and what is unseen in the city's ever-changing landscape.

I asked Stoltz if he ever mourned what he didn't get, the shots and sequences that got away, the missed opportunities—something that haunts many filmmakers. "The ideal in my mind is to be able to approach my own footage the same way I would approach found footage," he replied. "You're not precious about it. Because in theory, there's always more coming down the pipe. You can always find the things that you're looking for, or be surprised by the things you stumble upon, and work within that."

In essence, Stoltz is "happy to surrender to time," he says. Not time as a finite concept but as something that is vast and full of potential. For Stoltz, film is a tool not just for capturing moments but for bending them, reshaping them, and letting them unfold—long after the cut is made.

261

Peter Tomka

by David J. Getsy

Souvenir Views

Peter Tomka's photographs flirt with a loss of control. He has made things hard on himself, submerging the self-exposure he has built into his drawn-out and indirect material process. The resulting large-scale photographs remind us of what they do not show. Abrupt cropping, excessive grain, errant shadows, and blurred traces of motion compete with any recognizable image. They feel telescoped, as if we are looking at a distance or through a lens straining to capture and hold.

Such effects are a rejection of the assumed equation of photography with immediacy. Especially since the ubiquity of high-resolution digital photography, capturing an image has been quick, computer-aided, and addictive. We use photographs as the diaries of our lives, seeing them as an endless resource accumulating in our phones' albums. Tomka remarks, "Memory is so visual now, if you want to remember what you did a month ago, you can go through your pictures and say, 'A month ago, I was here.' You can remember where you were." Tomka has thought about

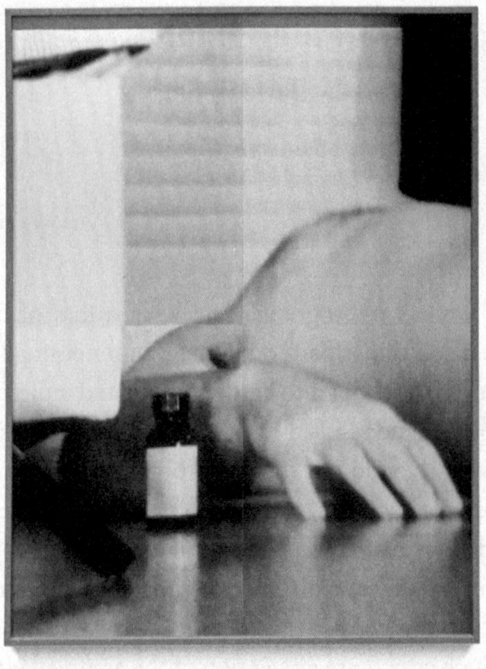

Peter Tomka, *Petite Mort*, 2024, from the series *Bachelor Suite*. Four gelatin silver prints. 44 × 33 ¼ in. (118.8 × 84.5 cm) each

264

this diary effect and how our lives are structured by the images we have taken—and collected. His work, however, breaks with the instant image and its wasteful accumulation, choosing to materialize a small selection of images as labor-intensive events on photographic paper.

Tomka works where he lives, and the physical confines of his domestic space form the material parameters of the photographs. He transforms his living area into a room-size darkroom. When printing on light-sensitive photographic paper, darkness is essential. In traditional processes, an intense light is shown through a film negative (itself a result of the exposure of light onto photosensitive celluloid inside the camera) onto paper that has been chemically treated to react to that light. A further chemical process "fixes" the paper to stop its light sensitivity, and a photographic print is created. This traditional "wet process" requires precision and control to master the light and chemicals in order to create the proper contrasts and depths. The darkroom is of equal importance to the act of taking the photograph; it is where the immaterial image becomes materialized. Tomka exaggerates this process to make large-scale prints with photosensitive paper attached to one of his walls. To block the light, he will upend his bed, with the only rays passing through a hole of about three inches in diameter that he's bored through the mattress. He has wryly compared the aperture to a glory hole—not inapposite given the source of his makeshift studio's "safe light," the specialized bulbs that photographers use to see in the darkroom without affecting the photo-sensitive paper. He explains:

> I live in a bachelor suite—technically that's just a room without a kitchen. I black out my windows. I set up the bed. I put the projector in the bed. I project onto the easel, which is where I put the paper, and there's kind of like a coat-rack mechanism where I'm opening the shutter to let in the light and then closing the shutter to stop the exposure. The safe light was a light bulb I had stolen from the bathroom in the Cock [a gay bar in New York]. (I was there one night, and I unscrewed it—and burned my hand.) I was using that as my safe light, but then I realized that it wasn't actually red light, it was just a painted light bulb.

Because of this disruptive domestic set-up, all of Tomka's prints are hard-won and unique. He has loosened control on the process through these ad hoc adaptions, fighting the light and its leaks. To expose the print and to fix it, he has to transform his bachelor suite entirely. The mattress is *his* mattress, and it will later be returned to a horizontal position to make his bed. As he concluded about this ritual, "I had driven myself to an edge in that printing process, but I think that was important."

The images Tomka chooses to project in this home-made darkroom come from many sources. They are digital images that have accumulated on his phone, selected

266

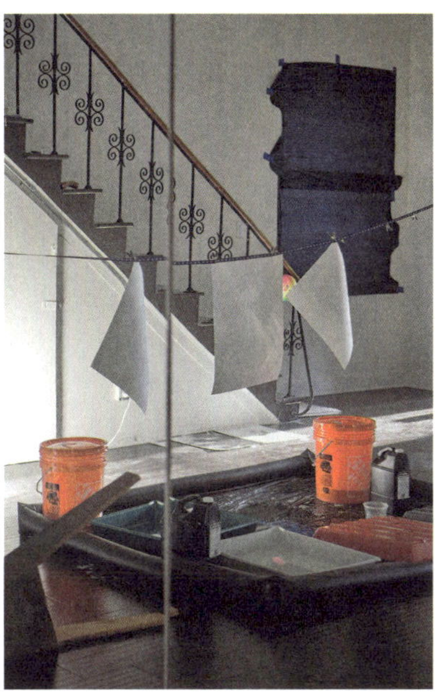

Peter Tomka, Test prints for *Watering Hole*.
Los Angeles, 2023

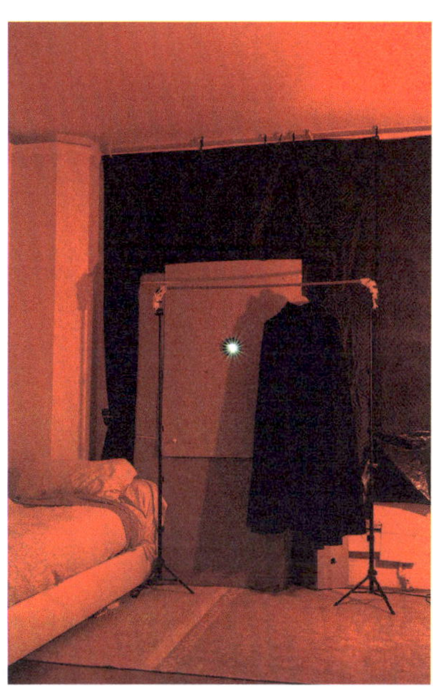

Peter Tomka, Projection mechanism for
Bachelor Suite. Los Angeles, 2024

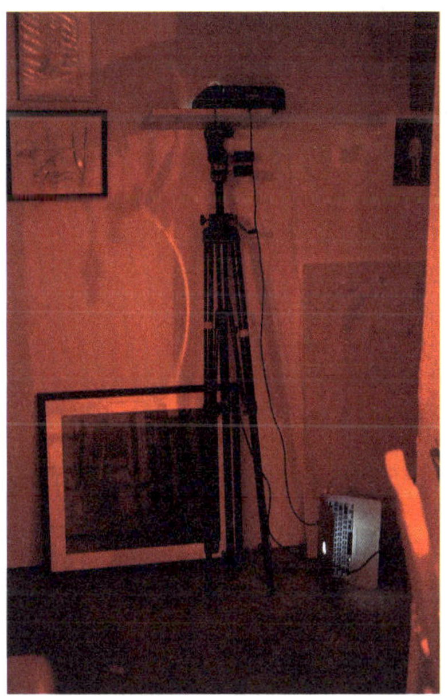

Peter Tomka, Projection mechanism for
Paternity Test. Los Angeles, 2021

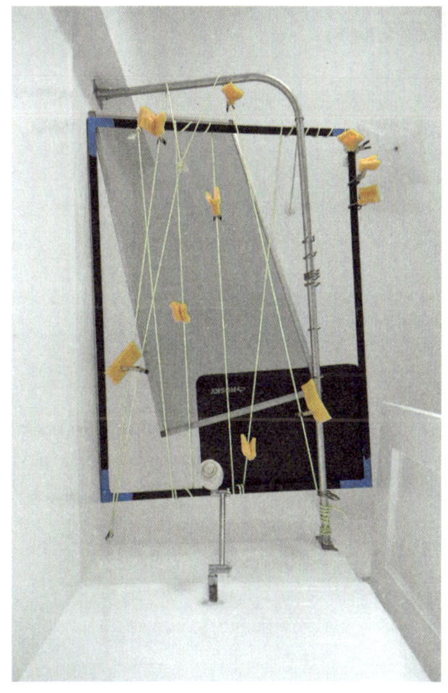

Peter Tomka, Drying rack for *Bachelor Suite*.
Los Angeles, 2024

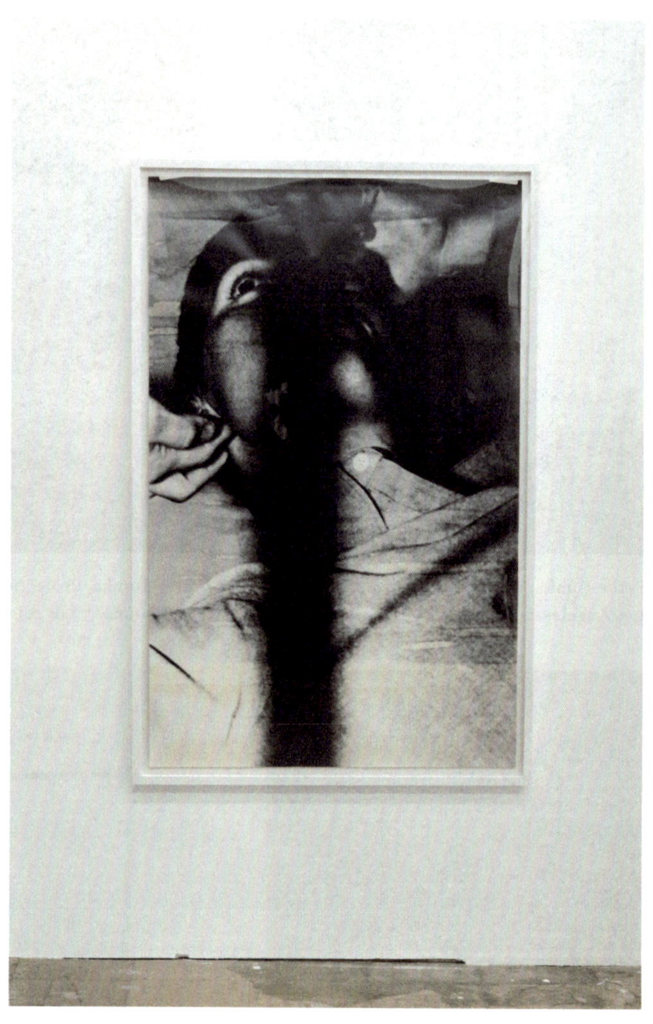

Peter Tomka, *Julius*, 2021, from the series *Paternity Test*. Gelatin silver print. 61 ⅞ × 41 ½ in. (157.5 × 105.4 cm)

268

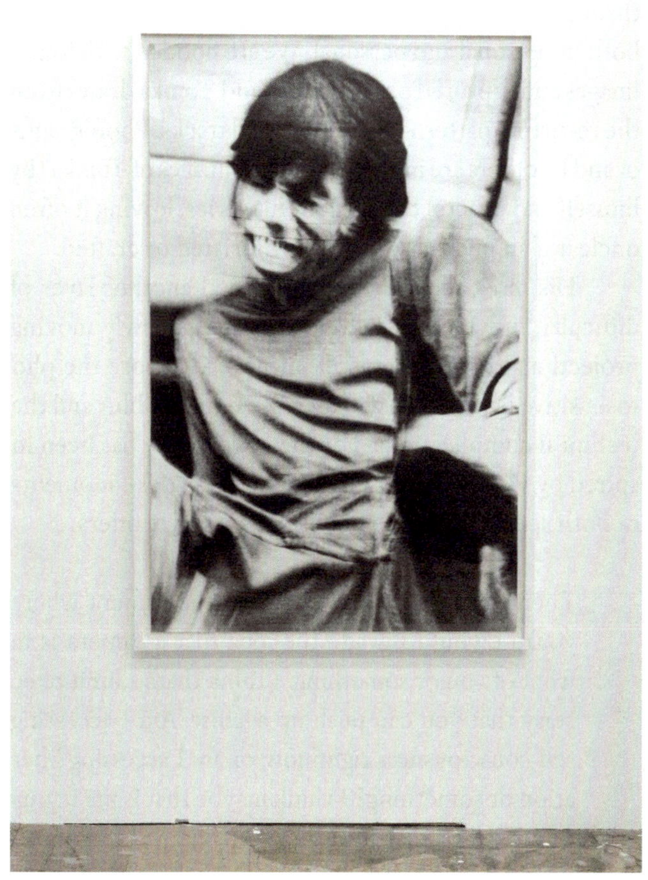

Peter Tomka, *Sean deLear*, 2021, from the series *Paternity Test*. Gelatin silver print. 61 ⅞ × 41 ½ in. (157.5 × 105.4 cm)

269

from thousands of photographs of his life, his friends, and also images he has encountered in his research. Many of his photographic series are the result of his tracking a theme through the image library, selecting and altering images both impersonal and personal. We are flooded with found images and captured photographs, and Tomka draws from the recurring patterns he discerns and tracks. Photographs of and by others are interspersed with images of Tomka (by himself and others) throughout his series, leaving it often unclear if an image has been appropriated or crafted.

His most recent work has added another layer of difficulty, in which he will now be using slowly moving projections (rather than still images) to expose the photosensitive paper. This will increase both the blur and the technical complications. For these works, he has been inspired by videos of himself dancing at parties—moments of both spectacle and self-consciousness. He offers:

> There was always a point with the camera where you're trying to evade the idea that a camera is in front of you or something. I think that's a limit of ecstasy that you can push up against. Am I accessing self-consciousness right now, or am I accessing liberation or something? I think maybe that is me trying to mix all of that into these.... The printed photographs will be still, but I want to have that movement, and I want to show that isolation and maybe that sincerity and that joy and somehow have it look like puzzle pieces that fit together.

270

Peter Tomka, *Bittencourt*, 2023, from the series *Watering Hole*. Four gelatin silver prints. 41 × 33 ¼ in. (104.1 × 84.5 cm) each

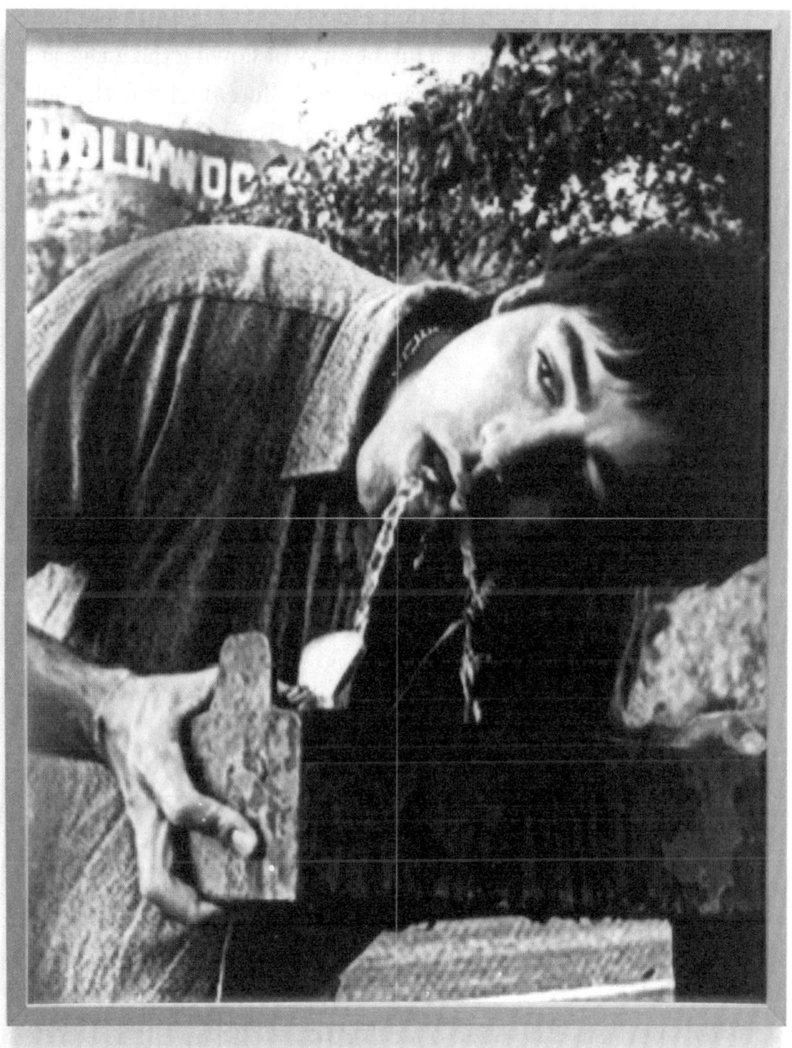

Tomka's conceptually and materially complex practice aligns itself with the amateur archivist and the home inventor. From the sea of collected and captured photographs, he finds the connections and patterns that congeal and won't let go. His domestically disruptive and self-made printing process is a further way of slowing the image and drawing out its strangeness and allure. Fighting the light to see the image made material, Tomka's work might be understood as a metaphor for the vertiginous ways that some images attach to us.

Freddy Villalobos

in conversation with Robeson Taj Frazier

Lost and Lookin': Processing Memory

Freddy Villalobos is a transdisciplinary artist whose practice includes sculpture, installation, photography, video, and mixed media. He explores questions of historical violence, urban space, and the power of memory and embodied knowledge in confronting uncomfortable truths and the darker facets of human experience—impermanence, vulnerability, and power.

ROBESON TAJ FRAZIER   Where did you grow up and when did you start creating things?

FREDDY VILLALOBOS   South Central L.A., on 89th Street and Broadway. As a kid I went to Sheenway School and Culture Center, at 102nd and Olive Streets. The director, Dolores Sheen (Aunt Dolores), really encouraged critical thinking, experiential learning, and cultural engagement. So, at a young age I was immersed in making and thinking creatively through plays, parades, dances, and other community activities.

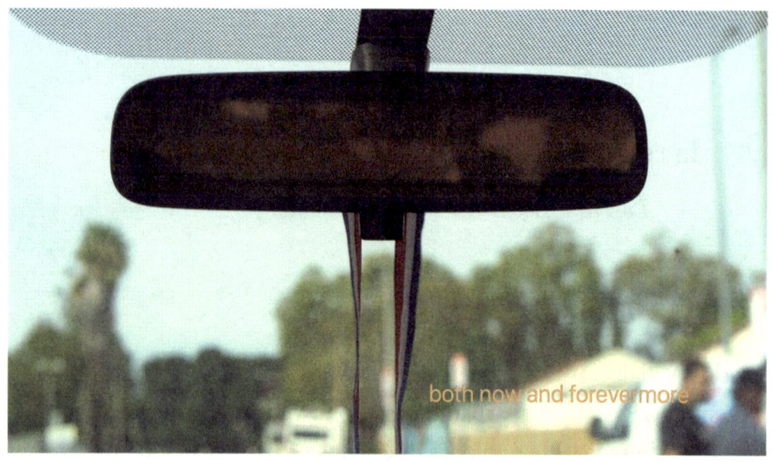

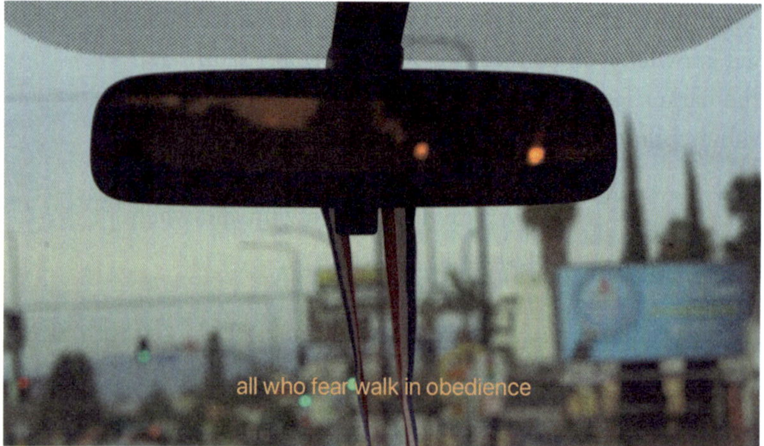

Stills from Freddy Villalobos's single-channel video installation *The Final Victory Lap with Songs of Ascent*, 2021

274

But a formative memory for my creative practice is when I was seven and my brother went to jail. His lawyer thought it would help his case if I drew something to give to the court that humanized him as a "good brother." What resulted was a crayon letter addressed to the USA that asked for my brother to be allowed to come home and which included a drawing of me and him playing at the park. Of course, it didn't work! [*Laughter.*] But when I think about it now, it's a political act, a political artwork. It's a document that gets used in a legal case and which is saved in the court's record, which is crazy. I didn't understand this as art at the time, but this way of making has shown up again in my practice.

R.F.   Most definitely. That's not "art for art's sake." It's testimonial, earnest, and urgent. When did you start to sense what art could be?

F.V.   Decades later, when I started taking art and critical theory classes at college and doing tattoos in my bedroom in my parents' house. I was commuting to school and being introduced to different concepts—negative dialectics, biopolitics, Afropessimism. But it was in my home and community that these ideas began to take real shape and truly felt at play.

I try not to talk about tattoos in the context of my artwork because it feels like they are two different practices. But there was something super vulnerable happening in my bedroom when I was tattooing. It's ninety degrees,

275

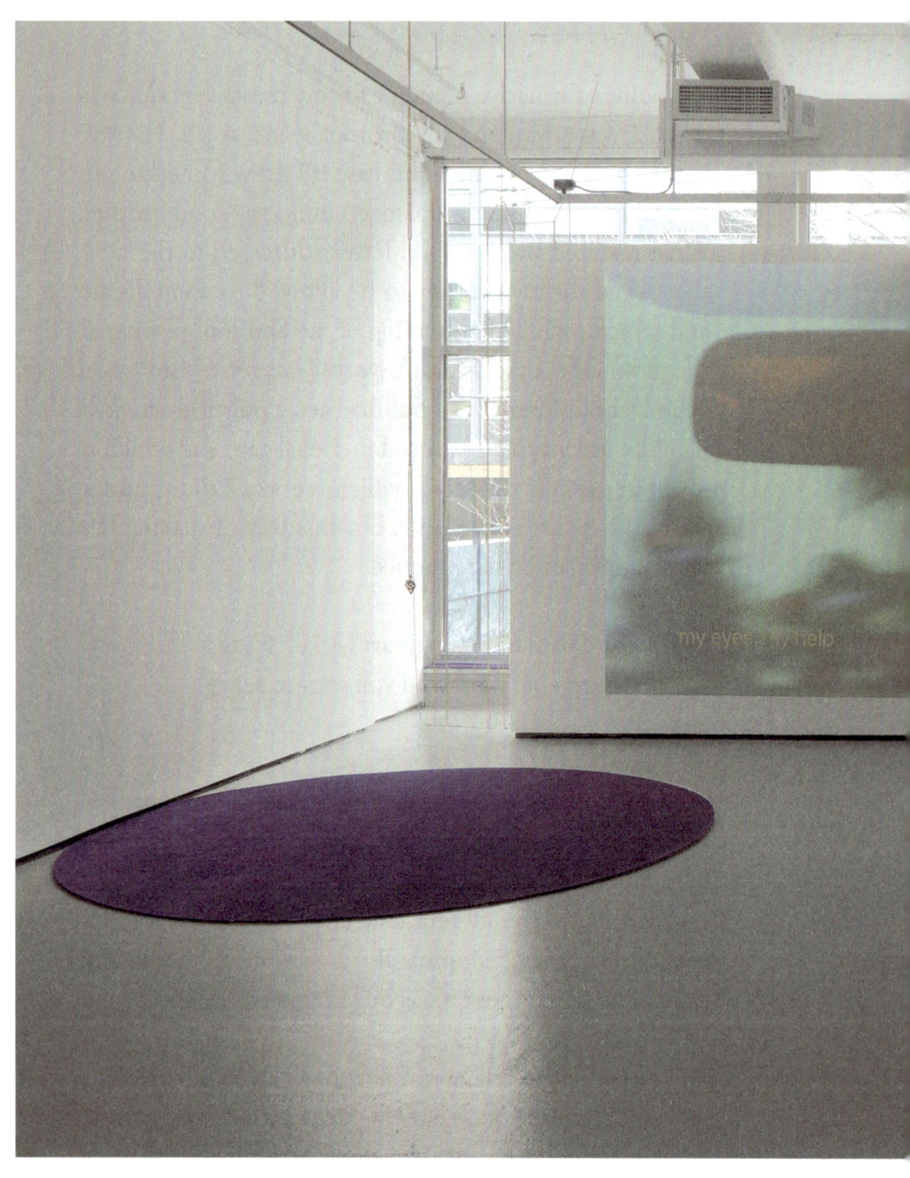

276

FREDDY VILLALOBOS

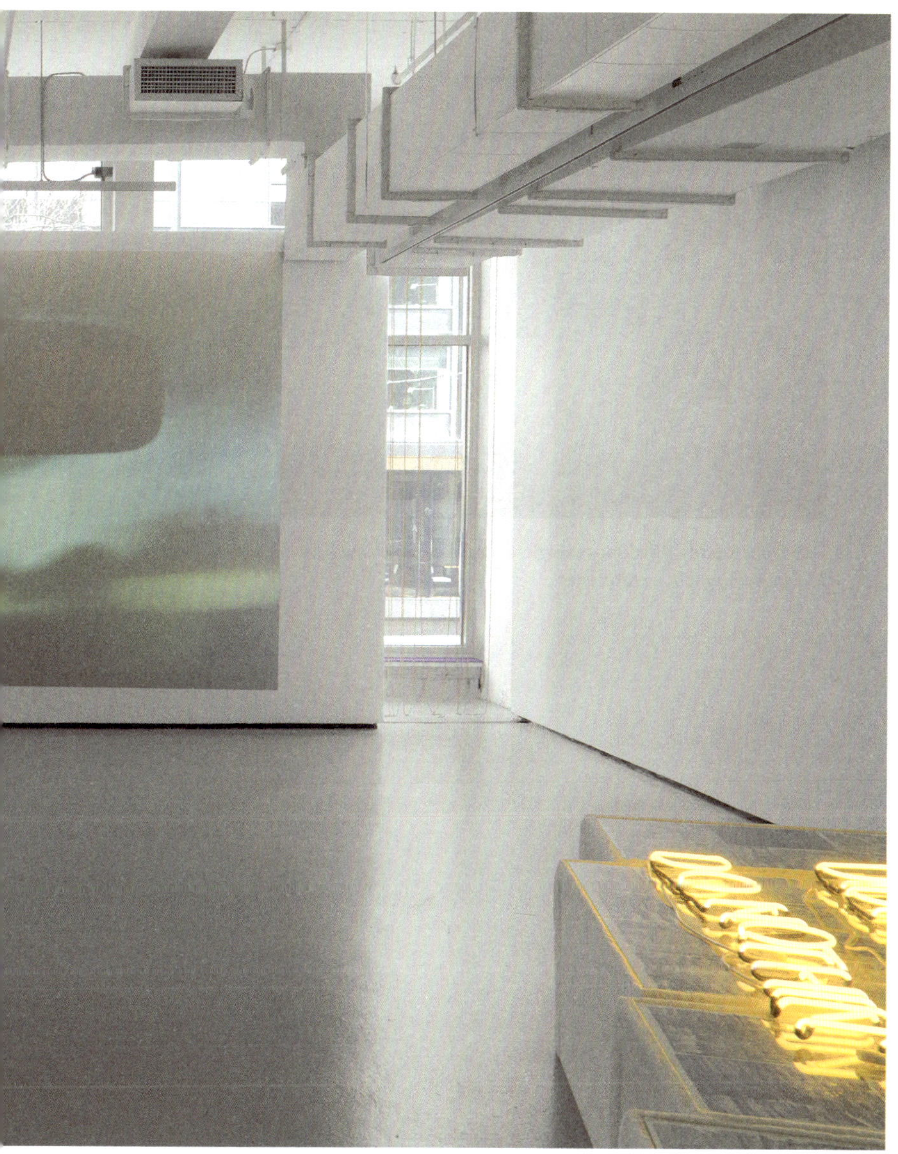

Freddy Villalobos, *I seek, I seek and can't find but a dream desublimated*, 2021. Mixed-media installation with video, sound, fake gold chains, carpet, carbon monoprints, fleece, MDF, acrylic, and neon. Dimensions variable. Installation view, *To Hear No Echo*, Green Hall Gallery, Yale School of Art, New Haven, CT, March 22–28, 2021

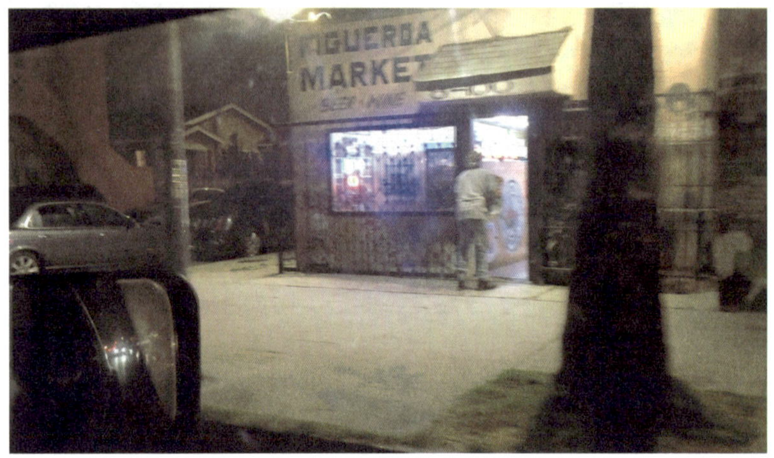

Still from Freddy Villalobos's single-channel video *waiting for the stone to speak, for I know nothing of aventure*, 2025

we have our shirts off for several hours, we're listening to music, and I'm tattooing people's stomachs and faces. When you tattoo a person's face, their eyes automatically tear up. They're literally crying! And we're chilling and laughing about it. A very close thing would happen because of that atmosphere. It made different conversations flow easier. Conversations become more existential. We start talking about loss, life, and purpose. About plans, or the idea of having no plans. That period was a mixture of a lot of things. Things I was learning at college that felt only theoretical. And then when I was in my bedroom, looking at the symbols people chose to adorn their bodies with and discussing with them the conditions and reasoning behind their life choices, the ideas behind the concepts were no longer theoretical. It was lived and experienced.

R.F.   The video from your installation *I seek, I seek and can't find but a dream desublimated* (2021), *The Final Victory Lap with Songs of Ascent*, stages this kind of intimate space for questioning, thinking, lingering, and feeling. But it's via the backseat of a car that is driven through South Los Angeles. Shot in a POV style, it re-creates the twenty-six-mile funeral procession route of hip-hop legend Nipsey Hussle. Embedded over the video are verses from the Songs of Ascents, psalms from the Bible sung by pilgrims on their journeys for worship, peace, and salvation. You create an interesting blend, at multiple levels. We experience the mixture of public and private spheres with the constant view of the streets from the interior of the vehicle. There's the

279

blending visually of what's ahead of the driver versus the rearview mirror's reminder of what's behind them—a temporal metaphor for where we've been and the unknown that lies before us. And then you're also blending the video with other objects and media.

F.V.   There is also sound in the installation that plays through MDF boxes underneath a neon sign that reads "Didn't Even Do Nothin'." The sound is the low-end frequencies, around 100 Hz down to below 20 Hz, pulled from songs that are culturally relevant in Los Angeles—my own take on the Songs of Ascents. I took away the vocals and the mids and I slowed everything down, so it's mainly heavy bass, distorted, chopped and screwed. Brown noise. Something that you feel. And which causes everything in the space of the installation and surrounding it to shake and rumble. It's reminiscent of driving a car with a shitload of bass, to the point that the trunk is rattling. And the feeling of when you pull up next to another car and they feel your trunk going crazy. That brief moment where the separation between the cars is broken by the loud guttural rumbling and vibration from the sound system, where your personal space bleeds into theirs and vice versa.

That feeling is a core memory for me. Being a kid, riding in the backseat of my brother's car, and then 2Pac's "Hail Mary" comes on. The bass was so loud! To the point where I felt like I could not breathe. Like the song's bass sucked the air from my lungs. There's something important in that. A feeling of breath, and air, and withholding

280

something. And also of staying in there, withstanding that feeling.

R.F.   It sounds like you're speaking about a rite of passage. Like there was a lesson you needed to get from that, the feeling of being overpowered. Of learning to hold your breath, or not to breathe at all, and trusting your lungs. Your project for Made in L.A. is similar, right? But it shifts the focus to singer Sam Cooke and Los Angeles's Figueroa Street. "Fig," as it's commonly known, is one of the city's longest streets, running north-south for more than thirty miles.

F.V.   Yeah, the new work restages the drive from the motel where Cooke was killed, on 92nd Street and Fig, to the morgue where his body was taken. It expands on this literal and conceptual death drive series that I've been creating. I'm interested in the historical context surrounding Cooke's death. The 1960s racial tension and struggles over housing discrimination and police brutality, the civil rights movement's belief that "a change is gonna come" (to quote his song of that title), and then also the demographic shifts that were taking shape in Los Angeles around freeway expansion. On Figueroa Street, you can go from seeing prostitution, gangs, and police outside your car window to seeing the University of Southern California, which is taking up way more space in the community than what I remember it taking up in the past. Next to USC is the L.A. Live entertainment complex. With both, there's an aesthetic

281

change, an architectural change, all of which is important to thinking about past-present-future legacies. So, while the video references Sam Cooke, it also uses the drive to consider what's happening in Los Angeles along this one route. There is a Sam Cooke song that I was listening to recently. It's called, "Lost and Lookin.'" It all feels very metaphorically aligned.

Kelly Wall

in conversation with Kate Durbin

Light Moves Through It

Kelly Wall's work is a menagerie of familiar objects transformed. Her stunning lawn-chair sculptures are made from woven stained glass, with cast-aluminum rats and other mischievous accoutrements, making Southern California's famous golden sunlight one of her primary materials. She places the transulcent pieces near windows or outdoors so that they change as the light changes. Often they consist of multiple chairs entangled or fused, giving them an uncanny anthropomorphism, like lovers hopelessly entwined. In other groups of works, Wall distorts mass-produced Americana from keychains to ashtrays, evoking collective and personal memories, witchily conjuring the emotions these common items carry. In her ongoing coffee-mug series, she cheekily tweaks sentimental, kitschy language—a scrawled red cursive *New Love* becomes *New Low*.

I spoke to Wall over Zoom in January 2025. Looking through the small window of my computer screen, I noticed her wood-paneled environment was filled with strange items, some of which turned out to be artworks and some of which were found objects that might become art in the future. At a glance it was hard to tell the difference, which felt apropos.

KATE DURBIN   Hi Kelly! Where are you? It looks like you're in a gift shop in the woods somewhere.

KELLY WALL   I think you'd be into this: It's a historically protected tract home from the 1940s in Mar Vista. Our house is like a pancake with windows, basically, and my studio is a converted garage that somebody wood paneled, probably in the 1970s.

K.D.   Oh my god—there's a giant fish on the wall behind you.

K.W.   My best friend's grandfather caught that in Long Beach in the 1970s. Let me show you some of the other things in here. When the local Rite Aid went out of business, my partner and I got all of their shelving. We got like 160 feet of it. Now I get to pretend "store."

K.D.   I love it. You have a postcard wheel, too.

K.W.   I also got that from the Rite Aid. I have these glass pieces that are cut into the shape of postcards and then I made them into a sunset gradient. I'm still figuring that piece out. Are you from L.A. originally?

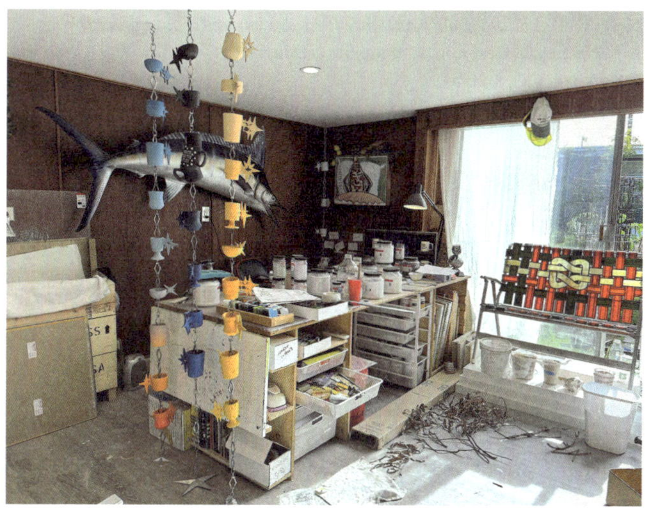

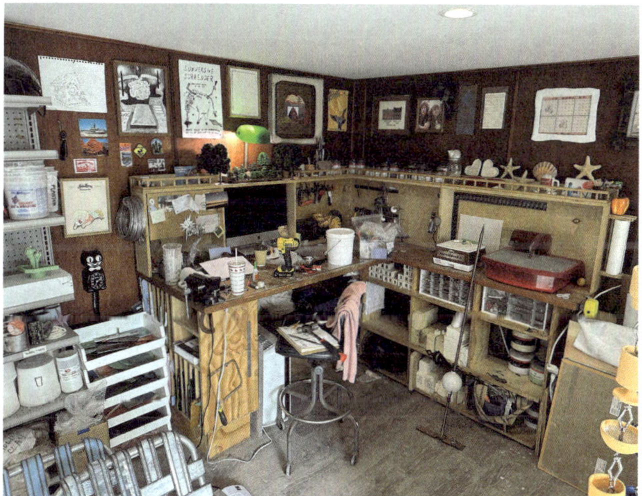

Views of Kelly Wall's studio. Los Angeles, March 2025

285

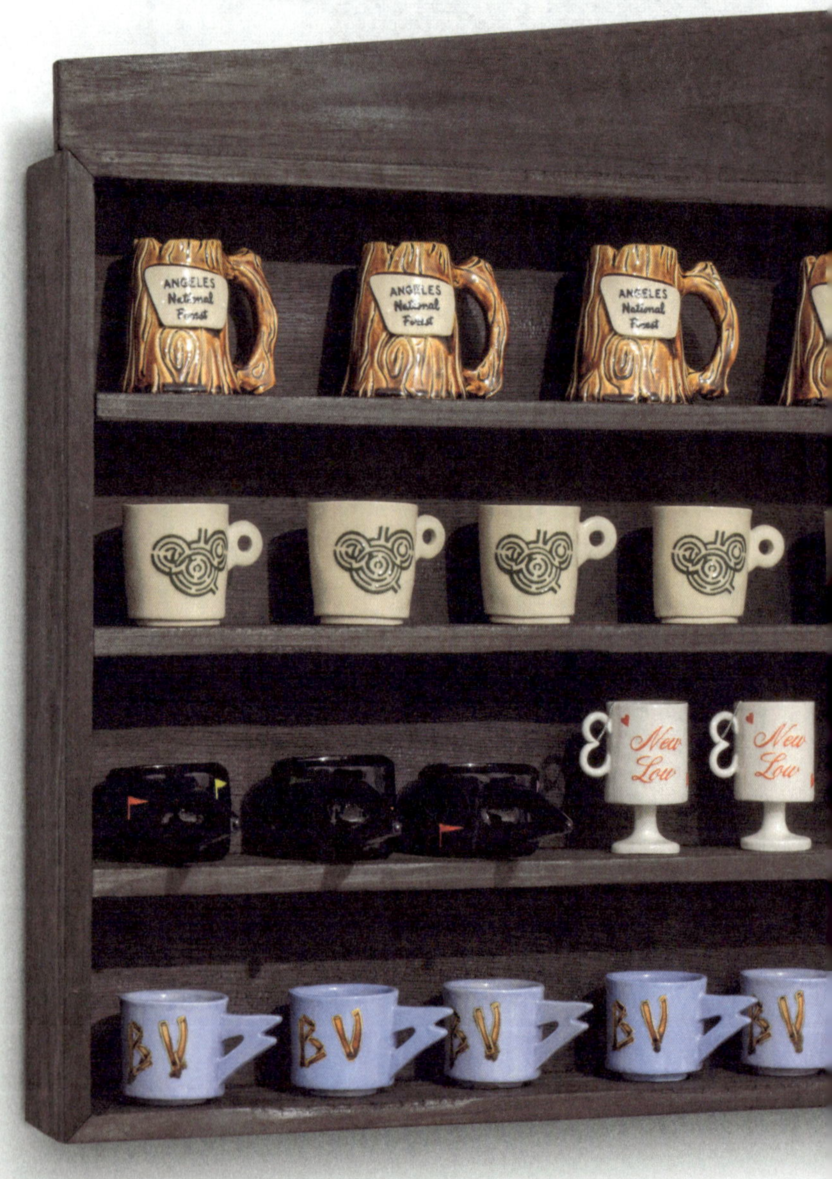

Kelly Wall, *I wish I could remember these dreams and what they're trying to tell me*, 2021. Ceramic, screenprint, resin, burnt wood. 31 × 54 ½ × 11 in. (78.7 × 138.4 × 27.9 cm)

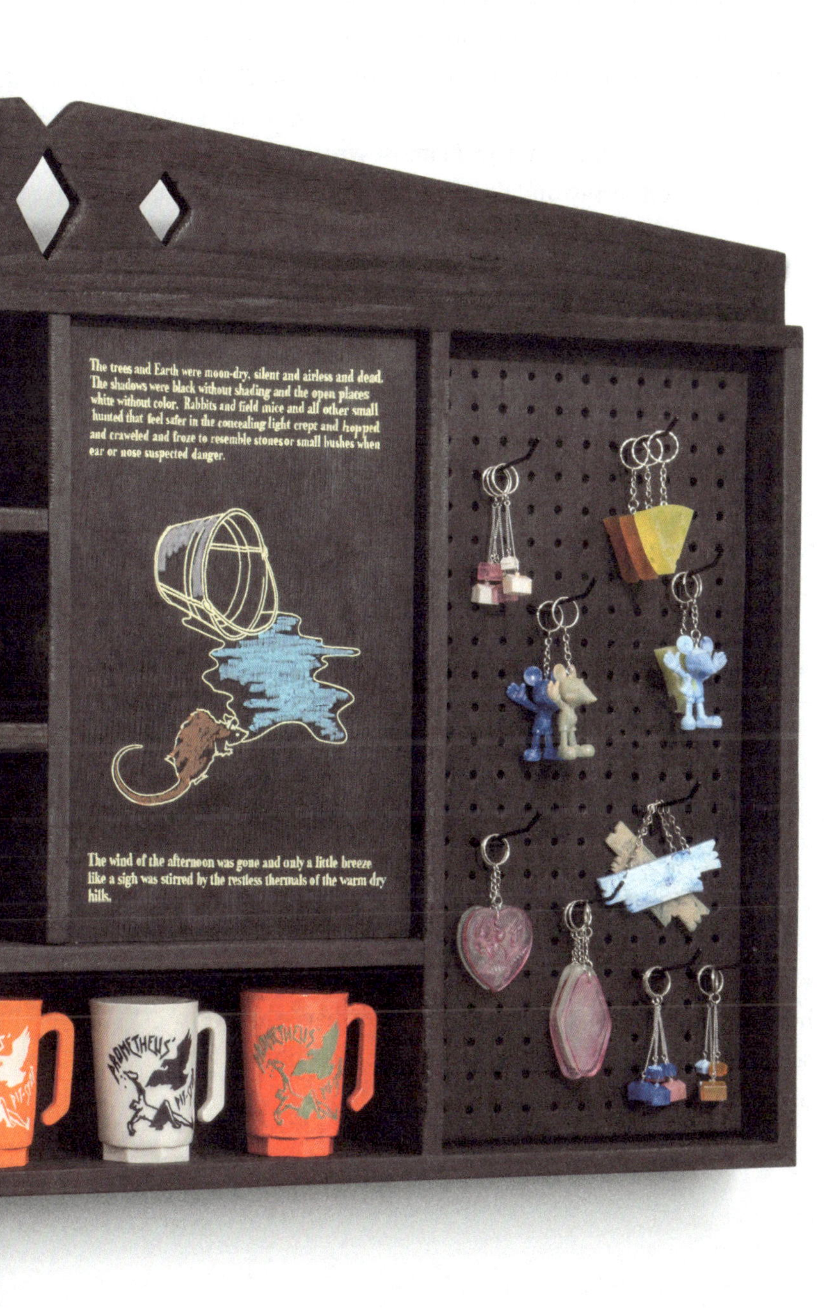

The trees and Earth were moon-dry, silent and airless and dead. The shadows were black without shading and the open places white without color. Rabbits and field mice and all other small hunted that feel safer in the concealing light crept and hopped and craweled and froze to resemble stones or small bushes when ear or nose suspected danger.
The wind of the afternoon was gone and only a little breeze like a sigh was stirred by the restless thermals of the warm dry hills.
PROMETHEUS
PROMETHEUS

K.D.   I grew up partly in San Juan Capistrano, in the OC.
I was noticing all the Mickey Mouses in your work. One
of my earliest memories of pure true love is Disneyland.

K.W.   I feel that too. I almost wrote my grad school admissions essay on Disneyland, because going through the Pirates of the Caribbean ride and seeing the analog way they created everything, where the fire is like a ribbon with a light on it…I love the way the park is put together and the level it's executed to. And I remember going to the Redwoods and thinking it looks like Disneyland, looking at the trees.

K.D.   It's interesting to think about in the context of your
work because you deal with perception and illusion a lot.
Do you feel like Disneyland has influenced your practice?

K.W.   I like things that have a slower rollout of understanding. If you look at it and you're like, "Oh, it's this thing," and then you realize, "Oh, wait, there's something off about it." Then it slowly unfolds. That then leads back to you thinking, "Whoa, how am I understanding things given my perspective or my emotional state?" I could definitely trace a lot of roots to Disneyland.

K.D.   I can't wait to see your chairs in person and watch
how the light moves through them. They have this great
sense of humor, and they're so anthropomorphic. I feel
like chairs are people.

K.W.   Chairs are people! I pick up things off the side of the road a lot, and I could fill storage units with random chairs that I get. Part of their draw for me is that they're an object where we really understand how we interact with it, and I'm interested in the slight variations of things that make them unique. Lately I've been working more with mugs. With mugs, there's endless variations of one form. Chairs are the same in that way. It's like an endlessly variability off of this one standardized form that we understand.

K.D.   How did you start working with stained glass?

K.W.   I took a class at Stained Glass Supplies in Pasadena, and I wanted to do something sculptural. One day I was thinking of making these glass lawn chairs. Glass is amazing in so many ways. It changes throughout the day, throughout different lighting and different settings. That's fun to play with because you can look at it twenty different ways.

One thing I love about it is that it starts at a really highly manufactured level, so that anything that I'm making that's glass is automatically at a highly manufactured level. Then the work can more easily play with trompe l'oeil effects of perception, because it can feel more mass produced.

I also really like that glass the material is the actual color, so you're not dealing with surface. It feels like the most pure sculptural thing, to only construct with material.

K.D.   Your stained-glass lawn chair sculptures are highly material, but they're also emotionally charged. Sometimes

289

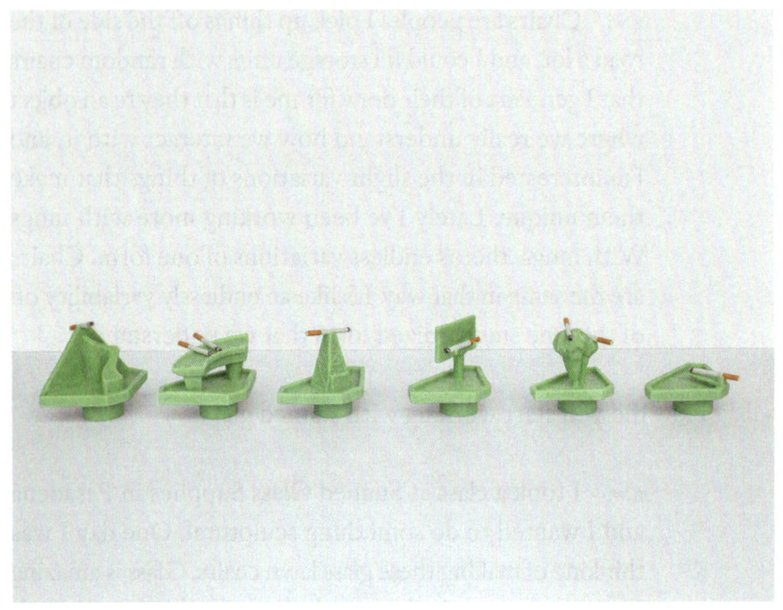

Kelly Wall, *Tell me stories in Angel's tongues*, 2023. Cast jadeite glass. 7 × 6 × 4 in. (17.8 × 15.2 × 10.2 cm) each

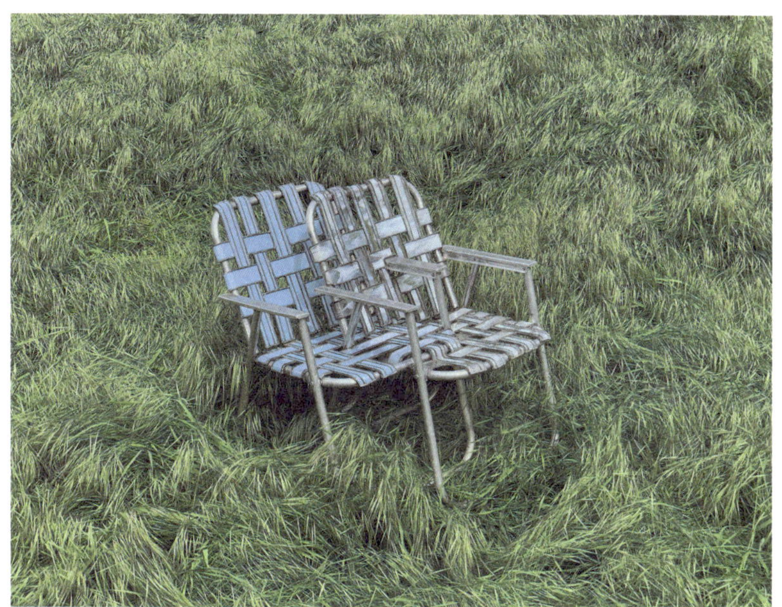

Kelly Wall, *Untitled (Phase One)*, 2022. Glass, lead, aluminum, steel. 31 × 31 × 28 in. (78.7 × 78.7 × 71.1 cm)

291

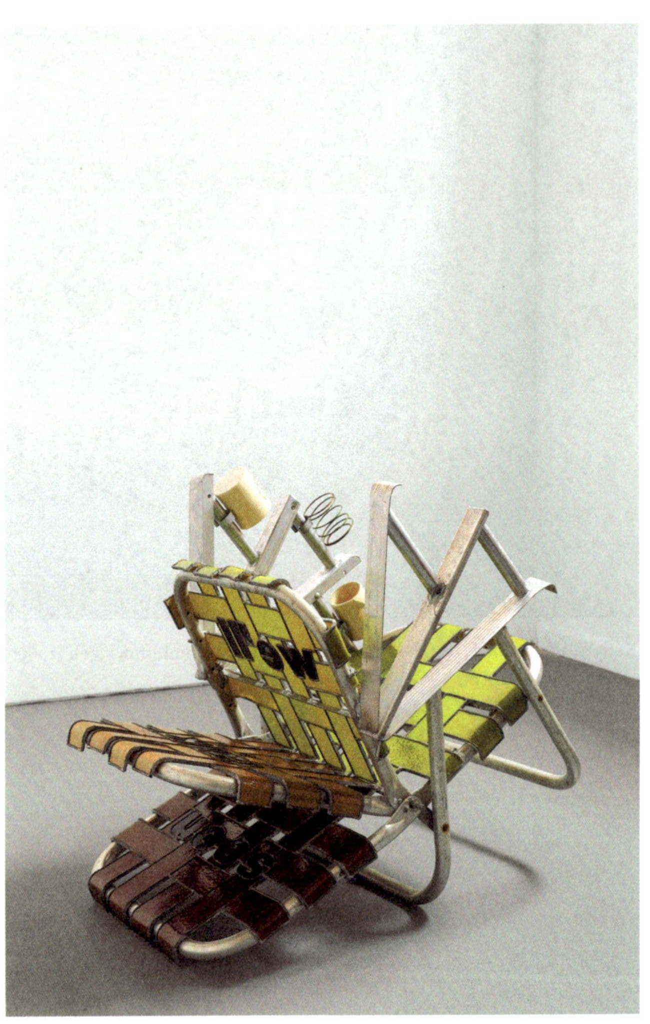

Kelly Wall, *The Fallback Plan*, 2023. Glass, lead, aluminum, steel, ceramic, "ugly old woman/beautiful young princess" optical illusion. 20 × 30 × 28 in. (50.8 × 76.2 × 71.1 cm)

292

you conjoin two chairs—they look like humans coupling. Even the solitary chairs look like they're feeling something. As the light changes throughout the day and filters through the glass, I imagine that evokes different moods, too.

K.W.   I'm an emotionally all over the place person, and oftentimes I wonder if I'm misreading a situation—"Did that person say that thing to me in that way?" My chair sculpture *The Fallback Plan* (2023) was a response to someone blowing me off.

K.D.   That's the precarious stack of three brown and green stained-glass chairs that says on the back, "We'll talk soon." What happened?

K.W.   I thought I was going to have an art thing, it didn't happen, and I was being emo. Basically, they said, "We'll talk soon." That's not an inherently bad sentence, but it felt like such a death blow. I'm like, "Was it even bad or am I making that up?" It's hard to say. I feel like that's why I'm into language, because there's so much space for misinterpretation.

K.D.   I'm glad you mentioned that, because I was thinking about how the use of language in your work is very layered. I had fun making a list of what I thought some of the references could be: apocalyptic religious texts, bumper stickers, graffiti, poetry, fables, semordnilaps, and the commercial and advertising text you see on buildings.

293

K.W. All of the things that you listed definitely resonate with where I'm pulling things from. If I feel stuck, I'll look up idioms and think, "Oh, is there any way that I can pull from these or change the language to mean something else?" I'm dyslexic and a terrible speller, so I accidentally change language a lot, too.

Earlier I sent you a photo of that mug that has the Morton Salt girl crying on it, which is about projecting your own issues onto something and how it can alter the surface. I feel like language can do that too. That's also why I like graffiti. The Basque people did sheepherding near Colorado, and they would carve into aspen trees. They would spend all this time alone, so it's mark making in a semi-unconscious way, where you're both trying to make your presence known but also your unconscious is coming out. In my work, the language is both conscious and unconscious at once.

Leilah Weinraub

by Terence Nance

Light on Sensor

I've noticed Leilah talks about posture quite often—the posture that is called for when addressing different types of "beings," the way one holds the body when walking and talking between realms and rooms. We all make these semi-conscious somatic calculations: What kind of energy do I want to emanate, given how I hold this body? I wonder—for Leilah—where this awareness comes from. Her posture is dynamic. She marks moments with poses and plays with her body in order to get at a point—a pause—and then her signature, "You know?" I do! And I do not.

I make films and am almost always thinking about a just-past or soon-to-arrive "shoot." This has me often thinking about the energy of the word *shoot* and more particularly *shooting*. I feel a part of some mid-aughts wave that tried to replace the word with *filming*, for maybe obvious reasons related to the parlance of war appropriated for the art ritual that is making a film. When I was younger my main job was documentary videography, so I found myself at concerts with a camera a lot and realized the level of endurance necessary to be there long enough to observe "the

295

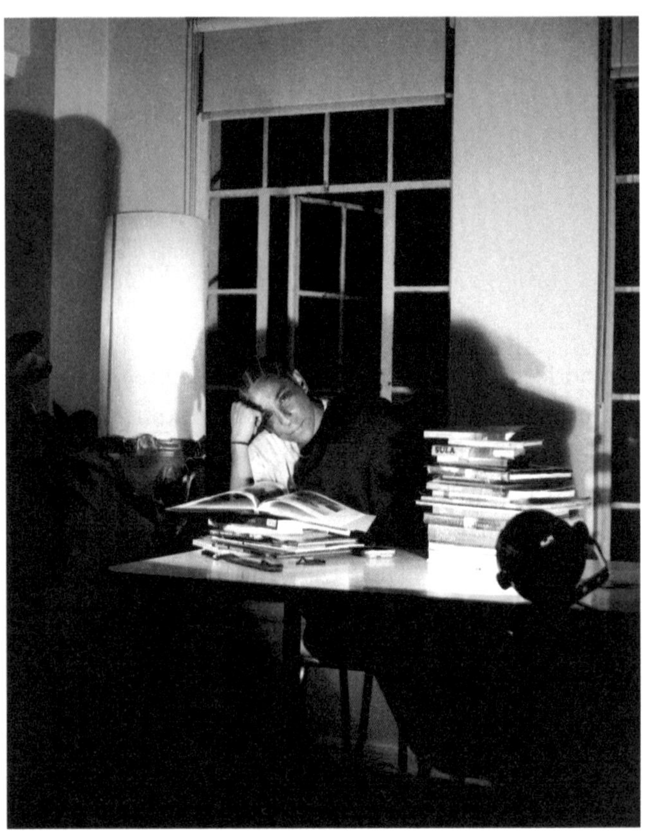

Leilah Weinraub, Los Angeles

296

moment." I particularly felt how much foot and lower back strength is necessary to do the long-term job. My dad was a news videographer, so I instantly understood the toll on his body given the weight of early news cameras. Leilah shot *Shakedown* (2018) with a Canon GL2 and was able to play with prosumer cameras of that era: light, small sensor, suspect lens build, complicated menus, kill-or-be-killed grain structure—somehow, our way out of the hood.

She played with "filming" in a way that is still very new to the concept of a motion-picture camera. The GL-2 is small and designed to act like a paintbrush and palette: a flick of the finger here and more motion blur, a flick of the finger there and the focal length changes from 28 to 70mm, push a few buttons and the ND filter is in. I don't think most people think of making cinema as *that* direct—as direct as painting (paint on canvas, light on sensor). That directness emanates from *Shakedown*.

It isn't always that way. Someone else often operates the camera for these types of films allowing Leilah to "direct." The result of her choice to keep the tool in her hand rendered a performance—evidence of a series of postures she assumed. I can watch the film and see her on the ground with the money, or straight up and down next to Egypt as she processes into her court, assuming these series of poses with and around the performers—together— conjuring the entities necessary to channel through the medicine of the moment.

Leilah told me that, in the early 2000s, she has chosen to omit violence from her palette. That the (moving)

297

picture of so-called violence is out of bounds for her. In television and opera, violence is a part of the lingua franca—a symbol of the stakes of life (death), a universalizing hungry ghost—easily signified with a splatter of blood, a lurch, a scream, a whack, a fall, a lifeless body. The catharses that violence begets have become cliché, old hat, and limited; there may be nothing else to learn from these symbols, exhausted. Violence has ironically lost its punch. Nevertheless, Leilah shared with me, violence is ever present in the process(es) that beget cinema. Namely, performance is a creative act that carries with it destructive subtractions from the being, from the scene, from the world that render a series of movements and sounds a performance—real, raw, and able to carry its own mass through space-time.

I asked her to name the spiritual practice that most accurately describes the performance discipline she's trained within—the one that's yielded her current project, *THE KIDS*. She answered with the above paradox—a nonviolent choice, a taboo, a thing the deities have forbidden her to do, up against an unchangeable law of the cosmos.

Her implication: The word *shoot* should stay as it is, given its accuracy. She said, "A gun is precise and powerful; maybe our cameras can work the same." I beg to differ. There is the matter of the tools themselves. Guns are not precise and often kill the people around the target. Cameras of all sizes see precisely what the eye misses. There is then the matter of the humans behind the tools. Snipers are trained to be precise, wielding the most selective

298

violence. Performers train to be unpredictable—out of the way of whatever is moving (through) the body they have on loan. And of course above all, the camera unlike the gun does not shoot anything; it receives light.

I asked her, "What character do you want to play?" What do you need your body to do that the Leilah spirit would need another spirit to help them with? She said, "A liar."

Bruce Yonemoto

by Jennifer Buonocore-Nedrelow

Imitations of Life

In February 2025, I met Bruce Yonemoto in Crestline, California, where he currently lives. At the entrance to his home was an interactive sculpture titled *La Vie Secrète* (1997), an homage to René Magritte. The work consists of a retractable home projection screen with a hole, slightly larger than a melon, excised from the middle. Bruce turned it on and instructed me to place my head in the void. As I did, I saw a small monitor at the base of the apparatus containing an image of the back of my head. I took part in an infinite regress of looking—viewing myself, viewing myself. Embodying Bruce's practice, this minimal, hybrid object caught me in an act of spectatorship, exposing the conditions that produced the image I was viewing and the reality behind it.

During nearly half a century living in Los Angeles, Bruce has produced a formally and thematically eclectic body of work blending the cinematic techniques and allusions of avant-garde and popular film with those of mass media formats like commercials and music videos. "Living in a one-industry town," he says, "we in Los Angeles best

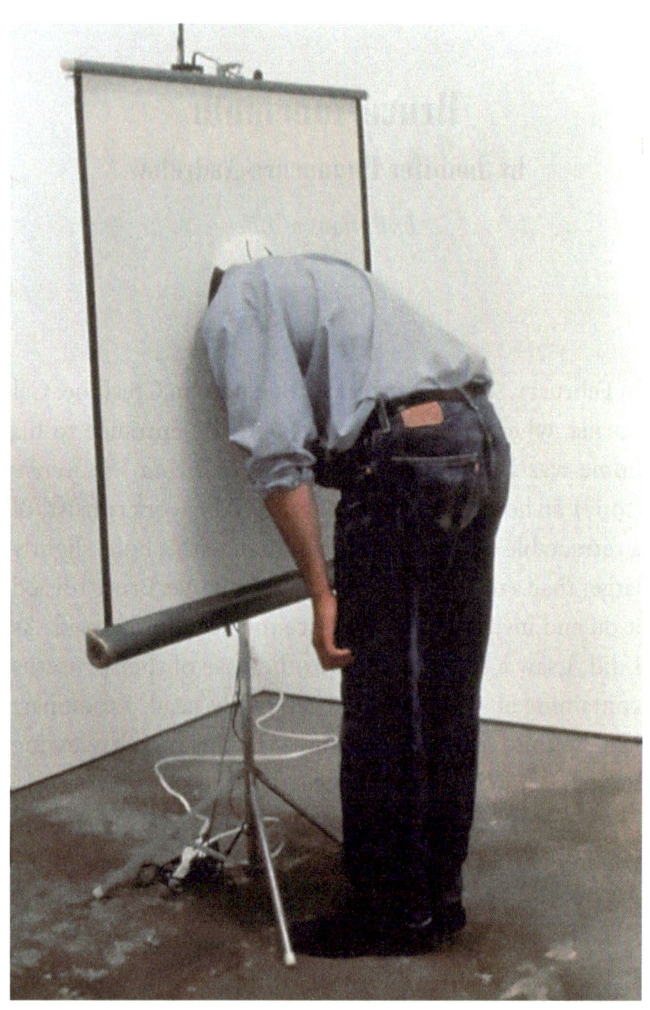

Bruce Yonemoto, *La Vie Secrète*, 1997. Altered screen, closed-circuit camera, and LED screen. 66 × 44 × 22 in. (167.6 × 111.8 × 55.9 cm)

302

understand the materiality of images," which feeds into a rich regional history of experimental video art. Through his work, he has assimilated the city's image-making culture as well as its expansive artistic and counterculture communities. Film and video are inherently collaborative mediums. As such, any quick inventory of Bruce's associations would be inadequate, likely including familiar names like artist Mike Kelley, underground film star Mary Woronov, and the pornographic film director Fred Halsted, perhaps omitting lesser or unknown ones like Robert Opel, mostly famed for his love of nudism, or Nikolai Ursin, the gifted UCLA-trained cinematographer behind a vast number of Yonemoto productions whose career was tragically cut short in the mid-1990s when he died of AIDS.

Bruce's older brother Norman was his longest-running collaborator. In the early 1970s, Bruce moved from the Bay Area to Los Angeles. Norman, an aspiring Hollywood director who had attended UCLA, was already there, making a living directing gay porn films, notably *Brothers* (1973), the first "anti–Vietnam War porno." In the mid-1970s, the pair embarked on a well-chronicled partnership, becoming pioneers in the nascent field of video art. Working both together and independently until Norman's death in 2014, their experimental work, largely narrative driven, critically appropriated the structures and conventions of commercial media, and thus broadly ran counter to the dominant tendency among their peers.

In the early 1970s, after studying at UC Berkeley and abroad in Japan, Bruce landed in Venice Beach: "A small

303

apartment, $250 a month. There were mostly junkies, drag queens, and artists." Already familiar with Goldie Glitters from the Cockettes, a psychedelic Bay Area queer theater troupe, Bruce ran into her at the Lafayette Café, a boardwalk hangout. He then started working in the video department of Santa Monica College, where Glitters was running for homecoming queen. After documenting her campaign, Bruce folded the footage into the campy midnight movie *Garage Sale* (1976), his first joint project with Norman and the last work they shot entirely on film. (Parts of *Made in Hollywood* [1990] and *Japan in Paris in L.A.* [1997] were shot on 16mm and 35mm.) With expectations of romantic love shaped by Hollywood, Goldie stars as a prudish woman navigating a loss of interest in her conventionally handsome husband, Hero.

After *Garage Sale* premiered at the Fox Venice Theater, Bruce enrolled at Otis College of Art and Design, studying with Germano Celant, the theorist behind arte povera, a late-1960s movement that emphasized everyday materials and their circulation. Celant asked his class "to consider art's impact on society," leading Bruce to reflect on all the movies he watched on television as a child in the 1950s. By strategically appropriating the conventions of movies and TV, treating moving images as material he could work with, he realized he could reveal mainstream media's role in shaping all kinds of social expectations and ideologies—gender, sexual, and racial stereotypes. He started making video "soap operas" with a Portapak recorder. At first, he says, "They didn't look like soap operas.

304

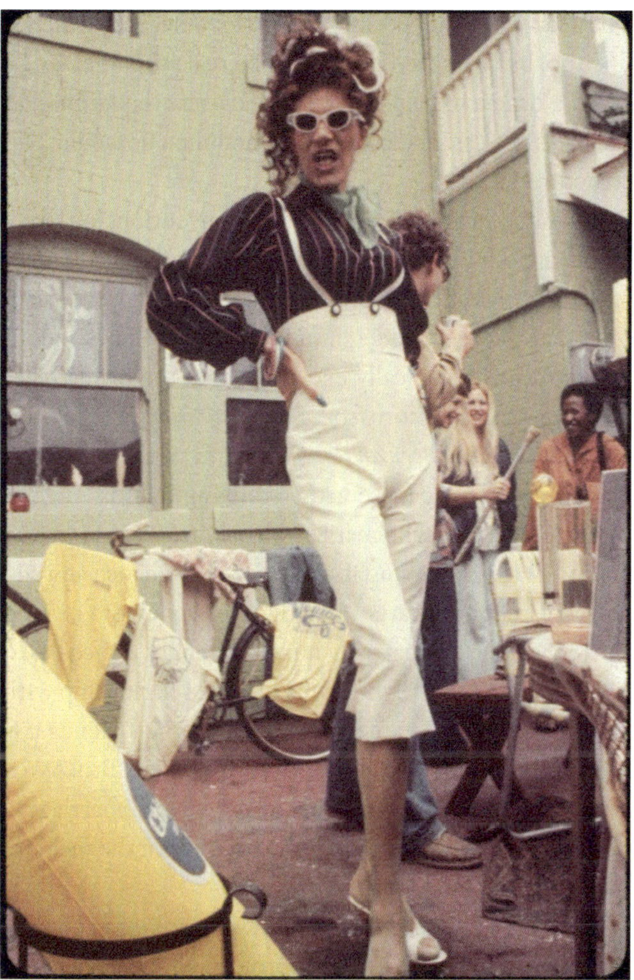

Bruce Yonemoto, Goldie Glitters on the set of Bruce and Norman Yonemoto's film *Garage Sale*, 1976

305

They looked like experimental video, video art, which is fine too, but I wanted it to look like real soap operas. . . . I asked Norman to help me. . . . I would write the scripts and the ideas and cast and all this stuff, and then he would help structure-edit."

While borrowing codes and conventions of Hollywood melodramas in the manner of made-for-TV movies and the Douglas Sirk films of the 1950s, the early soap operas also foregrounded immigrant experiences and minority histories typically excluded from the mainstream. Opening with the score from Sirk's *Imitation of Life* (1959), *Green Card: An American Romance* (1982) is the somewhat true story of a Japanese artist studying in Los Angeles, Sumie Nobuhara, who marries a local surfer to stay in the United States, believing it to be her only chance at a successful career in the arts. As with other Yonemoto productions, the storyline partially mirrored reality. Bruce based the script for *Green Card* on his real-life relationship with Nobuhara, whom he met at Otis, and other friends partook in the production. At the video's premiere, Bruce wed Nobuhara, entering into an actual green-card marriage, a performative event that candidly destabilized the melodrama's self-contained, imaginary world.

In the late 1980s, Bruce and Norman began conceptualizing another biographical project, about the mass incarceration of Japanese Americans during World War II, which affected their parents and grandparents. They were aware of films made by the War Relocation Authority, the federal agency responsible for creating the camps in the

306

1940s, in which prison life is portrayed as ordinary, even idyllic. After discovering the scripted and staged raw footage for these sham documentaries at the National Archives, they set out to expose their propagandistic aim. This led to the brothers' first video installation, *Framed* (1989), a darkened space containing a monitor overlaid by a two-way mirror. The monitor showed the WRA footage, while the partially transparent, two-way mirror glass presented a spectral succession of anxious and fearful faces—enlarged photographic stills the Yonemotos isolated from the same source. The result was a kind of in situ editing, as a friend of the pair described it, creating a montage that disrupted the original film's tactics of manipulation. For Made in L.A. 2025, Bruce continues his examination of intergenerational trauma with *Broken Fences* (2025). The multimedia diptych consists of side-by-side monitors presenting two propagandistic views of forced relocation and confinement during World War II: the WRA footage of the American Japanese internment camps and a Nazi film made at the Eastern European concentration camp of Theresienstadt. Assuming the appearance of documentary truth, both examples falsely idealized the camps. And yet neither set of images will be entirely visible to spectators, as Bruce has obscured the monitors with open-board fences treated with lacquer, a material long associated with Asian decorative arts and identity.

With a long-standing interest in international cinematic tradition and its role in the formation of cultural identity, Bruce earned a fellowship in the mid-1990s to

307

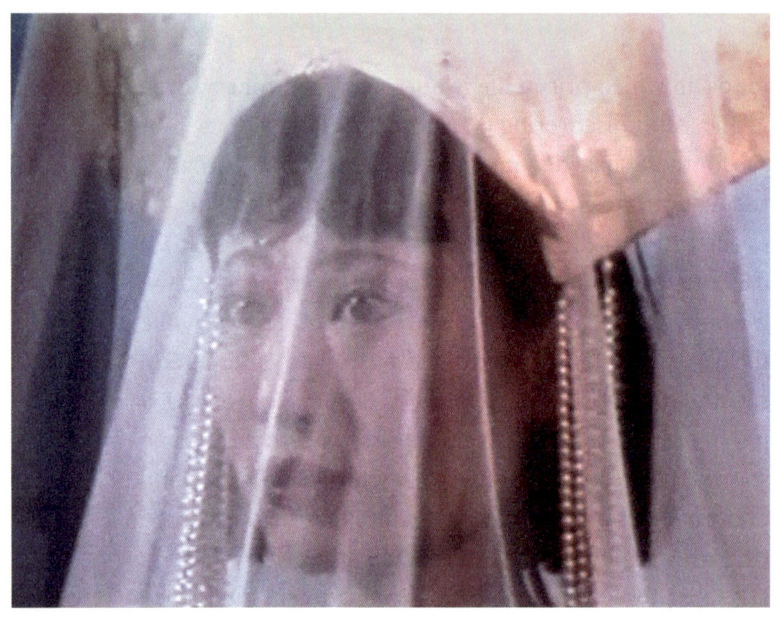

Stills from Bruce and Norman Yonemoto's single-channel video
Green Card: An American Romance, 1982

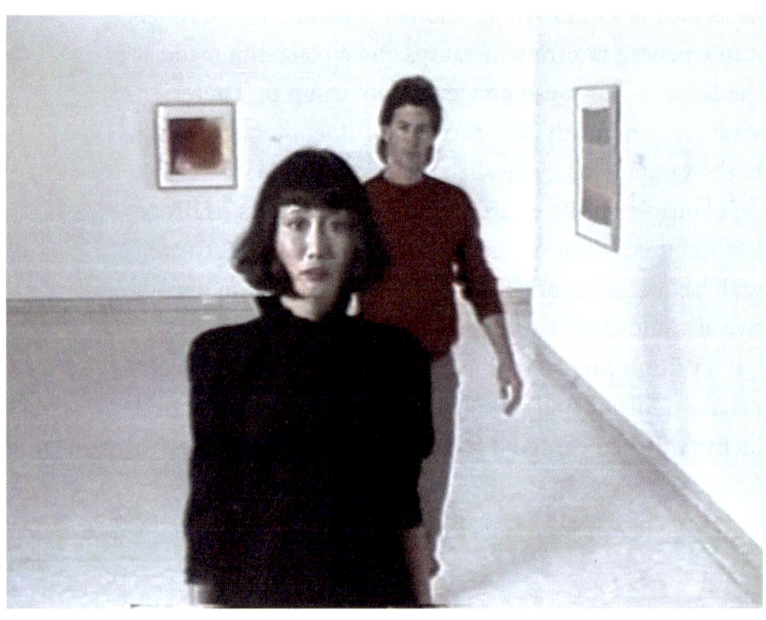

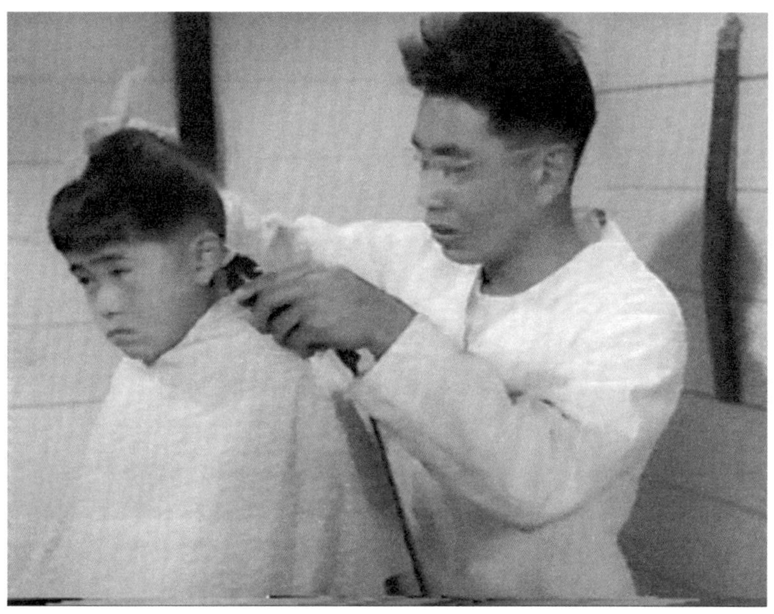

Stills from Bruce and Norman Yonemoto's two-channel video installation
Framed, 1989

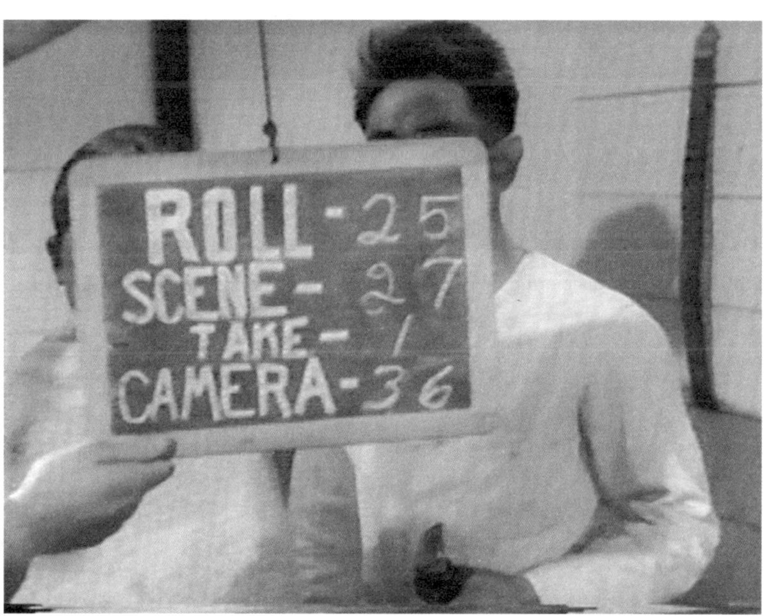

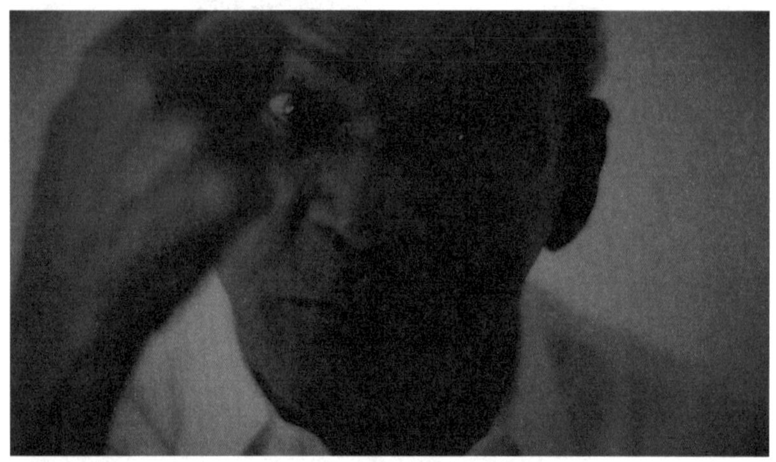

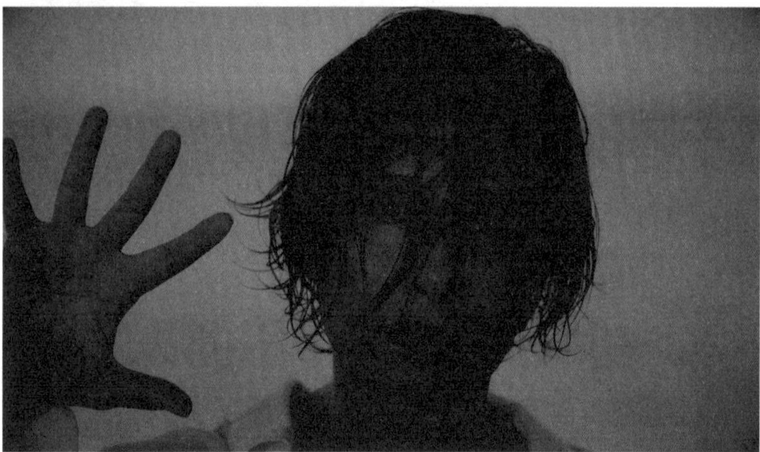

Stills from Bruce Yonemoto and Eder Santos's two-channel video installation *Barravento Novo*, 2017

310

research the movies made by the first wave of Japanese immigrants in Brazil. Later, in 2017, he embarked on a collaboration with Eder Santos, a Brazilian multimedia artist, to create a self-reflexive homage to Glauber Rocha's film *Barravento* (1962), a cornerstone of the Brazilian Cinema Novo movement. Starring Antonio Pitanga, a filmmaker, activist, and one of Brazil's first successful Black actors, the film tells the story of a character named Firmino's return to his hometown, a remote fishing village in the coastal region of Bahia. The fisherman in the village, most of whom are practitioners of the Afro-Brazilian religion of Candomblé, live in poverty, exploited by a wealthy white business owner. Determined to incite the fishermen to seek independence, uniting them in a twin revolt against their oppressive employer and tragic mysticism, Firmino eventually recruits the help of a young woman named Cota to seduce and discredit the devoted leader of their community, believing the others would be more inclined to rebel as a result.

On view in Made in L.A., Bruce's two-channel video installation *Barravento Novo* (2017) juxtaposes selections from Rocha's analog 35mm film with a new digital 4K video, overlaying two historical moments and modes of technology. In it, Antonia Pitanga's daughter, Camila Pitanga, famed tele-global soap opera star, adopts the personas of both Firmino and Cota. First, she reenacts a scene in which Firmino shouts at the fisherman, "Where is your independence?" Then she embodies Cota, performing movements intended to evoke Candomblé rituals. The images are inset, with Camilia appearing on a rear screen and

311

Antonio as Firmino on a projection screen in front. Projected simultaneously, Camila is placed in dialogue with Rocha's stark, filmic world as well as with her real-life father. As with the entirety of Yonemoto's production, *Barravento Novo* points outside itself, occupying a nebulous place between fiction and documentation, myth and reality.

DAVID ALEKHUOGIE

David Alekhuogie was born in 1986 in Los Angeles. Through research-based practice, Alekhuogie, a photographer and educator, explores the constructions of race, gender, and power. Recent solo exhibitions include Assembly, Houston (2023); Yancey Richardson, New York (2021); Kate Werble Gallery, New York (2020); Company Gallery, New York (2019); Commonwealth and Council, Los Angeles (2019); Los Angeles Municipal Art Gallery (2019); University of Wisconsin, Milwaukee (2018); Skibum MacArthur, Los Angeles (2017); and the Chicago Artists Coalition (2016). Recent group exhibitions include the Los Angeles County Museum of Art (2025); Carnegie Museum of Art, Pittsburgh (2024); Katonah Museum of Art, Katonah, NY (2024); High Museum of Art, Atlanta (2024); and the Museum of Modern Art, New York (2020). He is the recipient of honors including a Harvard University Radcliffe Institute Fellowship (2025); Rema Hort Mann Foundation Grant (2019); and an Ox-Bow LeRoy Neiman Foundation Summer Fellowship (2013). Alekhuogie earned a BFA from the School of the Art Institute of Chicago (2013) and an MFA from Yale University, New Haven, CT (2015).

BLACK HOUSE RADIO / MICHAEL DONTE

Michael Donte founded Black House Radio in 2023 in Los Angeles. Black House Radio is a live event series spotlighting Black DJs specializing in house music and a YouTube streaming platform. It aims to harness the power of house music to celebrate Black culture and create a welcoming place for all who share a passion for the genre. Donte has directed and produced films and media projects, including *The Spirit God Gave Us* (2022). He is the recipient of the NewFest Emerging Black LGBTQ+ Filmmakers Award and an Urbanworld Film Festival Best Young Creator award (both 2022).

Greg Breda was born in 1959 in Los Angeles. Often working on translucent surfaces, Breda paints intimate portraits suffused with symbolism and light. Recent solo and two-person exhibitions include Patron Gallery, Chicago (2024, 2021, 2018) and Patron Gallery, New York (2019). Recent group exhibitions include the African American Museum in Philadelphia (2024); Charles H. Wright Museum of African American History, Detroit (2024); Sean Kelly Gallery, Los Angeles (2024); Lubeznik Center for the Arts, Michigan City, IN (2022); Los Angeles County Museum of Art (2021); Columbus Museum of Art, OH (2021); Museum of Contemporary Art Chicago (2020); California African American Museum, Los Angeles (2019, 2017); Jeffrey Deitch Gallery, Los Angeles (2019); Xavier University of Louisiana Art Gallery, New Orleans (2018); and Advocate & Gochis Galleries, Los Angeles (2014).

WIDLINE CADET

Widline Cadet was born in 1992 in Pétion-Ville, Haiti. Through a practice rooted in photography, Cadet draws inspiration from her experience immigrating from Haiti to the United States to broadly address the complexities of Black diasporic life. Solo exhibitions include the Milwaukee Art Museum (2026); Nazarian/Curcio, Los Angeles (2025); PHotoESPAÑA, Case de América, Madrid (2024); Huis Marseille, Museum for Photography, Amsterdam (2023); and Deli Gallery, New York (2021). Recent group exhibitions include Pérez Art Museum, Miami (2025, 2024); Liverpool Biennial, England (2025); International Center of Photography, New York (2025); Los Angeles County Museum of Art (2024); El Museo del Barrio, New York (2024); Whitney Museum of American Art, New York (2023); Somerset House, London (2023); Museum of the African Diaspora, San Francisco (2023); Milwaukee Art Museum (2022); and MoMA PS1, Queens, NY (2021). Cadet earned a BA from the City College of New York (2013) and an MFA from Syracuse University, Syracuse, NY (2020).

CARL CHENG

Carl Cheng was born in 1942 in San Francisco. Through a genre-defying interdisciplinary practice, Cheng's explores the relationship between nature and technology, consumer culture, and racial injustice. Recent solo exhibitions include the Museum Tinguely, Basel, Switzerland (2025); Bonnefanten, Maastricht, Netherlands (2025); Institute of Contemporary Art, Philadelphia (2025); The Contemporary Austin (2024); REDCAT, Los

314

Angeles (2022); and Philip Martin Gallery, Los Angeles (2022, 2020). Recent group exhibitions include the Whitney Museum of American Art, New York (2025); the Aldrich Contemporary Art Museum, Ridgefield, CT (2024); Armory Center for the Arts, Pasadena, CA (2024); Chez Max et Dorothea, Los Angeles (2024); Another Space, New York (2020); Migos Museum of Contemporary Art, Zurich (2020); de Young Museum, San Francisco (2018); and the Los Angeles County Museum of Art (2018). Cheng earned a BA and an MA from the University of California, Los Angeles (1963, 1967).

ALONZO DAVIS

Alonzo Davis was born in 1942 in Tuskegee, AL, and died in 2025 in Largo, MD. Davis was an artist, educator, activist, and cofounder of the legendary Brockman Gallery, Los Angeles (1967–1990). Selected solo exhibitions include the Fisher Gallery, Schlesinger Center, Northern Virginia Community College, Alexandria, VA (2018); Prince George's African American Museum & Cultural Center, North Brentwood, MD (2018); United States Embassy, Freetown, Sierra Leone (2014–15); East Hawai'i Cultural Center, Hilo, HI (2006); East–West Center, Honolulu (1988); Triton Museum of Art, Santa Clara, CA (1987); Brockman Gallery, Los Angeles (1984, 1973); Watts Towers Arts Center, Los Angeles (1981); University of Southern California, Los Angeles (1980); William Grant Still Arts Center, Los Angeles (1978); Transition Gallery, Idaho State University, Pocatello, ID (1976); Bowers Museum, Santa Ana, CA (1975); Pomona Public Library, CA (1975); and Just Above Midtown, New York (1975). Selected group exhibitions include the Los Angeles County Museum of Art (2025, 1972); Lancaster Museum of Art, CA (2025); Washington Sculptors Group and the Phillips Collection, Washington, DC (2022); Saint Louis Art Museum (2019); The David C. Driskell Center, University of Maryland, College Park, MD (2017); Williams College Museum of Art, Williamstown, MA (2013); MoMA PS1, Queens, NY (2012); Hammer Museum, Los Angeles (2011); California African American Museum, Los Angeles (2011, 2005); Watts Towers Art Center, Los Angeles (2009); Studio Museum in Harlem, New York (1979, 1972); Otis Art Institute, Los Angeles (1977); Just Above Midtown, New York (1974); and the Brockman Gallery, Los Angeles (1967). Recent honors and awards include a Denbo Fellowship from the Pyramid Atlantic Art Center, Hyattsville, MD (2018) and a Lifetime Achievement Award from the James A. Porter Colloquium at Howard University, Washington, DC (2016). Davis earned a BA from Pepperdine University, Los Angeles (1964), and a BFA and an MFA from the Otis Art Institute, Los Angeles (1971, 1973).

315

Ali Eyal was born in 1994 in Baghdad. Trained as a painter, Eyal's multidisciplinary practice considers the entanglements of personal memory, political violence, and loss. Solo and two-person exhibitions include Visible Records, Charlottesville, VA; ChertLüdde, Berlin (2024); Bellyman, Los Angeles (2023); Brief Histories, New York (2022); and Saw Center, Ottawa, Canada (2022). Recent group exhibitions include the 18th Istanbul Biennial (2025); 14th Mercosul Biennial, Porto Alegre, Brazil (2025); Akademie der Künste der Welt, Cologne (2024); the Quebec City Biennale (2024); Bayt AIMamzar, Dubai, U.A.E. (2024); Chicago Cultural Center (2023); Arsenal—Institute for Film and Video Art, Berlin (2023); 22nd Biennial Sesc_Videobrasil, São Paulo (2023); Sharjah Biennial 15, U.A.E. (2023); 58th Carnegie International, Pittsburgh (2022); Documenta 15, Kassel, Germany (2022); Museum of Contemporary Art Metelkova, Ljubljana, Slovenia (2020); MoMA PS1, Queens, NY (2019); and Beirut Art Center, Lebanon (2018, 2019). He was a fellow in Ashkal Alwan's Home Workspace Program, Beirut (2016–17). Eyal earned a BFA from the Institute of Fine Arts, Baghdad (2015).

HOOD CENTURY/JERALD COOPER

Jerald "Coop" Cooper was born in 1983 in Cincinnati. Coop is an artist, designer, and the founder of Hood Century (@hoodmidcenturymodern), a new media agency researching, documenting, and educating the masses on African American legacies within modern architecture, design, and "the city." Through Hood Century and his own multidisciplinary practice, Coop explores the relationship between the Black lived experience and modernity as something "by design." Centering the Ghanaian tradition of Sankofa—meaning to gather, protect, and renew what is at risk of being left behind—Coop documents and proliferates the history of Black modernism through multimedia platforms and educational programming.

HANNA HUR

Hanna Hur was born in 1985 in Toronto. Recent solo exhibitions include Sweetwater, Berlin (2025); Doosan Art Center, Seoul (2024); Dracula's Revenge, New York (2024); Kristina Kite Gallery, Los Angeles (2023, 2021); Feuilleton, Los Angeles (2020); and Bel Ami, Los Angeles (2019). Recent group exhibitions include the Hammer Museum, Los Angeles (2025, 2022); XYZ collective, Tokyo (2025); Galeria Dawid Radziszewski, Warsaw (2024); Hannah Hoffman Gallery, Los Angeles (2024); Capc—Musée d'art contemporain de Bordeaux (2024); STARS Gallery, Los Angeles (2023); Gallery 12.26, Dallas (2023); Room 3557, Los Angeles (2023); Aspen Art Museum, CO (2022); Rachofsky House, Dallas (2022); Derosia, New York (2022); and the Institute of Contemporary Art, Los Angeles (2021). Hur earned a BFA from Concordia University, Montreal (2008), and an MFA from the University of California, Los Angeles (2019).

John Knight was born in 1945 in Hollywood and works in situ. Recent solo exhibitions include the Art Institute of Chicago (2024, 2015); Greene Naftali, New York (2024, 2015, 2011); O-Town House, Los Angeles (2024); Neuer Berliner Kunstverein façade, Berlin (2023); Cabinet, London (2022); The Intermission, Piraeus, Greece (2019); Ordet, Milan (2019); Center for Contemporary Art Kitakyushu, Fukuoka, Japan (2019); Établissement d'en face, Brussels (2018); S.M.A.K., Ghent, Belgium (2017); Cultuurcentrum, Strombeek, Belgium (2017); and REDCAT, Los Angeles (2016). His public artworks have been installed at the Art Institute of Chicago (2024); Bonner Kunstverein, Bonn, Germany (2021); Sculpture Garden, Geneva Biennale (2020); Skulptur Projekte Münster, Germany (2017); Whitney Museum of American Art, New York (2012); Museum of Contemporary Art, Los Angeles (2010); Hamburger Bahnhof—Nationalgalerie der Gegenwart, Berlin (2008); Storm King Art Center, Mountainville, NY (1998); Stroom, The Hague, Netherlands (1991); FRAC Centre, Orléans, France (1990); and FRAC Rhône-Alpes, Lyon, France (1989). He earned an MFA from the University of California, Irvine.

Kristy Luck was born in 1985 in Woodstock, Illinois. Drawing inspiration from personal experience, Luck creates abstract, cerebral paintings. Recent solo exhibitions include Franklin Parrasch, New York (2024); Philip Martin Gallery, Los Angeles (2023, 2021, 2020); and Mendes Wood DM, São Paulo (2022). Recent group exhibitions include Robilant + Voena, Milan (2025); Sidecar, Los Angeles (2024); Grimm, New York (2024); Analog Diary, Beacon, NY (2024); Marin Museum of Contemporary Art, San Rafael, CA (2024); Rachel Uffner Gallery, New York (2023); Philip Martin Gallery, Los Angeles (2023, 2022, 2020); Corbett vs Dempsey, Chicago (2019); and Torrance Art Museum, CA (2019). Luck earned a BFA from Rockford University, Rockford, IL (2010), and an MFA from the School of the Art Institute of Chicago (2014).

317

Patrick Martinez was born in 1980 in Pasadena, California. He makes paintings, reliefs, and sculptural installations from architectural materials such as ceramic tiles, cinder blocks, neon, window-security bars, and vinyl signs that mirror the urban landscape and visual culture of Los Angeles. Recent solo exhibitions include Dallas Contemporary (2024); Rubell Museum, Miami (2023); Institute of Contemporary Art, San Francisco (2023); Charlie James Gallery, Los Angeles (2022, 2018); Tucson Museum of Art (2021); Madison Museum of Contemporary Art, WI (2021); Arlene Schnitzer Gallery, Harvard-Westlake School, Los Angeles (2020); Fort Gansevoort, New York (2019); and the Vincent Price Art Museum, East Los Angeles College, Monterey Park, CA (2017). Recent group exhibitions include the Boston Public Art Triennial (2025); Whitney Museum of American Art, New York (2024, 2023); Palo Alto Art Center, CA (2024); Crystal Bridges Museum of American Art, Bentonville, AR (2024, 2022); Pérez Art Museum, Miami (2024); Jordan Schnitzer Museum of Art, Portland State University, OR (2024); The Broad, Los Angeles (2023); Brooklyn Museum (2023); Riverside Art Museum, CA (2023); Museum of Contemporary Art, Los Angeles (2023); Scottsdale Museum of Contemporary Art, AZ (2023); Long Beach Museum of Art, CA (2022); and El Museo del Barrio, New York (2021). He participated in the Atlantic Center for the Arts Residency, New Smyrna Beach, FL (2022); Robert Rauschenberg Foundation Residency, New York (2020); and the California Community Foundation Fellowship for Visual Artists, Los Angeles (2019). Martinez earned a BFA from ArtCenter College of Design, Pasadena, CA (2005).

BEAUX MENDES

Beaux Mendes was born in 1985 in New York. Rooted in materiality and the direct observation of nature, their fragmentary and abstract works are animated by latent apparitional figures. Recent solo exhibitions include Miguel Abreu Gallery, New York (2024, 2022); Galerie Barbara Weiss, Berlin (2023); STARS Gallery, Los Angeles (2021); and the New Wright Gallery, University of California, Los Angeles (2019). Recent group exhibitions include ProjecteSD, Barcelona (2025); High Art, Paris (2025); 15th Gwangju Biennale, South Korea (2024); MAMOTH, London (2024); Derosia, New York (2024); DREI, Cologne (2023); Tureen, Dallas (2023); and Meredith Rosen Gallery, New York (2022). Mendes earned a BA at Wesleyan University, Middletown, CT (2010), and MFAs from the University of California, Los Angeles (2019), and Bard College, Annandale-on-Hudson, NY (2021).

318

Na Mira was born in 1982 in Lawrence, Kansas. Incorporating film, video, mirrors, holographic materials, and radio transmitters, Mira's interdisciplinary work investigates perception, technology, and power. Recent solo and two-person exhibitions include Doosan Art Center, Seoul (2024); Museum of Contemporary Art Tucson (2023); Paul Soto, Los Angeles (2023, 2019); Croy Nielsen, Vienna (2023); Midway Contemporary Art, Minneapolis (2022); Company Gallery, New York (2022); and The Kitchen, New York (2021). Recent group exhibitions include 19th MOMENTA Biennale d'art contemporain, Montreal (2025); Museum of Contemporary Art Chicago (2025); 12th SITE Santa Fe International (2025); 15th Gwangju Biennale, South Korea (2024); Institute of Contemporary Art, Los Angeles (2024); Kunsthalle Zurich (2024); Art Sonje Center, Seoul (2024, 2023); 60th Venice Biennale (2024); Blaffer Art Museum, University of Houston (2023); Whitney Museum of American Art, New York (2022); Museum of Contemporary Art, Los Angeles (2022); Das Weisse Haus, Vienna (2022); ArtSpace, Sydney (2021); National Museum of Modern and Contemporary Art, Seoul (2020); La Casa Encendida, Madrid (2020); and the Institute of Contemporary Arts, London (2019). Mira is an Assistant Professor in the Department of Art at the University of California, Irvine. She earned a BFA from the School of the Art Institute of Chicago (2006), and an MFA from the University of California, Los Angeles (2013).

NEW THEATER HOLLYWOOD / CALLA HENKEL AND MAX PITEGOFF

Calla Henkel and Max Pitegoff established New Theater Hollywood in a historical, forty-nine-seat black box theater on Santa Monica Boulevard in Hollywood in 2024. Before relocating to Los Angeles, they ran a series of influential bar and theater spaces in Berlin, including TV Bar (2019–22), Grüner Salon at the Volksbühne (2017–18), New Theater (2013–15), and Times Bar (2011–12). Recent solo exhibitions include Fluentum, Berlin (2024); O-Town House, Los Angeles (2023); Reena Spaulings Fine Art, New York (2023); Galerie Isabella Bortolozzi, Berlin (2022); MAMCO, Geneva (2022); zaza', Milan (2022); Friart Kunsthalle, Berlin (2020); and The Downer, Berlin (2020). Recent group exhibitions include PLATO, Ostrava, Czech Republic (2025); Fitzpatrick Gallery, Paris (2024); Sadie Coles HQ, London (2024); Reena Spaulings Fine Art, New York (2022); FRONT International, Cleveland (2022); Hamburger Bahnhof—Nationalgalerie der Gegenwart, Berlin (2021); Pinchuk Art Centre, Kyiv, Ukraine (2021); Museum Morsbroich, Leverkusen, Germany (2021); Museum im Bellpark, Kriens,

Switzerland (2021); Neuer Berliner Kunstverein, Berlin (2020); and Manifesta 13, Marseille, France (2020). Henkel and Pitegoff earned BFAs from the Cooper Union School of Art, New York (2011).

PAT O'NEILL

Pat O'Neill was born in 1939 in Los Angeles. Long known as a pioneer in experimental film and visual effects, O'Neill has also produced a distinctive body of sculpture using postwar industrial materials such as fiberglass, plexiglass, resin, and aluminum. Selected solo exhibitions include Curatorial Exhibitions at The Reef, Los Angeles (2025); Mitchell-Innes & Nash, New York (2021, 2015); San Francisco Museum of Modern Art (2019); Philip Martin Gallery, Los Angeles (2018); Berkeley Art Museum and Pacific Film Archive (2016); Monitor, Rome (2016); VeneKlasen/Werner, Berlin (2016); Cherry and Martin, Los Angeles (2015, 2013); Academy of Motion Picture Arts and Sciences, Los Angeles (2011); and the Santa Monica Museum of Art, CA (2004). Selected group exhibitions include Huntington Beach Art Center, CA (2024); Philip Martin Gallery, Los Angeles (2023); Fowler Museum, University of California, Los Angeles (2021); Martos Gallery, New York (2019); Villa Arson, Nice, France (2018); Whitney Museum of American Art, New York (2016, 2008, 1991); Carnegie Museum of Art, Pittsburgh (2015); Les Abattoirs, Musée – Frac Occitanie Toulouse, France (2014); Fellows of Contemporary Art, Los Angeles (2011); Centre Pompidou, Paris (2010, 2008, 2006); Museum of Contemporary Art, Los Angeles (2009); Haus der Kunst, Munich (2008); and Tate Liverpool, England (2006). Honors and awards include a Creative Capital Grant (2015); a California Community Foundation Fellowship for Visual Artists (2013); First Prize in Film at FLEX Fest, Tampa (2011); a Rockefeller Foundation Grant (1997); the Maya Deren Award for Independent Film and Video, American Film Institute (1993); and a Guggenheim Fellowship (1992). O'Neill earned a BA (1962) and an MA (1964) from the University of California, Los Angeles.

WILL RAWLS

Will Rawls was born in 1978 in Boston. A choreographer and visual artist, he creates performances and installations that incorporate dance, video, sound, text, printmaking, and animation to explore the intersection of visibility, erasure, and language. Solo exhibitions include the Institute of Contemporary Art, Los Angeles (2025); Adams and Ollman Gallery, Portland, OR (2022); and the Henry Art Gallery, University of Washington, Seattle

320

(2021). Recent group exhibitions include the 12th SITE Santa Fe International (2025) and Counterpublic Triennial, Saint Louis (2023). Performances include the 12th SITE Santa Fe International (2025); REDCAT, Los Angeles (2025, 2021); MoMA PS1, Queens, NY (2025); Whitney Museum of American Art, New York (2024); 35th Bienal de São Paulo (2023); The Momentary, Bentonville, AR (2023); Museum of Contemporary Art Chicago (2023, 2018); Portland Institute for Contemporary Art, OR (2023, 2017); On the Boards, Seattle (2023); Pace Live, Los Angeles (2022); Henry Art Gallery, University of Washington, Seattle (2021); Hessel Museum of Art, Bard College, Annandale-on-Hudson, NY (2019); ISSUE Project Room, Brooklyn (2019, 2018); Institute of Contemporary Art, Boston (2019); Walker Art Center, Minneapolis (2019); Yale Repertory Theater, Yale University, New Haven, CT (2019); and the Museum of Modern Art, New York (2019). Recent honors and awards include grants from the Mellon Foundation (2023, 2022); a Creative Capital Award (2021); a National Dance Project Production Grant (2020); the Herb Alpert Award in the Arts (2022); and a Guggenheim Fellowship (2017). Rawls is an Associate Professor of Choreography and Interdisciplinary Practice at the University of California, Los Angeles. He earned a BA from Williams College, Williamstown, MA (2000).

BRIAN ROCHEFORT

Brian Rochefort was born in 1985 in Lincoln, Rhode Island. Drawing inspiration from excursions to remote landscapes such as the Amazon, Rochefort works with clay to create abstract, organic sculptures. Recent solo exhibitions include Bernier/Eliades Gallery, Athens (2025, 2021); Sean Kelly Gallery, Los Angeles (2024); Van Doren Waxter, New York (2024, 2022, 2019); The Little House, Los Angeles (2023); SOCO Gallery, Charlotte, NC (2023); Massimo de Carlo, Hong Kong (2022), Milan (2021), and London (2019); Museum of Contemporary Art Santa Barbara, CA (2019); Sorry We're Closed Gallery, Brussels (2018); and the Mistake Room, Guadalajara, Mexico (2019). Recent group exhibitions include Sean Kelly Gallery, New York (2025); Jeffrey Deitch, Los Angeles (2025, 2023, 2021); Kasmin Gallery, New York (2023); Patricia Low Contemporary, Gstaad, Switzerland (2023); The Pit, Los Angeles (2023); Massimo de Carlo, Beijing (2023); Fondation Villa Datris, L'Isle-sur-la-Sorgue, France (2022); Montpellier Contemporain, France (2022); Tristan Hoare, London (2021); Blum & Poe, Los Angeles (2021); Nouveau Musée National de Monaco, Villa Sauber, Monaco (2020); Crocker Art Museum, Sacramento (2019); and Craft Contemporary, Los Angeles (2018). Rochefort earned a BFA from the Rhode Island School of Design, Providence (2007).

321

Amanda Ross-Ho was born in 1975 in Chicago. Ross-Ho considers her artistic practice a form of experimental archival research, driven by impulses to commemorate and analyze life's intimacies. Selected solo exhibitions include ILY2, Portland, OR (2023); Abroms-Engel Institute for Visual Art, University of Alabama, Birmingham, AL (2024); Mitchell-Innes & Nash, New York (2017); Bonner Kunstverein, Bonn, Germany (2017); Vleeshal Center for Contemporary Art, Middelburg, Netherlands (2016); The Approach, London (2014); and the Museum of Contemporary Art, Los Angeles (2012). Selected group exhibitions include Commonwealth and Council, Los Angeles (2025); Institute of Contemporary Art, Los Angeles (2025, 2018); Museum Kunstpalast, Düsseldorf, Germany (2024); Henry Art Gallery, University of Washington, Seattle (2024, 2022, 2017); Bel Ami, Los Angeles (2023); Aargauer Kunsthaus, Aarau, Switzerland (2019); Kunsthall Stavanger, Stavanger, Norway (2019); 33rd Ljubljana Biennial of Graphic Arts, Ljubljana, Slovenia (2019); EXILE, Vienna (2019); Orange County Museum of Art, Costa Mesa, CA (2017); Walker Art Center, Minneapolis (2016); and the Whitney Museum of American Art, New York (2008). Her public art commissions include Carnegie Mellon University, Pittsburgh (2024); Public Art Fund, New York (2015); and the Museum of Contemporary Art, Chicago (2013). Ross-Ho is the recipient of numerous honors including the Marciano Art Foundation's Artadia Award (2025); an Anonymous Was a Woman award (2023); a California Community Foundation Visual Arts Fellowship (2017); and a Joan Mitchell Foundation Painters & Sculptors Grant (2013). Ross-Ho is a Professor of Sculpture at the University of California, Irvine. She earned a BFA from the School of the Art Institute of Chicago (1998), and an MFA from the University of Southern California, Los Angeles (2006).

GABRIELA RUIZ

Gabriela Ruiz was born in 1991 in the San Fernando Valley. Her interdisciplinary practice explores surveillance capitalism, mass consumerism, and the intersection of technology, memory, and fantasy. Solo exhibitions include the Institute for the Humanities Gallery, University of Michigan, Ann Arbor, MI (2023); Palm Springs Art Museum (2022); Anat Ebgi Gallery, Los Angeles (2022); LaPau Gallery, Los Angeles (2021); and the Vincent Price Art Museum, East Los Angeles College, Monterey Park, CA (2019). Recent group exhibitions include the Pérez Art Museum, Miami (2024); Jeffrey Deitch, Los Angeles (2024, 2021); Cheech Marin Center for Chicano Art &

Culture, Riverside Art Museum, CA (2023); VETA Galeria, Madrid (2023); Museum of Contemporary Art Santa Barbara, CA (2022); Museo de las Artes, Universidad de Guadalajara, Mexico (2019); Museum aan de Stroom, Antwerp, Belgium (2019); One Gallery, West Hollywood, CA (2019); and the Institute of Contemporary Art, Los Angeles (2018). Performances have been presented at Anat Ebgi, Los Angeles (2022); Museum aan de Stroom, Antwerp, Belgium (2019); REDCAT, Los Angeles (2019); Centro Cultural Clavijero, Morelia, Mexico (2019); Institute of Contemporary Art, Los Angeles (2018); and the Roski School of Art and Design, University of Southern California, Los Angeles (2018). Ruiz was a recipient of the California Community Foundation's Fellowship for Visual Artists (2024).

ALAKE SHILLING

Alake Shilling was born in 1993 in Los Angeles. Wrought with dark humor and nostalgia, Shilling's ceramics and paintings resonate with a millennial generation familiar with the designs of Lisa Frank, only her fantastic cartoon creatures and landscapes take on unsettling dispositions. Recent solo exhibitions include the Palm Springs Art Museum, CA (2024); Jeffrey Deitch, Los Angeles (2023, 2021); 356 Mission, Los Angeles (2018); and Maitland Foley, Los Angeles (2016). Recent group exhibitions include Jeffrey Deitch, Los Angeles (2025, 2023, 2021, 2019); Sargent's Daughters, New York (2024); Somerset House, London (2024); Charlie James Gallery, Los Angeles (2024); CONTROL Gallery, Los Angeles (2024); Fondation Vincent Van Gogh, Arles, France (2023); Museum of Arts and Design, New York (2023); Public Access, New York (2022); Sow & Tailor, Los Angeles (2020); NSU Art Museum, Fort Lauderdale, FL (2019); Loyal Gallery, Stockholm (2019, 2018); Hammer Museum, Los Angeles (2019); Rubell Family Collection, Miami (2018); Karma International, Los Angeles (2018); Josh Lilley Gallery, London (2018); and Night Gallery, Los Angeles (2018). Shilling studied at the School of the Art Institute of Chicago and Los Angeles City College.

NICOLE-ANTONIA SPAGNOLA

Nicole-Antonia Spagnola was born in 1991 in Los Angeles. A multimedia artist with a practice rooted in film, Spagnola draws inspiration from a wide range of sources, including the history of computational media and 1980s Italian hardcore music. Recent solo and two-person exhibitions include Commercial Street, Los Angeles (2025, 2021); Schaufenster, Kunstverein München, Munich (2024); Ivory Tars, Glasgow, Scotland (2024); Felix

Gaudlitz, Vienna (2023); Stadtgalerie Bern, Bern, Switzerland (2023); The Wig, Berlin (2023); Reena Spaulings Fine Art, New York (2023); 100 Bell Towers, Montreal (2022); Artists Space, New York (2022); and Full Haus, Los Angeles (2017). Recent group exhibitions include The Wig, Berlin (2024); Galerie Hussenot, Paris (2024); Sgomento Zurigo, Zurich (2024); Ivory Tars, Glasgow, Scotland (2024); 3236RLS, London (2024); Bel Ami, Los Angeles (2024); Felix Gaudlitz, Milan (2024) and Vienna (2023); and Galerie Neu, Berlin (2023). Spagnola earned a BFA at the California Institute of the Arts (2016), Valencia, CA, and an MA at the University of California, Los Angeles (2018). She is currently a PhD candidate at the University of California, Los Angeles.

MIKE STOLTZ

Mike Stoltz was born in 1981 in Miami. An experimental filmmaker, he works directly with the tools of cinema—images, sound, and time—to probe the medium of film. Recent presentations and screenings include Los Angeles Filmforum (2023); Stove Works, Chattanooga, TN (2022); Artist Film Workshop, Melbourne, Australia (2019); LaborBerlin (2018); WORM, Rotterdam, Netherlands (2018); Cavia, Amsterdam (2018); La Lumière Collective, Montreal (2018); Milwaukee Underground Film Festival (2018); Headroom Cinema, Iowa City, IA (2017); Microlights Cinema, Milwaukee (2017); Nightingale Cinema, Chicago (2017); A.P.E. Gallery, Northampton, MA (2017); Sight Unseen Cinema, Baltimore (2017); and No Nothing Cinema, San Francisco (2016); Recent festivals include Light Field, San Francisco (2025); International Film Festival Rotterdam, Netherlands (2024); Museum of the Moving Image, Queens, NY (2024); Los Angeles Festival of Movies (2024); Edinburgh International Film Festival, Scotland (2024); Artist Film Workshop, Melbourne, Australia (2024); Milwaukee Underground Film Festival (2024); Moviate Underground Film Festival, Harrisburg, PA (2024); Winnipeg Underground Film Festival, Canada (2024); Media City Film Festival, Windsor, Canada (2024); and Anthology Film Archives, New York (2023). Stoltz is the recipient of numerous honors and awards including a Mike Kelley Foundation for the Arts Artist Project Grant via the Echo Park Film Center (2016); Best Experimental Film award at the Athens International Film and Video Festival (2015); and Top Prize Award at the Milwaukee Underground Film Festival (2011). He earned a BA from the University of Florida, Gainesville, FL (2011), and an MFA from the California Institute of the Arts, Valencia, CA (2014).

Peter Tomka was born in 1989 in Des Moines. Tomka is a photographer and the founder of the artist-run program No Moon LA. By manipulating rigorous technical and material processes, Tomka creates large-scale—partial, blurred, cropped, and grainy—photographs that are queer in form and content. Recent solo and two-person exhibitions include Webber Gallery, Paris (2024); O-Town House, Los Angeles (2024); the Fulcrum Press, Los Angeles (2023); and No Moon LA, Los Angeles (2021). Recent group exhibitions include O-Town House, Los Angles (2024, 2023); Galerie Wood, Los Angeles (2024); Webber Gallery, Los Angeles (2024); and Giovanni's Room, Los Angeles (2023). Performances include L.A. Dance Project (2019) and Human Resources, Los Angeles (2018). Tomka earned a BA at the University of Iowa, Iowa City, IA (2011), and an MFA at the University of California, Riverside (2020).

FREDDY VILLALOBOS

Freddy Villalobos was born in 1989 in Los Angeles. He is an interdisciplinary artist whose work interrogates states of vulnerability, disruption, and becoming. Solo and two-person exhibitions include International Waters, Brooklyn (2021); Mandujano Cell, Inglewood, CA (2018); and Catalyst Gallery, University of California, Irvine (2015). Group exhibitions include International Objects, Brooklyn (2023); White Cube, London (2021); Green Hall Gallery, Yale School of Art, New Haven, CT (2021, 2020, 2019); Vincent Price Art Museum, East Los Angeles College, Monterey Park, CA (2018, 2017); CB1 Gallery, Los Angeles (2017); Human Resources, Los Angeles (2017); Los Angeles Contemporary Exhibitions (2017); Underground Museum, Los Angeles (2017); and the University Art Gallery, University of California, Irvine (2016). He is the recipient of honors and awards including a Shandaken Governors Island Project Residency, New York (2023); a residency at the Skowhegan School of Painting and Sculpture, Madison, ME (2022); the AIM Fellowship, Bronx Museum of the Arts, NY (2022); and a Graduate and Professional School Research Fellowship, Beinecke Rare Book and Manuscript Library, Yale University, New Haven, CT (2021). Villalobos earned a BA at the University of California, Irvine (2016), and an MFA at Yale University, New Haven, CT (2021).

Kelly Wall was born in 1990 in Los Angeles. With a recent focus on stained glass, Wall creates meticulously crafted sculptures that resemble nostalgic, mass-produced objects such as ashtrays, beach chairs, and souvenir mugs. Solo exhibitions include Various Small Fires, Los Angeles (2024); New Low, Los Angeles (2023, 2021); California Institute of the Arts, Valencia, CA (2019); and Industry Gallery, West Hollywood, CA (2016). Recent group exhibitions include OCHI Gallery, Los Angeles (2025); Noon Projects, Los Angeles (2025); Pio Pico, Los Angeles (2025, 2023); Wolford House, Los Angeles (2025); Alabaster Projects, Los Angeles (2024); The Hole, Los Angeles (2024); Chez Max et Dorothea, Los Angeles (2023); Praz-Delavallade, Los Angeles (2022); Aspen Art Museum, CO (2022, 2021); Human Resources, Los Angeles (2019); JOAN, Los Angeles (2019); and François Ghebaly, Los Angeles (2018). Wall earned a BFA from Otis College of Art and Design, Los Angeles (2013), and an MFA from the California Institute of the Arts, Valencia, CA (2019).

LEILAH WEINRAUB

Leilah Weinraub was born in 1979 in Los Angeles. An artist, film director, and performer, Weinraub is best known for the underground documentary *Shakedown* (2018). Her latest film, *Seek No Favor* (2025), codirected with Elle Clay, premieres at the BlackStar Film Festival. Weinraub recently held a residency at New Theater Hollywood, where her performance work evolved in dialogue with her cinematic practice. Recent solo presentations include Gavin Brown's Enterprise, New York (2018) and What Pipeline, Detroit (2018). Group exhibitions include the 35th Bienal de São Paulo (2023); Centre d'Art Contemporain, Geneva (2021); Kunsthall Stavanger, Stavanger, Norway (2021); Performa, New York (2021); Sullivan Galleries, School of the Art Institute of Chicago (2019); Gavin Brown's Enterprise, New York (2018); and the Whitney Museum of American Art, New York (2017). Weinraub studied at Antioch College, Yellow Springs, OH, and the Milton Avery Graduate School of Arts at Bard College, Annandale-on-Hudson, NY.

BRUCE YONEMOTO

Bruce Yonemoto was born in 1949 in San Jose. A pioneer in the field of video art, over the last half century Yonemoto has produced a formally and thematically eclectic body of film, video, photography, and sculpture. Selected solo and two-person presentations include Kunstverein in Hamburg

(2023); O-Town House, Los Angeles (2022,2023); Anthology Film Archives, New York (2022); Tate Modern, London (2017, 2012); Imperial Palace, Rio de Janeiro (2017); Museum of Modern Art, New York (2017); The Luckman, California State University, Los Angeles (2017); Hong-Gah Museum, Taipei, Tawain (2015); c.nichols Project, Los Angeles (2016); Art Gallery, Kanazawa College of Art, Ishikawa, Japan (2012); LAXART, Los Angeles (2011); Saint Louis Art Museum (2010); Convento de Santo Domingo, Qorikancha, Cusco, Peru (2006); MIT List Visual Arts Center, Cambridge, MA (2001); Institute of Contemporary Art, Philadelphia (2001); ICC Intercommunication Center, Tokyo (1999); Japanese American National Museum, Los Angeles (1999); and the Wexner Center for the Arts, Columbus, OH (1997). Selected group exhibitions include the Institute of Contemporary Art, Los Angeles (2024); Institute of Contemporary Art, San Jose (2024); Galerie Quynh Contemporary Art, Ho Chi Minh City, Vietnam (2023); Yuz Museum, Shanghai (2020); Los Angeles County Museum of Art (2020); Qatar Museums, Doha, U.A.E. (2020); Chi-Wen Gallery, Taipei, Taiwan (2018, 2017); Los Angeles Contemporary Exhibitions (2014); Stedelijk Museum, Amsterdam (2014); Centre Pompidou, Paris (2014); MoMA PS1, Queens, NY (2014); Museum of Contemporary Art, Los Angeles (2014, 2011); and the Museum of Modern Art, New York (2011). Honors and awards include a Guggenheim Fellowship (2022); a Rockefeller Foundation Intercultural Film/Video/Multimedia Fellowship (1998); and a Maya Deren Award from the American Film Institute (1993). He earned a BA from the University of California, Berkeley (1972), and an MFA from Otis College of Art and Design, Los Angeles (1979).

TAYLOR RENEE ALDRIDGE

Taylor Renee Aldridge is a writer, curator, and cofounding editor of *ARTS. BLACK* Journal. She is based in Detroit.

SAMPADA ALDRIDGE

Sampada Aranke is a teacher, curator, and writer whose work examines how artists theorize systems of power and enable us to imagine alternative ways of living.

GIAMPAOLO BIANCONI

Giampaolo Bianconi is the Dittmer Associate Curator of Modern and Contemporary Art at the Art Institute of Chicago, where he shapes the museum's exhibitions, acquisitions, and programs with a focus on conceptual practices and global contemporary art.

ANNIKA BOHANEC

Annika Bohanec is a curatorial assistant in the Department of Modern and Contemporary Art at the Art Institute of Chicago, with a research focus on contemporary sculpture and the intersections of race and gender. She holds an MA from the Courtauld Institute of Art, London, and BA and BS degrees from Loyola University Chicago.

JENNIFER BUONOCORE-NEDRELOW

Jennifer Buonocore-Nedrelow is an art historian and curator with expertise in interdisciplinary art since 1960. She holds a PhD from the Institute of Fine Arts, New York University.

Kate Durbin is a writer and artist based in Los Angeles. Her most recent book, *Hoarders* (Wave Books, 2021), was named a best book of 2021 by National Public Radio, Lit Hub, and Electric Literature.

DOUGLAS FOGLE

Douglas Fogle is an independent curator and writer based in Los Angeles. Fogle has nearly thirty years of experience as a museum curator focusing on exhibitions and publications devoted to contemporary art, film, architecture, fashion, and design. Previously, he held curatorial positions at the Walker Art Center, Minneapolis; Carnegie Museum of Art, Pittsburgh; Hammer Museum, Los Angeles; and Anderson Ranch, Snowmass Village, CO.

ROBESON TAJ FRAZIER

Robeson Taj Frazier is an award-winning writer, arts and humanities curator, and producer of docuseries and documentary film. He is the host of two PBS productions (*Hip Hop and the Metaverse* [2023] and *Outside the Lyrics* [2024]), and the author of multiple books, including *KAOS Theory: The Afrokosmic Ark of Ben Caldwell* (Angel City Press, 2023). He is an Associate Professor of Communication at the University of Southern California, Los Angeles.

DAVID J. GETSY

David J. Getsy is the Eleanor Shea Professor of Art History at the University of Virginia, Charlottesville, VA. His books include *Abstract Bodies: Sixties Sculpture in the Expanded Field of Gender* (Yale University Press, 2015/2023), *Queer* (MIT Press, 2016), and *Queer Behavior: Scott Burton and Performance Art* (University of Chicago Press, 2022), which received the Robert Motherwell Book Award for outstanding publication in the history and criticism of modernism in the arts.

ESTI GIORDANI

Esti Giordani is a writer and producer for film and television. She has written for series on AppleTV+, Amazon, and Starz, as well as for Nicolas Winding Refn's upcoming feature film, *Her Private Hell*. Giordani lives in Los Angeles with two Chihuahuas.

Essence Harden is curator of the Focus section for Frieze Los Angeles (2024–26) and has curated exhibitions in Los Angeles at Art + Practice, the California African American Museum, and Los Angeles Contemporary Exhibitions as well as at the Orange County Museum of Art, Costa Mesa, CA; Museum of the African Diaspora, San Francisco; and the Oakland Museum of California, among others.

CHINAKA HODGE

Chinaka Hodge is a poet, playwright, and screenwriter. Her screenwriting credits include *Rise* (NBC), *Snowpiercer* (HBO/Max), *Amazing Stories* (AppleTV+), and *The Midnight Club* (Netflix). Hodge is Head Writer/Executive Producer of Disney+/Marvel's forthcoming series, *Ironheart*, which focuses on the adventures of Black girl tech genius, Riri Williams. She holds an MFA from the School of Cinematic Arts at the University of Southern California, Los Angeles. She lives in Los Angeles and is also a mom to a brilliant four-year-old.

SUZANNE HUDSON

Suzanne Hudson is an art historian and critic based in Los Angeles. She is a Professor of Art History and Fine Arts at the University of Southern California, Los Angeles.

SUMMER KIM LEE

Summer Kim Lee is an Assistant Professor of English at the University of California, Los Angeles. She is the author of *Spoiled: Asian American Hostility and the Damage of Repair* (Duke University Press, 2025).

TODD LEREW

Todd Lerew is Director of Special Projects at the Library Foundation of Los Angeles, curating eclectic exhibitions and programs in support of the Los Angeles Public Library. He is the author of *Also On View: Unique and Unexpected Museums of Greater Los Angeles* (Angel City Press, 2024). Lerew is also a composer of experimental music and inventor of musical instruments, and serves as a volunteer fire lookout in the San Bernardino National Forest.

Ali Liebegott is a writer and painter. She has published four books: *The Beautifully Worthless* (Suspect Thoughts Press, 2006), *The IHOP Papers* (Carroll & Graf, 2007), *Cha-Ching!* (City Lights, 2013), and *The Summer of Dead Birds* (Feminist Press, 2019). In 2022, her paintings featured in a solo exhibition at OCHI Gallery, Los Angeles.

HENOCH MOORE

Henoch Moore is an artist, music executive, and archivist. He is the Head of Artists & Repertoire at Warp Records, London, and co-runs L.A. Club Resource with his longtime collaborator, Delroy Edwards.

TERENCE NANCE

Terence Nance (also known as Terence Etc.) is an artist, filmmaker, and musician. In 2023 alone, he created the score for director Tayarisha Poe's *The Young Wife*, directed an accompanying visual film for musician André 3000's album *New Blue Sun*, and presented his first solo exhibition at the Institute of Contemporary Art, Philadelphia. His first feature film, *Oversimplification of Her Beauty* (2012), premiered at the Sundance Film Festival, Park City, UT, and he went on to create the Peabody Award-winning HBO series *Random Acts of Flyness* (2018–22). Recent albums include *V O R T E X* (2022) and *Things I Never Had* (2020).

KATE NESIN

Kate Nesin is an art historian, writer, and curator-at-large for the Department of Modern and Contemporary Art at the Art Institute of Chicago. Her current research focuses on image- and audio-description practices, and her recent writing includes essays on artists Nairy Baghramian, B. Ingrid Olson, and Lutz Bacher.

PAULINA POBOCHA

Paulina Pobocha is an art historian, writer, and Chair and Curator of Modern and Contemporary Art at the Art Institute of Chicago.

Leigh Raiford is a Professor of African American and African Diaspora Studies at the University of California, Berkeley, where she teaches, researches, curates, and writes about race, gender, justice, and visuality. Raiford is the author of *When Home Is a Photograph: Blackness and Belonging in the World* (forthcoming 2026); *Imprisoned in a Luminous Glare: Photography and the African American Freedom Struggle* (University of North Carolina Press, 2011); co-author with Ariella Aïsha Azoulay, Wendy Ewald, Susan Meiselas, and Laura Wexler of *Collaboration: A Potential History of Photography* (Thames & Hudson, 2024); and series editor with Sarah Elizabeth Lewis and Deborah Willis of the Vision and Justice Series, a book imprint of Aperture.

HEIDI SCHRECK

Heidi Schreck is a writer and performer based in Brooklyn. Her critically acclaimed play, *What the Constitution Means to Me*, played a sold-out run on Broadway in 2019. The play was nominated for two Tony Awards and was a finalist for the Pulitzer Prize.

Page 121: Courtesy of the artist and
ChertLüdde, Berlin. Photo: Marjorie
Brunet Plaza
Pages 122–123: Courtesy of the artist and
Carnegie Museum of Art, Pittsburgh.
Photo: Sean Eaton
Page 138: Courtesy of the artist. Photo:
Jason Mandella
Pages 140–141, Page 142 (top): Courtesy
of the artist. Photos: Paul Salveson
Page 142 (bottom): Hammer Museum,
Los Angeles. Purchased with funds
provided by anonymous donor, 2024
Page 144: Photos: Euirock Lee
Page 147 (postcard): Courtesy of the
Chesapeake Bay Program. Photo:
Will Parson
Pages 151–152: Courtesy of the artist and
Franklin Parrasch Gallery, New York
Pages 158–159, Page 164: Courtesy of the
artist. Photos: Ed Mumford
Pages 162–163: Courtesy of the artist.
Photo: Kevin Todora
Page 172: James Maltz Collection,
London. Photo: Stephen Fraught
Page 173: Courtesy of the artist and
Miguel Abreu Gallery, New York.
Photo: Stephen Fraught
Page 174: Collection of Gaby and
Wilhelm Schürmann, Herzogenrath,
Germany. Photo: Stephen Fraught
Pages 193–195: Courtesy of the artist
and Philip Martin Gallery, Los
Angeles. Photos: Brian Forrest
Pages 200–204: Courtesy of the artist.
Photos: Julieta Cervantes
Pages 206–207: Courtesy of the artist.
Photo: Jared Sorrells

Page 208 (top): Courtesy of the artist
and Portland Institute for Contempo-
rary Art. Photo: Mario Gallucci
Page 208 (bottom): Courtesy of the
artist and Institute of Contemporary
Art, Los Angeles. Photo: Jeff McLane
Pages 215–216: Courtesy the artist and
Massimo De Carlo Gallery. Photos:
Marten Elder
Pages 221–222: Courtesy of the artist.
Photo: Jeff McLane
Pages 224–225: Courtesy of Chang
Mathieu Collection. Photos: Robert
Wedemeyer
Page 229: Courtesy of the artist. Photo:
Dorian Ulises López Macías
Page 232 (bottom): Courtesy of the
artist. Photo: Ruben Diaz
Pages 234–235: Courtesy of Vincent
Price Art Museum, Monterey Park,
CA. Photo: Monica Orozco
Pages 238–239: Courtesy of the artist
and Jeffrey Deitch, Los Angeles
and New York. Photo: Charles White/
JW Pictures
Page 240: Collection of Shio Kusaka and
Jonas Wood. Photo: Evan Bedford
Page 244: Collection of Jeffrey Deitch.
Photo: Elon Schoenholz
Page 264: Courtesy of Webber Gallery,
Los Angeles
Pages 268–269: Courtesy of No Moon
LA, Los Angeles
Page 271: Courtesy of The Fulcrum
Press, Los Angeles. Photo: Josh
Schaedel
Pages 276–277: Courtesy of the artist.
Photo: Jackie Furtado

Pages 286–287: Courtesy of the artist.
  Photo: Josh Schaedel
Page 290, Page 292: Courtesy of the
  artist. Photo: Julia Saltzman
Page 296: Photo: Calla Henkel and
  Max Pitegoff

Lenders to the Exhibition:
Miguel Abreu Gallery, New York
Collection of Jeffrey Deitch
Jeffrey Deitch, Los Angeles
parrasch heijnen, Los Angeles
James Maltz Collection, London
Philip Martin Gallery, Los Angeles
Darren and Candice Romanelli
Collection of Gaby and Wilhelm
  Schürmann, Herzogenrath, Germany
Collection of Shio Kusaka and
  Jonas Wood

Made in L.A. uniquely touches every staff member at the Hammer, and we would like to acknowledge them in the following list.* Additional gratitude to all the part-time and student staff who contributed to this exhibition.

Shira Abramsohn
Javier Acuna
Bryan Alfaro
Evelyn Aquino
Vanessa Arizmendi
Karina Arzate-Arenivaz
Cheyenne Assil
Marvin Barrios
Adriana Bastida
Sara Beattie
Erica Benson
Brooke Berlin
Nicole Berry
Claudia Bestor
Reshma Bishnoi
Jennifer Buonocore-Nedrelow
Cynthia Burlingham
Bacilio Castillo
Michelle Castro Bastida
Erin Christovale
Nathalie Chybik
Henry Clancy
Paula Condo-Porto
Lauren Coryell
Monica Cruz
Shannon Cynowa
Lisa Davis
Lionel Deatherage
Mary Delgado
Julie Dickover
Jessi DiTillo
Ramon Espinosa
Tim Ferris

Jim Fetterly
Teresa Fleming
Kevin Folk
Elena Francisco
Nyah Ginwright
Renato Gontijo
Lauren Graycar
Beth Harker
Sophie Helm
Madicyn Herbst
Esteban Hernandez
Susan Hersey
Matt Hutchinson
Silvia Jacome
Malaya Johnson
Alice Kaufman
Harrison Keenan
Aiza Keesey
Isabella Kefgen
Dylan King
Hannah Kirby
Wee Kong
Ashley Kruythoff
Philip Leers
Ryan Lenhardt
Randy Luna
Jeffrey Marroquin
Leticia Martinez
Portland McCormick
Mo McGee
Kelin Michael
Michael Monahan
Kai Monet
Tara Morris
Aram Moshayedi
Daniel Munoz
Michael Nock
Gabriel Noguez Ibarra
Brennen Ogawa

Santiago Pazos
Adam Peña
Marta Peña
Juan Perez
Angelica Perez-Aguirre
Elizabeth Powers
Jason Pugh
Todd Quinn
Pablo José Ramírez
Courtney Raterman Casal
Rachel Regalado
Weijun Robertson
Marc Rodrigues
Emma Rudman
Maribel Ruiz
Zoë Ryan
Hallie Scott
Juan Manuel Silverio
Michelle Soliman
Muhammed Sonko
Angeline Sun
Nicholas Swing
Naoko Takahatake
Scott Tennent
Michael Terzano
Alexis Tongue
Phon Tran
Emma Vale
Diana Vasquez
Maribel Villegas
Jennie Waldow
Jade Wisansky
Ebony Wyatt
Fred Yeries
Esther Zeilig Bonilla
Chris Zickefoose

*As of June 1, 2025

This book was published on the occasion of Made in L.A. 2025, organized and presented by the Hammer Museum, Los Angeles, October 5, 2025–March 1, 2026.

Made in L.A. 2025 is organized by Essence Harden, independent curator, and Paulina Pobocha, Chair and Curator of Modern and Contemporary Art, Art Institute of Chicago, and former Hammer Museum Robert Soros Senior Curator, with Jennifer Buonocore-Nedrelow, curatorial assistant.

The exhibition is made possible by the Mohn Family Foundation and members of the Hammer Circle. Major support is provided by The Billy and Audrey L. Wilder Foundation, Miky Lee, and Mark Sandelson. Generous support is provided by The Fran and Ray Stark Foundation; Bill Hair; Susan Genco and Mitch Kamin; J.P. Morgan; Dori Peterman Mostov and Charles Mostov; and Orange Barrel Media. Additional support is provided by The Buddy Taub Foundation, Dennis A. Roach and Stephanie Roach, Directors; McCrea Foundation; the Pasadena Art Alliance; The Rhonda S. Zinner Foundation and Jonathan Segal; and Michael Silver.

Published in 2025 by the Armand Hammer Museum of Art and Cultural Center, Inc., and DelMonico Books • D.A.P.

341

Hammer Museum
10899 Wilshire Boulevard
Los Angeles, CA 90024-4201
310-443-7000
hammer.ucla.edu

DelMonico Books available through
ARTBOOK | D.A.P.
75 Broad Street, Suite 630
New York, NY 10004
artbook.com
delmonicobooks.com

Design:
Folder Studio

Editor:
Domenick Ammirati

Copy editor:
Anthony Carfello

Proofreader:
Rachel Walther

Director, exhibition and
publication management:
Michael Nock

Project manager:
Jennifer Buonocore-Nedrelow

Color separations:
Echelon, Santa Monica

Printer:
die Keure, Bruges, Belgium

The book is typeset in Eden CT and Adobe Kis, and printed on 80 gsm Munken Pure and 250 gsm Remake Carapace CR Smoke paper.

Printed and bound in Bruges, Belgium.

ISBN:
978-1-63681-169-7

Library of Congress Control Number:
2025937783